PRAISE FOR *Cheese and Culture*

"In this painstakingly researched yet passion-laced book, Paul Kindstedt shows us how cheese, from its rudimentary beginnings to today's manufacturing, is inextricably linked to culture and, no less, to our future. *Cheese and Culture* is essential reading for anyone who loves cheese and, equally, cares about the future of food itself."

—Laura Werlin, author, *Laura Werlin's Cheese Essentials*

"All honor and respect to Aristaeus—the Greek god who taught us to make cheese—and to Paul Kindstedt, who in *Cheese and Culture* teaches us its glorious history ever since."

—Rob Kaufelt, proprietor, Murray's Cheese NYC

"From the Garden of Eden to the dairy industries of today, Paul S. Kindstedt unfolds the monumental story of cheese. Vast in scope, rich in detail, *Cheese and Culture* is a casein-inspired epic."

—Eric LeMay, author, *Immortal Milk*

"*Cheese and Culture* is the book both cheese professionals and cheese geeks have been waiting for. Professor Kindstedt gives us the mostly untold history of cheese and its societal import from 6500 BC to the present, answering all my cheese questions—even the ones I didn't know I had. *Cheese and Culture* is the most comprehensive cheese book ever written by an American, a great addition to our collective cheese library."

—Gordon Edgar, cheese buyer, Rainbow Grocery Cooperative, and author, *Cheesemonger: A Life on the Wedge*

"This book will fascinate anyone who loves cheese. With a sweeping perspective, from the earliest prehistoric domestication of goats and sheep to the present, it chronicles how social, technological, and political developments gave rise to the vast array of cheeses we know and love."

—Sandor Ellix Katz, author, *The Art of Fermentation*, *The Revolution Will Not Be Microwaved*, and *Wild Fermentation*

"Given the vast amount that's been written about cheese down the centuries, the surprising absence of a scholarly work on the history of cheese is all the more remarkable. With *Cheese and Culture*, noted dairy scientist and author Paul Kindstedt has admirably filled this gap to an extent that should satisfy even the most avid cheese geek."

—Kate Arding, cofounder, *Culture* magazine

"No cheese lover or cheesemaker's education will be complete without reading of the epic journey of cheese as it influences and is influenced by human civilization. Paul Kindstedt steers the reader through a vast sea of history with the steady, inspired hand and confidence of a seasoned captain of his subject. What a gift to the world of cheese!"

—Gianaclis Caldwell, cheesemaker, Pholia Farm,
and author, *The Farmstead Creamery Advisor*

"Paul Kindstedt has fashioned a remarkable book about one of humankind's most distinctive foods. Drawing upon comprehensive evidence from archaeology to contemporary artisan cheese making, Dr. Kindstedt shapes the complex story of cheese. He examines the impact of geography and climate, religion, social status and wealth, transportation and commerce . . . to describe and explain the 8,500-year evolution of cheese from Neolithic humans to present-day America. From archaeologists and anthropologists and historians to cheesemakers and consumers who want to deepen their understanding and appreciation of cheese, Dr. Kindstedt's book will enlighten, entertain, and reveal the fascinating history and culture of cheese. *Bravissimi e complimenti!*"

—Jeffrey Roberts, New England Culinary Institute
and author, *The Atlas of American Artisan Cheese*

"I love this book—accessible in its prose and style with the breadth and depth of an academic work. All those interested in the role that cheesemaking has played in the development of the world we live in will come away after reading this book with context and understanding, and an intellectual appreciation of why cheese appeals to so many people at an emotional level. Paul Kindstedt has produced a seminal work in *Cheese and Culture.*"

—Mateo Kehler, cheesemaker, Jasper Hill Farm

"Dr. Kindstedt's love and passion for the artisan cheese movement is inspiring. In his latest book, he has presented a beautiful and historically rich mosaic of the history of cheese on our little green planet. With reference to the past, and detailed attention paid to the present, as well as extrospection for the future, Dr. Kindstedt has created an amalgamation of artisan cheese reference the like of which has not been attempted before."

—Matt Jennings, co-owner/executive chef, Farmstead/La Laiterie

"Only a true scholar could weave together the complexity of history, anthropology, language, geography, religion, and science to inform and enlighten our understanding of the evolution of cheese making throughout the millennia. Kindstedt, first and foremost with his discerning scientific mind, helps historians inform the heretofore mysteries in the cheese-making continuum."

—Catherine Donnelly, PhD, codirector, Vermont Institute for Artisan Cheese

CHEESE

and

CULTURE

CHEESE
and
CULTURE

A History of Cheese and Its
Place in Western Civilization

PAUL S. KINDSTEDT

CHELSEA GREEN PUBLISHING
WHITE RIVER JUNCTION, VERMONT

Scripture taken from the HOLY BIBLE, NEW INTERNATIONAL VERSION®, copyright © 1973, 1978, 1984 by the International Bible Society. Used by permission of Zondervan Publishing House. All rights reserved.

The "NIV" and "New International Version" trademarks are registered in the United States Patent and Trademark Office by the International Bible Society. Use of either trademark requires permission of the International Bible Society.

Cover painting by Clara Peeters (Flanders, Antwerp, circa 1594–after 1639/before 1657)
Still Life with Cheeses, Artichoke, and Cherries, circa 1625
Painting, oil on wood, 18 ⅜ × 13 ⅛ in. (46.67 × 33.34 cm)
Gift of Mr. and Mrs. Edward W. Carter (M.2003.108.8)
European Painting and Sculpture Department.
Los Angeles County Museum of Art, Los Angeles, U.S.A.
Digital Image © 2012 Museum Associates/LACMA. Licensed by Art Resource, NY

Project Manager: Patricia Stone
Editorial Contact: Ben Watson
Copy Editor: Laura Jorstad
Proofreader: Ellen Brownstein
Indexer: Lee Lawton
Designer: Peter Holm, Sterling Hill Productions

Printed in the United States of America
First printing March, 2012
10 9 8 7 6 5 4 3 2 1   12 13 14 15 16

Our Commitment to Green Publishing
Chelsea Green sees publishing as a tool for cultural change and ecological stewardship. We strive to align our book manufacturing practices with our editorial mission and to reduce the impact of our business enterprise in the environment. We print our books and catalogs on chlorine-free recycled paper, using vegetable-based inks whenever possible. This book may cost slightly more because it was printed on paper that contains recycled fiber, and we hope you'll agree that it's worth it. Chelsea Green is a member of the Green Press Initiative (www.greenpressinitiative.org), a nonprofit coalition of publishers, manufacturers, and authors working to protect the world's endangered forests and conserve natural resources. *Cheese and Culture* was printed on FSC®-certified paper supplied by Thomson-Shore that contains at least 30% postconsumer recycled fiber.

Library of Congress Cataloging-in-Publication Data
Kindstedt, Paul.
   Cheese and culture : a history of cheese and its place in western civilization / Paul Kindstedt.
     p. cm.
   ISBN 978-1-60358-411-1 (hardback) — ISBN 978-1-60358-412-8 (ebook)
    1. Cheese—History. 2. Cheese making—History. 3. Cooking (Cheese)—History. 4. Cheese industry—History.
5. Civilization, Western—History. I. Title.
SF270.4.K56 2012
637'.309--dc23
                                                      2011047819

Chelsea Green Publishing
85 North Main Street, Suite 120
White River Junction, VT 05001
(802) 295-6300
www.chelseagreen.com

To my parents,
Ed and Amy Kindstedt,
who fought the good fight and
remained faithful to the end.

CONTENTS

Preface | ix

Introduction | 1

1 | *Southwest Asia and the Ancient Origins of Cheese* | 3

2 | *Cheese, Religion, and the Cradle of Civilization* | 17

3 | *Bronze, Rennet, and the Ascendancy of Trade* | 40

4 | *Greece, Cheese, and the Mediterranean Miracle* | 63

5 | *Caesar, Christ, and Systematic Cheese Making* | 81

6 | *The Manor, the Monastery, and the*
Age of Cheese Diversification | 116

7 | *England, Holland, and the Rise of*
Market-Driven Cheese Making | 158

8 | *The Puritans, the Factory, and the*
Demise of Traditional Cheese Making | 185

9 | *The Cultural Legacy of Cheese*
Making in the Old and New Worlds | 212

Acknowledgments | 227

Bibliography | 229

Index | 245

Ten years ago I took a sabbatical leave to write a book that I hoped would become a useful resource for the new generation of artisan cheesemakers that had recently taken America by storm. Although the primary goal of *American Farmstead Cheese* was to distill the complex science of cheese making down to accessible, user-friendly principles for artisan cheesemakers, I also decided to include a couple of chapters on cheese history to provide context for the amazing rebirth of farmstead cheese making in America.

Four months into my sabbatical I found myself still working on the two history chapters and realized with growing alarm that I could easily spend the entire year working on chapters 1 and 2. The material was so captivating that I resolved then and there to eventually resume the historical research and develop an undergraduate course at the University of Vermont that would integrate cheese science and technology into the interpretation of cheese history. That course, Cheese and Culture, was first piloted in 2005. Student reaction was immediately positive, and I continued to teach and refine the course over the next couple of years, finalizing it as a permanent offering in 2008.

Around this same time, I found myself increasingly involved with far-reaching policy issues relating to cheese safety regulations (especially raw-milk cheese safety), intellectual property rights pertinent to traditional cheese names, and the role that public values should (or shouldn't) play in the shaping of our food system, regulations, and policies. Many of these issues were being played out at the international level under free-trade agreements, and I was particularly struck by the gulf that exists between US policies and those of the European Union on a whole range of food and agricultural issues. I also was struck by the different trajectories that cheese history has followed in United States as compared with the EU. It seemed that cheese history could provide useful insight into the origins of some of the great international policy disputes that have arisen over cheese and food more broadly. This, too, became an element of Cheese and Culture.

Thus, my course Cheese and Culture has been the inspiration for this book from the start, but the book also has taken on a life of its own. As the research unfolded I found it necessary to continually widen my circle of interest beyond the fragments of available information about cheese in a particular time and place to the larger happenings of the world that surrounded the cheesemaker. This intersection of cheese history with the larger story of world civilization and especially western civilization cuts both ways. Cheesemakers and their cheeses were often profoundly influenced by the great events and stages of western civilization; cheesemakers and their cheeses, in turn, influenced the unfolding of western civilization, at times in significant ways. This book, therefore, is as much about the place of cheese in western civilization as it is about cheese history per se.

As a cheese scientist I admit that I have been stretched by this book project; various lines of inquiry have led down many avenues of scholarship that are far afield of my specialization and expertise. My goal has been to access the best scholarship available and follow wherever it leads. I take sole responsibility in the event that I have inadvertently misinterpreted the excellent work of the many scholars whom I reference. As I wrestled to make sense of various fragments of potentially useful information I often pondered what it would be like to work with a team of historians, archaeologists, anthropologists, geneticists, climatologists, linguists, classics specialists, and other scholars with complementary expertise. My great hope, perhaps naive, is that this book will stimulate scholars in diverse fields to join ranks as interdisciplinary teams dedicated to reconstructing and interpreting cheese history. There is still much work to be done—and what fun we could have!

INTRODUCTION

W e who live in the twenty-first century cannot fully appreciate the
spectacular array of cheeses that have been handed down to us
without delving into the distant past and exploring the historical contexts
within which various groups of cheesemakers developed their unique products. There is a story behind every traditional cheese, and by examining the
world of the cheesemaker and applying a few simple principles of cheese
science and technology it is often possible to begin to understand why
cheesemakers responded to the world around them in the ways they did,
and why their cheeses took on their peculiar characteristics, shaped by and
tailored to the surrounding environment of the time. Therefore, the first
objective of this book is to integrate cheese science and technology into the
interpretation of cheese history in order to better understand the environmental cues that inspired cheesemakers to develop their diverse cheeses.

There is also a larger story, a grand narrative that binds all cheeses together
into a single history, that started with the discovery of cheese making, and
that is still unfolding. This book endeavors to tell that nine-thousand-year
story while acknowledging that to do so is like putting together an enormous jigsaw puzzle from which half the pieces are missing. Many wonderful cheeses and cheese-making regions have been left out of this work, not
because they lack importance but because the archaeological, historical,
anthropological, and other research that is needed to adequately reconstruct their cheese-making past has yet to be conducted and published or is
not readily accessible.

Nevertheless, we are about to embark on a journey that begins at the
awakening of humankind as a species unlike any the earth had witnessed
before and then winds its way through the ensuing centuries to the present.
In the process we shall pass through some of the pivotal periods in human
prehistory and ancient, classical, medieval, Renaissance, and modern
history that have shaped western civilization, for these periods also shaped

the lives of cheesemakers and the diverse cheeses they developed. Thus, the second objective of this book is to examine the many points of intersection between cheese history and the larger story of western civilization.

The traditional cheeses that took shape in various locations over the centuries, along with other traditional foods that arose alongside them, shaped the surrounding culture. Thus, in regions of the world that share long histories of cheese making, especially southern and central Europe, one finds the deep cultural imprints of these cheeses and other traditional foods embedded in the human landscape to this day. This stands in striking contrast with the United States, where cheese history spans fewer centuries and where the American experience with cheese in particular, and food and agriculture in general, has differed vastly from the European. The chasm in food culture that has arisen out of our different histories has become a source of perpetual friction between the United States and European Union since 1994 when the creation of the World Trade Organization (WTO) under the General Agreement on Tariffs and Trade (GATT) ushered in the current global trading system.

Contentious issues involving intellectual property rights (such as the right to use or protect traditional product names), food-safety regulations (such as those governing the use of unpasteurized milk in cheese making), and policies governing new agricultural and food-processing technologies—including genetically modified organisms (GMOs), hormone use in milk and meat production, and perhaps, in the near future, animal cloning—have repeatedly pitted the United States and European Union against one another in trade negotiations and WTO litigation, with no end in sight. Why do American industry leaders and trade negotiators and their European counterparts view the food system so differently, and how did we get to this state of intense disagreement? The final objective of this book is to use cheese history as a lens through which to consider the divergent paths of food culture in America and Europe that have led to the sharply contrasting food systems of our time.

CHAPTER ONE

Southwest Asia and the Ancient Origins of Cheese

Adam lay with his wife Eve, and she became pregnant and gave birth to Cain. She said, "With the help of the Lord I have brought forth a man." Later she gave birth to his brother Abel. Now Abel kept flocks, and Cain worked the soil.

Genesis 4:1–2

In the biblical account of human origins, the story of Cain and Abel includes the intriguing though often overlooked detail that Abel kept flocks while Cain worked the soil. Thus, Genesis links the emergence of humankind as a species different from all others (made in the image of God) with the mastery of crop cultivation and animal husbandry, and the occurrence of an environment that was favorable to agricultural pursuits. It turns out that the Genesis account is not as far-fetched as some might suppose. Agriculture first arose in southwest Asia about eleven thousand years ago, at around the same time and in the same geographic neighborhood where Genesis places Cain and Abel, and the beginnings of agriculture did indeed coincide with changes among human populations that were truly extraordinary and placed humans along a pathway that is unique among species (Cauvin 2000). The origins of cheese making stretch back almost to the beginnings of agriculture. Therefore, we will begin our journey at this amazing period in the story of humanity, which provides the context for the ancient origins of cheese making and all that would follow.

Paleolithic Beginnings

The emergence of anatomically modern humans as a distinct species known as *Homo sapiens* has been estimated through genetic analyses to have occurred around two hundred thousand years ago from a small "founding population" that lived in Africa (Bogucki 1999). These peoples survived by hunting wild game, fishing, and gathering wild plants; they were perpetually on the move in search of food following seasonal patterns of migration. They lived in loosely defined communal groups or bands, within which the sharing of food and resources was apparently universal and institutionalized as an enforced sharing ethic that prevented individuals or small groups within the band from accumulating resources (Bogucki 1999). They left limited evidence of their activities because their primitive, transient way of life produced little to contribute to the archaeological record of the period. This was Paleolithic man (*paleo* meaning old, ancient; *lithic* pertaining to the use of stone implements) of the Old Stone Age. For almost two hundred thousand years Paleolithic man showed only faint glimmers of the human potential for creativity and innovation, intellectual achievement, social complexity, artistic acuity, and spiritual awareness that we now take for granted.

Prior to about eleven thousand years ago the earth's climate was dramatically different from the stable and hospitable climate that has largely prevailed since. During the last ice age, which commenced around thirty-five thousand years ago and peaked around 18,000 BC, glacial sheets of ice covered a significant swath of the Northern Hemisphere, and the earth in general was much colder and drier than today—far too cold and dry to support agriculture. This was followed by a time of wildly fluctuating global temperatures that included some warmer and wetter periods as the glaciers retreated, but overall the earth remained colder and drier than the present. The unstable climatic conditions continued until about 9500 BC, throughout which the earth's climate remained either too cold and dry, or too subject to extreme variations to sustain human agricultural innovations (Bellwood 2005; Barker 2006).

Beginning around seventeen thousand years ago, however, the onset of post-glacial global warming began to intermittently establish a characteristic weather pattern in the Mediterranean region of hot dry summers and cool wet winters that would ultimately prevail and become the stable climate that we know today. Wild cereals such as wheat, rye, and barley, along with legumes like beans, peas, and lentils, became genetically adapted to thrive in this "Mediterranean" climate. Eventually extensive stands of wild cereals were established in an elongated swath extending from the Jordan River Valley northward through inland Syria into what is now southeastern Turkey.

Around 12,000 BC populations of hunter-gatherers established seasonal (and in some cases continuously occupied) settlements in this region to take advantage of the natural harvests of wild cereals, legumes, and fruits (Bellwood 2005). These people, the Natufians, became increasingly dependent on harvesting wild plant foods. In the process they developed a more sedentary lifestyle and experienced a rudimentary blossoming of artistry. They also underwent a transformation in culture suggesting that the family replaced the communal band as the basic residential and social unit for the first time (Barker 2006; Cauvin 2000). This may not seem like a major step in the human story, but in the context of Paleolithic man it represented a startling cultural development. Thus, the term Mesolithic (*meso* meaning middle) is used to distinguish these peoples from their Paleolithic forebears and the Neolithic peoples (*neo* meaning new) who would soon follow. Between 11,000 and 9500 BC, however, the earth plunged into one last cycle of extreme cooling, and the Natufians all but disappeared (Barker 2006).

The Neolithic Revolution

Then around 9500 BC an extraordinarily rapid and intense episode of global warming occurred, during which the average annual temperature increased by as much as 13°F (7°C) within a couple of generations. This was followed by slow but steady warming over the next two millennia, culminating about ten thousand years ago in climatic conditions that were similar to those that we enjoy today. Even more remarkable was the high degree of climatic stability that followed this period of warming, resulting in the establishment of the warmer, wetter global conditions that have persisted for the past ten thousand years, interrupted periodically by only very small (though, as we shall see, very influential) temperature oscillations. This new temperate environment with predictable weather patterns and seasonality was exceptionally human-friendly, for it opened the door to cultivation and domestication of food crops and became the ultimate enabler of agriculture. It also coincided with a stunning new phase in human development, Neolithic man (Bellwood 2005).

Cultivation refers to the deliberate gathering and storing of seeds from the previous harvest, sowing of the seeds in anticipation of the next growing season, and caring for the crops until harvested. *Domestication* is the intentional selection and planting of specific genetic strains of crops that possess desirable characteristics, or the breeding of specific genetic strains of animals in the case of livestock. Mastery of cultivation and domestication were pivotal in human development because they opened the door to the earth's productive capacity for both plant and animal foodstuffs. The advent of comparatively abundant and secure food supplies in turn afforded humankind a new freedom and luxury to live and behave differently, for better or for worse. To use biblical imagery, Cain and Abel had no idea of the vast power that lay within their mastery of crop cultivation and animal husbandry.

The archaeological record contains clear evidence of domesticated plants in the Fertile Crescent beginning around 9000 to 8500 BC (Barker 2006; Lev-Yadun et al. 2000; Simmons 2007). *Fertile Crescent* refers to the comparatively well-watered swath of land that runs from the Jordan River Valley of the southern Levant northward through inland Lebanon and Syria to the southeastern corner of the Anatolian peninsula (modern Turkey) and northern Iraq, then arching southeast along the foothills of the Zagros Mountains in western Iran, parallel to the alluvial plains of the Euphrates and Tigris Rivers (figure 1-1).

Cultivation of field crops by sedentary Neolithic villagers in the Fertile Crescent likely attracted goats and sheep, especially near mountainous regions that serve as their natural habitat. The gregarious nature of goats and sheep and their frequent presence around the new agricultural communities presented the inhabitants with a novel opportunity to secure a stable supply of meat and animal products such as skin and fiber. Goats in

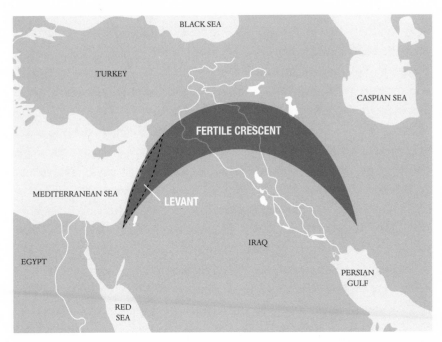

Figure 1-1. Agriculture and the Neolithic Revolution first began around 9000 BC in the Fertile Crescent of southwest Asia. Neolithic development was especially intense in the Levant, located along the western arch of the Fertile Crescent (indicated by the dashed lines).

particular were uniquely suited by temperament for domestication because they were accustomed to living in the confined spaces of mountain caves. Thus, it is not surprising that the first herding and domestication of goats and then sheep occurred in the foothills of the Taurus Mountains of southwest Anatolia and the Zagros Mountains of western Iran around 8500 BC, very soon after the beginning of crop cultivation and domestication (Barker 2006; Hole 1989, 1996).

The first evidence for cattle domestication occurred somewhat later in central Anatolia (modern Turkey), around 7000 BC (Cauvin 2000), by which time a mixed farming model based on crop cultivation and ovocaprine (sheep and goat) husbandry had become widespread throughout the Levant and beyond, to the islands of Cyprus and Crete to the west, northern Iraq and Iran to the east, and the Anatolian peninsula to the north. By 7000 BC the entire region also had experienced dramatic population growth, triggered by the growing abundance of food and the adoption of sedentary lifestyles that decreased birth spacing and infant and elderly mortality (Bellwood 2005).

The development of mixed farming and the rapid growth in population between 9500 and 7000 BC also brought profound cultural changes that marked a turning point in human prehistory: the blossoming of the Neolithic or New Stone Age (Bellwood 2005). Settlements became much larger and permanently occupied. Architectural innovation gave rise to the classic multi-roomed, rectilinear structural forms that have dominated Old World domestic architecture ever since. The use of crude unpolished stone implements gave way to a more sophisticated array of fully polished stone tools. Perhaps most important was the blossoming of artistic expression and the onset of a newfound spiritual awareness, as evidenced by the sudden widespread appearance of religious symbols, such as clay figurines of deities, and the construction of shrine-like buildings (Cauvin 2000; Banning 2003). These changes unequivocally differentiated the species *Homo sapiens* from all others; humans had moved beyond the status of a slightly revised and more efficient version of the biological eating and breeding machines that had preceded them. To use biblical language, humans were made "in the image of God."

Cultivation and domestication, the construction of permanent homes and settlements, and the relentless advancement in technology that commenced with the Neolithic represented a fundamental change in humanity's relationship to nature. Now humans were beginning to exercise new and significant control over nature rather than simply responding to the natural world, as had been the case up to this point. The onset of spirituality had even greater implications, for now humans possessed a unique perception of their place in the world and, with it, a unique potential to alter the world. This blossoming spiritual dimension of humanity also had profound implications for dairying and cheese making; cheese would soon become an important component of early religious expression and cultic practices. Indeed, the spiritual thread of western civilization and cheese history would intersect often and remain intertwined right down to the present.

Dairying and the Birth of Cheese Making

Shortly after 7000 BC two prerequisites for cheese making that had hitherto been lacking—namely, the availability of surplus milk, and also of suitable containers to collect, store, and coagulate the milk, then separate the resulting curd from the liquid whey—suddenly fell into place. Although widespread domestication of sheep and goats had occurred throughout the Fertile Crescent by 7000 BC, the age and gender distribution of bone specimens indicate that up to that point the animals were raised for meat, not for milk production (Barker 2006). It must have taken generations of selective breeding to genetically transform the wild strains of sheep and goats, which had little capacity to produce milk beyond what was needed for their newborns, into dedicated milk-producing stock. It was also necessary for herders to learn how to persuade the animals to let down their milk to a human milker (Sherratt 1981).

The first definitive evidence for substantial shifts from meat to milk production occurred around 6500 BC in western Anatolia, as indicated by shifts in the bone distributions of domesticated animals, and more definitively by the presence of milkfat residues in pottery shards (Evershed et al. 2008). By this time population growth throughout the entire Levant had reached a tipping point, and widespread environmental degradation due to soil depletion, deforestation, and erosion was threatening the survival of Levantine communities. The move toward pastoralism (that is, primary reliance on livestock grazing) and milk production was probably a response to these troubled times (Bellwood 2005).

Pastoralism enabled peoples who were threatened by crop failures and hunger to take advantage of surrounding unused marginal land that was unsuitable for crop cultivation but could support sheep and goat grazing (Zarins 1990). This in turn encouraged the movement of pastoral populations in search of new land, which soon erupted into mass migrations that led to the settlement of northwest Anatolia around this time. There, along the fertile shores of the Sea of Marmara, the settlers shifted their pastoral emphasis from small ruminants to cattle, and the production of cow's milk commenced probably for the first time (Evershed et al. 2008).

Neolithic man's first efforts at harvesting milk were probably targeted toward the feeding of infants and young children, for whom milk was an invaluable food, rather than toward the adult population. Why? Because milk contains a high concentration of lactose or milk sugar, the digestion of which requires the production of the enzyme lactase in the gut. All mammals including humans naturally produce lactase at birth, which enables the newborns to digest their mothers' milk. However, lactase production normally declines in mammals after weaning and does not persist into adulthood. Therefore, when adult humans consume milk, the lactose remains undigested and disrupts the gut microflora, triggering a number of noteworthy side effects such as explosive diarrhea, flatulence, and bloating.

Today, of course, many adults, especially those of northern European descent, remain lactose-tolerant into adulthood because their ancestors eventually acquired the genetic capacity to produce lactase (and thus digest lactose) into adulthood. Recent genetic research strongly suggests that adult lactase persistence did not become widespread in human populations until around 5500 BC, and that the genetic capability was first developed among Neolithic peoples in the northern Balkan peninsula and central Europe who had migrated from southwest Asia (Itan et al. 2009). Thus, when milk began to be harvested in Anatolia between 7000 and 6500 BC, adult lactose intolerance was probably near universal within the human population, and its effects likely presented a strong disincentive to adult milk drinking.

Almost immediately after dairying commenced in southwest Asia, however, technologies for making cheese and butter were discovered that rendered the nutritional value of milk accessible to adult populations. Pivotal to the development of cheese making was the period of around 7000 to 6500 BC, when the discovery of pyrotechnology (the application of high temperature to materials) ushered in the Neolithic era of ceramics and pottery. The development of pottery was an enormous step forward from the standpoint of food storage, processing, transport, and culinary capability in general.

The arrival of pottery and the concurrent shift toward dairying meant that surplus milk could now be collected and stored in ceramic pots. In the warm climate of southwest Asia, stored milk would have fermented quickly and coagulated spontaneously due to the production of lactic acid by bacteria that are always naturally present in milk environments. The fragility of the coagulated milk and its tendency separate into solid curds and liquid whey when stirred would have become quickly evident, and it was only a matter of time before Neolithic pastoralists discovered that adults were able to consume the curds in modest amounts without developing the symptoms that they experienced when they drank milk. The reason behind this is that much of the lactose in milk is either fermented to lactic acid or removed with the whey when milk spontaneously coagulates and the whey is drained from the curds. Therefore, the concentration of lactose in the resulting cheese is much lower than it is in fluid milk, rendering the cheese more digestible for adults who are lactase-deficient.

Once this was recognized, the Neolithic pastoralists had a strong incentive to develop an efficient means to separate the curds from whey, and their newly acquired expertise in pottery afforded an innovative solution in the form of perforated ceramic containers that served as sieves, the remnants of which are abundantly evident in archaeological strata (Banning 1998; Bogucki 1984; Ellison 1984). Pottery sieves were probably also used for a variety of other purposes; scholars have speculated that they might have served as braziers, honey strainers, strainers used in beer making, and even pyrotechnic devices akin to the Bunsen burner (Banning 1998; Bogucki 1984, 1988; Wood 2007). However, the very strong association between the appearance of perforated sieves in the archaeological record and the arrival of dairying in the Near East and then Europe, along with the strong ethnographic record of the continued use of ceramic sieves in cheese making into the modern era, almost certainly mean that the major use for such sieves from the beginning was in cheese making. Indeed, as recently as the early twentieth century ceramic sieves were still being used in the traditional making of acid-coagulated cheeses in central Europe (Bogucki 1984).

Woven baskets also may have been used to separate curds from whey, though not surprisingly there is little supporting evidence because these materials are fragile and far less likely than ceramic pottery to survive in the archaeological record.

The joint availability of surplus milk, pottery, and perhaps basket weaving, therefore, opened the door to acid-coagulated cheese making on a regular basis. The enormous value of milk processing and the competitive advantages that it offered must have been recognized very quickly because cheese making (and butter making) became common throughout the Fertile Crescent shortly after the beginning of dairying. Analyses of organic residues (specifically lipids) on pottery shards recovered from the archaeological strata corresponding to around 6500 to 6000 BC have confirmed that pots from this period were widely used to store dairy products. Furthermore, the nature of the residues indicates that the pots contained processed dairy products, probably cheese and butter or ghee (butter oil), rather than unprocessed raw milk (Evershed et al. 2008).

What were the first Neolithic cheeses like? We'll never know for certain, but it seems likely that they were soft, acid-coagulated types similar to traditional varieties that are still produced in the Near East today, such as Çökelek cheese (Kamber 2008a). In addition, early Neolithic cheesemakers probably stumbled on coagulation caused by the combined action of acid and heat, which is the principle behind ricotta-type cheeses. The advent of pottery had made it possible to heat liquids over an open fire, which inspired new techniques in cooking and probably led to much experimentation with the heating of various foodstuffs, as evidenced by the presence of soot and pyrolytically formed organic residues (that is, organic residues formed through extensive heating) in pottery (Evershed et al. 2008; Barker 2006). Attempts at heating partly soured milk, or whey that remained after cheese making, eventually would have produced the right combination of acidity and temperature to cause the coagulation of milk proteins, hence the discovery of acid/heat-coagulated cheeses, which to this day are widely produced in the Near East (Kamber 2008a).

Acid-coagulated and acid/heat-coagulated cheeses are very high in moisture content and therefore spoil rapidly due to uncontrolled microbial degradation, especially in the hot climate of southwest Asia. Therefore, these early cheeses were probably consumed fresh, as is often still the case in the Near East. However, even these very perishable cheeses can be preserved for extended periods if they are salted, packed tightly in airtight packaging, and shielded from high temperatures. In Turkey, for example, traditional acid-coagulated and acid/heat-coagulated cheeses, such as Çökelek and Lor, are still sealed in airtight ceramic pots that are buried in the ground to preserve and ripen the cheese and shield the contents from the searing heat (Kamber 2008a). Thus, it is possible that cheese residues found on pottery sherds dating to 6500 BC were acid-coagulated or acid/heat-coagulated types that had been packed, then as now, into sealed pots to store and preserve. Bags made from animal skins also may have been used to store and ripen soft cheeses, as is still practiced traditionally in Turkey today (Kamber 2008a), but the archaeological record is silent concerning whether this more perishable form of packaging was used at this early stage. Still another preservation alternative for fresh curd was drying in the sun—also still widely practiced today in the Near East—which results in a highly stable, very hard dried cheese that is well suited for grating into soups. Small ceramic sieves that contain very rough interior surfaces, found somewhat later in the archaeological strata, may have served as cheese graters that were used for this purpose (Ellison 1984).

What about rennet-coagulated cheese making? Did Neolithic cheesemakers also experiment with this more complex form of cheese? We'll never know for certain, but it seems possible that the technology for coagulating milk using animal rennet (the tissue material derived from the stomachs of kids, lambs, or calves, or a brine extract thereof) may have been appreciated fairly soon after the harvesting of milk commenced. Specifically, it would have been obvious to Neolithic herders that the stomachs of kids, lambs, and calves that died naturally or were slaughtered while still suckling were filled with coagulated milk. Thus, there was ample opportunity for the association between the stomach, milk coagulation, and cheese curd to take root. The first experiments with rennet coagulation may have involved the addition of clotted milk gathered from the suckling's stomach to fresh milk, a practice that dates back to antiquity and continued up until at least the eighteenth century in England and America. At some point the actual stomach material was added to milk, which delivered a much more concentrated source of coagulating enzymes and thus improved coagulation. Once the coagulating value of the stomach was recognized, efforts to preserve stomachs for future use by salting likely followed, leading to the development of a reliable and steady supply of rennet.

Another possibility for the discovery of rennet coagulation is the often-cited myth of the nomadic traveler who filled his canteen, consisting of a bag made from the stomach of a goat or sheep (or other mammal), with fresh milk at the beginning of his journey, only to find that the milk had coagulated when he stopped to take a drink. This scenario seems less likely, however, because it presupposes that the milk-drinking adult nomad was lactose-tolerant. As noted earlier, the development of lactase persistence among adult populations likely did not occur for at least a thousand years after Neolithic humans began to harvest milk and produce cheese and butter. Thus, there is growing scholarly consensus that cheese and butter making long preceded the development of adult consumption of milk and, indeed, enabled dairying to spread much more rapidly than otherwise would have been possible given the barrier posed by adult lactose intolerance (Evershed et al. 2008).

In other words, it was cheese and butter making that enabled dairying to gain a foothold among Neolithic populations and allowed the genetic selection for adult lactase persistence to take place eventually. Bottom line: It seems unlikely that our mythical nomadic traveler would have been drinking milk on his trip unless cheese and butter making had been already well established for a thousand years, in which case there would have been ample time for rennet coagulation to have been discovered already. Of course, if our mythical nomad had been carrying milk in the stomach bag for his young child, that's a different story. But this is all very speculative, and definitive historical evidence for rennet coagulation would not occur until much later.

In summary, the discovery of cheese making during the seventh millennium BC was a huge step forward for Neolithic man because it transformed the extraordinary nutritional value of the milk into a vital food that was suited for both young and old, and that could be stored for later use. All of this was taking place at a time when the agricultural system of the Fertile Crescent was failing catastrophically due to rising populations and environmental degradation. The value of cheese making was not lost on these peoples, and they would carry this knowledge with them and continue the craft of cheese making wherever they journeyed and settled during the many centuries to come.

The Neolithic Expansion

About the time that pottery took off and pastoralism and milk produc-tion began to assume importance in the Near East economy, the stresses caused by rising population and environmental degradation prompted mass movements of peoples from their Fertile Crescent homelands in all directions (figure 1-2). Migrations to the southeast led to the settlement of the Mesopotamian lowlands along the southern reaches of the Tigris and Euphrates Rivers by the Ubaid people. By 6000 BC the Ubaid had created a new culture based on irrigation farming, laying the foundation for the great Mesopotamian civilizations that would soon follow. Migrations to the southwest through the Sinai Peninsula reached Egypt about 5000 BC, where another new civilization, also based on irrigation farming, would arise along the Nile River. To the east, population migration moved progressively through Iran, Afghanistan, and Pakistan, reaching the Indus River Valley

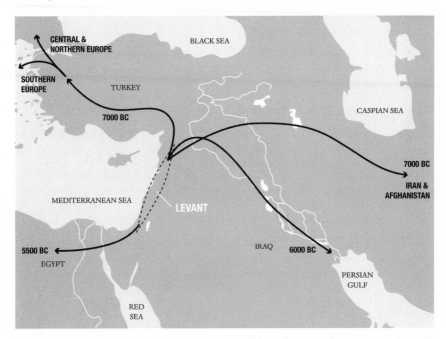

Figure 1-2. Rising population and environmental degradation in the Levant and Fertile Crescent eventually prompted mass movements of Neolithic peoples in all directions. Wherever they migrated they brought a mixed agricultural way of life that included dairying and cheese making.

that forms the boundary between Pakistan and India by around 6500 BC. There the great Harappan civilization would flourish eventually. Cheese making would become an important component of the Mesopotamian and Egyptian civilizations, and perhaps also the Harappan.

And finally, migration to the north and west would follow two separate routes. One route proceeded by land through Turkey into Thrace and the Balkan peninsula, then northward along the Danube and Rhine Rivers, reaching the North Sea and England by around 4500 BC. The second route proceeded westward by sea from the Levantine coast through the northern Mediterranean coasts of Greece, Italy, France, and Spain. Analyses of animal bone distributions and pottery shards confirmed that wherever these Neolithic farmers migrated, they brought with them a characteristic Near East culture based on mixed farming that included milk production and butter and cheese making (Copley et al. 2003, 2005a, b; Craig et al. 2005; Evershed 2005; Evershed et al. 2008; Spangenberg et al. 2006).

By around 4500 BC Neolithic Near East culture dominated the Mediterranean basin, most of Europe, and the Middle East, extending all the way to the gateway of India. Even more important from the standpoint of cheese history, wherever these peoples migrated cheese making followed, and humanity was now one step closer to the development of a dizzying array of diverse cheeses.

CHAPTER TWO

Cheese, Religion, and the Cradle of Civilization

The Lord appeared to Abraham near the great trees of Mamre while he was sitting at the entrance to his tent in the heat of the day . . . So Abraham hurried into the tent to Sarah. "Quick," he said, "get three seahs of fine flour and knead it and bake some bread." Then he ran to the herd and selected a choice, tender calf and gave it to a servant who hurried to prepare it. He then brought some curds and milk and the calf that had been prepared and set these before them. While they ate, he stood near them under a tree.

Genesis 18:1, 6–8

According to the biblical account in Genesis, it was out of the southern Mesopotamian city of Ur that Abraham, a pastoral nomad who became the patriarch of the three great monotheistic religions of Judaism, Christianity, and Islam, was called by God to migrate to the Promised Land in the southern Levant around the start of the second millennium BC. Mesopotamia, comprising the alluvial floodplains formed by the Tigris and Euphrates Rivers as they flow through Syria and Iraq to the Persian Gulf, is considered the "cradle of civilization," and the great city of Ur stood at the center of Mesopotamian civilization during the third millennium BC (Chavalas 2005). At its peak, Ur's population was estimated to range as high as sixty-five thousand, probably making it the world's largest city of the time. Ur was also a center for cheese and butter making according to detailed accounts compiled by temple scribes on clay cuneiform tablets.

After leaving Ur, Abraham eventually settled in Hebron near the west bank of the Jordan River in the land of Canaan. It was here that the eighteenth chapter of Genesis described a frantic Abraham when he suddenly realized that three newly arrived visitors were in fact the Lord God and two angels. How could he extend an appropriate level of honor and hospitality to such esteemed guests? Keeping his cool under pressure, Abraham hastily arranged a fitting reception that included freshly baked bread, tender veal, curds (or fresh cheese), and milk. The account is intriguing on the one hand because it implies that adult lactose tolerance by this time had become widespread in Abraham's homeland of Mesopotamia, and that milk had risen to the status of a revered beverage. Consistent with this, archaeological findings from southern Mesopotamia indicate that cow's, goat's, and sheep's milk were all consumed as beverages, primarily by the pastoral nomadic members of Mesopotamian society but also by the royal elite (Bottéro 2004; Limet 1987).

Even more interesting from the standpoint of cheese history is the observation that Abraham saw fit to include curds, or fresh cheese, in this banquet given in honor of the Lord. This was by no means the first recorded occasion on which cheese was offered up in an act of worship. By this time, cheese had been an integral element of religious practice in Abraham's Mesopotamian homeland for more than a thousand years. Indeed, institutionalized cultic rites that included daily offerings of cheese and butter were commonplace in temples throughout Mesopotamia during the third millennium BC. The system of religious ideology that spawned these rites played a central role in the creation of humankind's first civilization, which in turn influenced nearly every civilization to follow in the Near East and eventually even Greece and Rome (Kramer 1969). Amazingly, cheese was there at the beginning as an integral element of the religious mythology and cultic expression that helped to initiate a domino-like progression of great civilizations that ultimately shaped western culture.

But now we're getting ahead of ourselves. Chapter 1 ended during the waning years of the Neolithic Age around 6000 BC, by which time overpopulation and widespread environmental degradation had prompted a surge in pastoralism and great migrations of Levantine peoples in all directions. We now return to that story, for out of those troubled times would emerge the world's first civilizations—and yes, cheese would play a role in this saga.

The Rise of Mesopotamia

By the sixth millennium BC, the southward migration of Neolithic peoples along the Tigris and Euphrates had resulted in the settlement of two societies, the Halaf to the north and the Ubaid to the south (Bogucki 1999). In the highlands to the north there was sufficient rainfall to support agriculture without having to resort to irrigation, and the Halaf founded a network of small farming communities, much as their ancestors had throughout the Neolithic. To the south however, in what is now southern Iraq, Ubaid communities were completely dependent on small systems of irrigation that tapped into the life-giving waters of the Euphrates River, enabling them to grow crops in otherwise desert-like conditions.

For more than fifteen hundred years Ubaid villages grew but slowly and remained small rural communities, yet out of those humble beginnings there arose around the start of the fourth millennium BC a startling new development in the human story that has been termed the "urban revolution" (Chavalas 2005). This was the beginning of Sumerian civilization, the world's first, which was marked by the abrupt arrival of large complex cities that functioned as independent city-states. These new city-states, among which Uruk was preeminent, were built upon sophisticated and highly centralized systems of governance and administration that created a new order of socioeconomic stratification, along with impressive technological and architectural advances, a revolution in shared religious ideology and communal worship, and a stunning new form of communication: writing.

Sumerian civilization in its various periods would last for nearly two thousand years and would continue to influence subsequent Mesopotamian civilizations (early Babylonian, Assyrian, late Babylonian) as well as Egyptian, Hittite, and ultimately Greek and Roman civilizations (Kramer 1963b, 1969). Why this quantum leap in human society happened first in the inhospitable environment of southern Iraq, ahead of anywhere else in the world, remains "one of the most fascinating unsolved riddles of antiquity" (Foster and Foster 2009). Nevertheless, recent archaeological and anthropological findings have brought this critical period into scholarly focus, and an intriguing story has emerged that directly intersects with our journey through cheese history.

The urban revolution that accompanied the rise of Sumerian civiliza-tion was itself a product of another revolution, which has been termed the "secondary products revolution" (Sherratt 1983, 1981). This was a period, beginning probably in the fifth and culminating during the fourth millen-nium BC, when innovative new uses for domestic animals for traction and transport, as well as for intensive wool and milk production, were developed and put into widespread practice, first in Mesopotamia and then spread-ing rapidly throughout the Near East and eventually Europe. A critical component of the secondary products revolution was the invention of the plow. Cattle thrived in the marshy delta region of southern Mesopotamia where the Tigris and Euphrates Rivers empty into the Persian Gulf, and the Ubaid peoples there were apparently the first to harness the powerful traction capacity of the ox via the invention of the plow. The use of the plow in combination with intensive irrigation enabled the Ubaid to greatly increase their cultivation of fertile alluvial lands along the banks of the Euphrates, far beyond what had been previously possible using only the hoe. Consequently, the banks of the Euphrates became intensively culti-vated and very productive, which enabled the Ubaid to thrive for more than a millennium and even produce agricultural surpluses, as evidenced by the widespread construction of communal agricultural storage facilities.

As the amount of land under Ubaid cultivation increased during the fifth millennium BC, the stubble that remained in the fields after the harvest, along with fallow fields that were withheld from cultivation periodically to replenish their fertility, offered excellent grazing for sheep and goats, which in turn provided a rich source of fertilizer for the fields in the form of manure. Sheep and goat herding had long been practiced nomadically in the marginal lands on the fringes of the Mesopotamian floodplain (Zarins 1990), and especially in the well-watered valleys of the Zagros Mountains to the east (Flannery 1965). During the fifth millennium BC, goat and especially sheep herding began to concentrate heavily along the alluvial plains of the Euphrates River under Ubaid cultivation. This in turn created a heightened need for alternative grazing lands for the livestock during the growing season when the cultivated fields were off-limits. The nomadic herders responded by developing a system of *transhumance* (the seasonal movement of livestock) that involved the movement of animals to distant grazing sites scattered throughout the surrounding wastelands and the Zagros Mountains, and their return to the alluvial plains after the harvest (Flannery 1965; Pollock 1999). Transhumance enabled sheep pastoralism to flourish, and this in turn encouraged a new, more intense emphasis on wool production and textiles manufacture, and on milk production and its preservation in the form of cheese and butter or ghee (Sherratt 1981, 1983). Ghee is a purified butter oil with improved keeping qualities, produced by melting butter and removing the water and protein fractions. This was perhaps the first instance of cheese making becoming integrally linked to systematic transhumance, a model that would be repeated often throughout the history of cheese making.

Another striking development of Ubaid culture was the appearance of the village temple, a community building that served as the focal point of shared religious ideology. Religious practice in the Neolithic Near East, though ubiquitous, had hitherto been confined primarily to the family or household shrine. At the Ubaid city of Eridu, a total of eighteen temples were built successively on the same site over a fifteen-hundred-year period beginning around 5000 BC (Dickin 2007). Over time the temples became progressively larger and more elaborate, and by the end of the fifth millennium BC the local temple had taken on a significant economic function by providing communal storage facilities and administrative oversight for the growing surpluses of grain and, eventually, wool textiles that were accruing as the plow and intensive irrigation opened up new land for cultivation and grazing. Wool textiles, in turn, provided Ubaid communities with a precious resource that could be traded with distant communities for raw materials and goods they lacked, such as timber and stone for building projects, and precious stones including obsidian, a glassy volcanic crystal that was highly prized for its use in ornaments and for its ability to maintain sharp cutting surfaces on implements. Hammered and cast copper, the development of which occurred in Anatolia during the sixth millennium BC, was also increasingly sought after for its use in a range of implements. During this same period the wheeled cart coupled to domestic animals such as oxen and donkeys made its debut in southern Mesopotamia, as did the use of domestic animals (donkey, horse) for riding and pack transport (Sherratt 1983). This newfound capacity to transport goods and people encouraged the expansion of Ubaid trading networks.

Thus, by the fourth millennium BC the conjunction of expanding Ubaid populations that employed irrigation and plow agriculture to produce growing surpluses of crops and wool, their newfound capacity to engage in long-distance trade using animal transport, and the flowering of the community temple and shared religious ideology set the stage for a new chapter in the human story that was about to occur in the great city of Uruk. The Uruk period was characterized by a massive increase in the number of settlements on the alluvium of southern Mesopotamia, followed by a demographic implosion as the countryside became relatively depopulated and tens of thousand of people were gathered into Uruk and a handful of other towns that would become major cities (Bogucki 1999; Yoffee 1995). These towns apparently drew in large segments of the population that had been living in the countryside, such that by the second half of the fourth millennium BC five great cities had arisen—Uruk, Eridu, Ur, Nippur, and Kish—of which Uruk was by far the largest. These were mankind's first true cities, indeed city-states, which heralded the birth of Sumerian civilization.

In stark contrast with Ubaid villages—which had remained small in size (under 2.47 acres, or 1ha) for more than a millennium—Uruk grew rapidly into a massive walled city of about 620 acres (250ha) with a population of up to forty thousand (McMahon 2005). The skyline was dominated by two large temple complexes, one dedicated to An, the sky god, and the other to Inanna, the lady of heaven, that towered over the surrounding landscape and could be seen for miles across the flat plains (Foster and Foster 2009). Uruk had a sophisticated economy, centralized rule and administration, and a stratified social structure all dominated by the secular ruling elite working in close partnership with the temple hierarchy. The power of the ruling elite extended not only throughout the city itself but also to the surrounding countryside, from which heavy tribute was exacted in the form of agricultural produce. Just how the ruling elite and temple priests were able to acquire such far-reaching control over such large populations, both urban and rural, quickly enough to account for the extraordinary growth in the size and sophistication of Uruk is still debated by scholars. However, it is widely accepted that shared religious ideology and monumental temple architecture were important elements that the ruling elite used to win over the hearts and minds of the people and unify them under the control of the city-state (Liverani 2005). The religious mythology, cultic practices, and temple complexes that arose from the Uruk period became powerful underpinnings for centralized rule in Uruk and its sister Sumerian city-states. Those religious underpinnings would subsequently be borrowed and reshaped by other civilizations throughout the Near East.

Inanna, Queen of Heaven and Lover of Cheese

Central to the religious pantheon of Uruk was the goddess Inanna, the Queen of Heaven, who took the form of the morning and evening star (not a true star, but the planet Venus). Inanna was the goddess of fertility and erotic love, and of the seasons and the harvest through her role as guardian of the communal storehouse where agricultural surpluses were held (De Shong Meador 2000; Kramer 1969, 1972). Of all the Sumerian deities she was arguably the most closely involved in the affairs of humankind, because she oversaw the natural cycle of the seasons on which the harvest depended. The unprecedented power wielded by the ruling elite and temple priests of Uruk derived in part from their close relationship to Inanna and their perceived ability to secure her goodwill and protection. The special relationship between the king and Inanna became institutionalized through the Inanna mythology and cultic rites, which probably originated during the Uruk period and then passed down to the Sumerian and Akkadian dynasties that subsequently ruled Mesopotamia during the third millennium BC. Eventually the myths and rites were written down during the Ur III dynasty, around 2300 to 2100 BC, in the form of clay cuneiform tablets, many of which have been recovered and translated (Kramer 1963a).

In the myth of Inanna's sacred marriage, for example, Inanna is about to choose a human spouse when she finds herself in conflict with her brother, the sun god Utu (Kramer 1969). Utu wants Inanna to marry Dumuzi, the shepherd, but Inanna prefers Enkimdu, a farmer who is able to provide her with grain, over Dumuzi, who offers her milk and cream. Dumuzi then confronts Inanna, demanding to know why she prefers the farmer. He presents an impassioned comparison of the products that the farmer has to offer, such as bread, beans, and dates, with his own products, including rich milk, fermented milk (yogurt), churned milk (butter or ghee), and honey cheese and small cheeses. He ends with a boast that he produces so much cream and milk that his rival the farmer could live off the leftovers (Kramer 1969). Dumuzi's argument carries the day, and Inanna agrees to marry the shepherd.

In another related myth, Inanna appoints her new husband Dumuzi to the "godship of the land" and Dumuzi becomes king of Uruk. Once the married couple is happily settled, Inanna makes a deal with Dumuzi. She pleads with the new king to supply her with rich fresh milk, cream, and cheese, and in return promises repeatedly to watch over and preserve the king's storehouse and its prosperity (Kramer 1969).

This was the origin of the Dumuzi-Inanna cult, which in its various forms remained influential in Mesopotamia for more than two thousand years. The cult had as its central rite the sacred marriage ceremony, which was performed annually at the beginning of the new year, when the reigning monarch symbolically married Inanna, probably represented by a surrogate priestess (Kramer 1969). The king of Uruk thus became symbolically identi-fied with Dumuzi, Inanna's true husband, and was assured of Inanna's bless-ing in the coming year, provided of course that he fulfilled Dumuzi's end of the bargain and continued to keep the queen of heaven well provisioned with cheese and cream, which in practice took the form of butter or ghee. In the eyes of the people, this special relationship between king and goddess, consummated annually with the sacred marriage rite, elevated the king to near-divine status. Keeping Inanna happy and securing her blessing on the harvest was a rallying call that the common people could comprehend and embrace. It made voluntary submission to the will of the king and ruling elite psychologically palatable (Liverani 2005). Thus vested with unprec-edented authority and prestige by Inanna herself, the ruling elite of Uruk were empowered to organize a city-state that became the wonder of the world and was soon copied.

Evidently the idea that Inanna's favor could be won through marriage was so appealing that the sacred marriage rite was adopted by other Sumerian cities such as Nippur, Ur, and Isin, each of which had its own patron god, yet still looked to Inanna for protection and prosperity (De Shong Meador 2000; Kramer 1969; Reisman 1973). Over time the rite also evolved into different forms in different cities and time periods. In one Akkadian variant practiced in the city of Ur around 2300 BC, the sacred marriage rite involved Inanna's parents Nana and Ningal, the moon god and goddess. The annual marriage of Nana (represented by the king of Ur) and Ningal (represented by the high priestess of Nana's temple) secured continuing fertility of the land in the coming year (De Shong Meador 2000). Like her daughter Inanna, Ningal demanded daily offerings of cheese and butter. Other known variations on the theme of the sacred marriage rite included the deities Ningirsu and Bab, and Nanse and Nindar (Selz 2008). Eventually the Dumuzi-Inanna cult became the Tammuz-Ishtar cult, the Semitic-Akkadian counterpart that would persist in Mesopotamia up until the beginning of the Christian era. Ishtar would eventually be renamed Astarte in the Levant and become the infamous goddess of love and fertility who repeatedly seduced the Israelites, and even the great King Solomon in the Old Testament. The Phoenicians also worshipped Astarte and would later introduce her cult to the Greeks, who evidently renamed her Aphrodite and adopted her into their pantheon as the goddess of love and fertility sometime around 900 BC (Sansone 2009). Such was the reach of Inanna across time and space.

Inanna's choice of the shepherd Dumuzi and her call for ewe's-milk products not only set into motion the daily offering of cheese and butter by the temple elite, but also had important implications for the broader economy of Uruk and other Mesopotamian civilizations to follow. Inanna's constant demand for cheese and butter meant that the temple needed to control sheep production; in the process the temple gained control of wool production as well (Liverani 2005). Wool-producing sheep were an innovation of breeding that probably occurred between about 4000 and 3500 BC. Before this, sheep were covered with long coarse hair called *kemp* that could not be woven into textiles (Anthony 2007). The advent of wool-bearing sheep made possible the production of superior woolen textiles, and Uruk was among the first cities, perhaps *the* first, to capitalize on the tremendous potential of wool. Uruk's textiles became famous and served as a precious export product that was used to build a far-flung network of trade colonies.

Inanna's symbol has been found on Uruk seals depicting herds of sheep and various stages in the textile-production process, indicating that the temple had gained control over wool and textile production by the fourth millennium BC (Algaze 2008). The breeding of sheep and goats for the production of wool underwent tremendous increases under temple management during the Uruk period, to the extent that wool textiles employed an estimated five to six thousand workers and generated great wealth for Uruk and her sister city-states (Algaze 2008; Liverani 2005). Thus, it would seem the Inanna mythology provided the ruling elite with a shrewd opportunity to gain control over sheep production, ostensibly to furnish the cheese and butter that Inanna demanded, but also solidifying control over wool production.

Large-scale production of wool textiles continued in Mesopotamia long after the decline of Uruk, eventually encompassing millions of sheep and an estimated fifty to sixty thousand workers employed in massive state-sponsored textile manufacturing facilities (Algaze 2008). Wool textiles were the major economic driver of Sumerian civilization during the fourth and third millennia BC, and it would seem that Inanna unwittingly, or perhaps not so unwittingly, helped to kick-start this economy through her insatiable appetite for sheep's-milk cheese and butter.

The logistical challenges associated with keeping Inanna adequately provisioned with offerings of cheese, butter, and other agricultural products evidently played an important role in the development of writing. The Uruk temple complex was massively enlarged during the fourth millennium BC as cultic rites expanded in scale and frequency. Daily offerings and special rites demanded a constant stream of agricultural products, including dairy products, which meant that storerooms became larger and administrative oversight more complex. Clay tokens were used initially to keep track of the products used for offerings. The tokens, each of which represented a unit of goods, were placed in a hollow clay ball, which was then closed and stamped with an official seal using a carved stone token. Temple storerooms and vessels used to store goods also were sealed routinely with clay sealings. The wet clay of the sealing was stamped with a carved stone token or rolled with an engraved stone cylinder that left an imprint identifying the contents and ensuring against tampering. Numerous such seals containing Inanna's symbol have been recovered from the area surrounding Inanna's temple in Uruk (figure 2-1).

As the burden of keeping track of ever-larger inventories of agricultural

Figure 2-1. Uruk-period cylinder seal, circa 3300–3000 BC (right), and clay sealing (left) depicting a priest feeding Inanna's sacred ewes. Inanna's symbol, an upright bundle of reeds capped by a flowing headdress, is depicted three times in the sealing. (Photo courtesy of the British Museum; © The Trustees of the British Museum. All rights reserved.)

products increased, temple administrators evidently decided that it would be easier to depict the goods and their quantities on a clay tablets rather than with tokens (Dickin 2007). Thus, they developed an accounting system using signs scratched into wet clay tablets. This was a proto-cuneiform form of writing that would evolve into the Sumerian cuneiform language, the world's first written language (Kramer 1963a). The earliest evidence of proto-cuneiform writing consists of pictographic signs on clay tablets dated from around 3300 BC, which were recovered from the area around Inanna's temple in Uruk (Bogucki 1999). Around fifty-eight hundred such clay tablets, dating from the end of the fourth millennium BC, have been recovered from the Uruk temple complexes as well as a few other sites (Foster and Foster 2009).

The complexity of the record keeping maintained by the priestly administrators of Inanna's temple was amazing. Proto-cuneiform clay tablets recovered from Uruk provide annual reports for the herds of sheep, goats, and cows that supplied dairy products to Inanna's temple (Green 1980). The temple apparently contracted out Inanna's sacred herds to the care of professional herders, who provided an accounting for all the animals at the end of the year. The tablets record the number of adult male and female animals in the herd, the number of male and female offspring, and the quantities of dairy products that were produced during the year.

The contract hiring of shepherds (and goatherds and cowherds) became a common practice in the ancient Near East in later times. Typically herders were assigned annual quotas of cheese and butter that they were expected to deliver to the temple (Finkelstein 1968; Gelb 1967; Gomi 1980). The vast number of seals and tablets that have been recovered from Inanna's temple, which undoubtedly represents only a small fraction of the original documents, indicates that keeping Inanna provisioned with cheese and other dairy products had become a big business, and writing was a handy administrative tool for keeping track of the growing priestly empire. Other Sumerian city-states would follow the example of Uruk and keep extensive temple accounting records of sheep's-, goat's-, and cow's-milk products (Green 1980; Gomi 1980; Martin et al. 2001).

A detailed account of daily offerings from the city of Ur near the end of the third millennium BC was recovered from the temple of the goddess Ningal, the patron goddess of Ur and mother of Inanna (Figulla 1953). A total of sixty-seven clay cuneiform tablets, the surviving remnants of a much larger collection of temple archives, were recovered from the temple and spanned a period of about a hundred years. The tablets contain records of the products received by the priests from the temple storehouses for daily offering to Ningal, Inanna, and other deities. All of the tablets contain the same three basic commodities of butter (or ghee), cheese, and dates, with the occasional inclusion of milk, fine oil, and lubricant oil. The amounts of butter and cheese that were offered daily, always in equal amounts, were remarkably constant over the hundred-year period, ranging from 7.65 gallons (29

Figure 2-2. Cast of a limestone-on-bitumen relief from Tell Al-'Ubaid in southern Mesopotamia, circa 2500 BC, depicting a dairy-processing scene in which two cows are being milked on the right, while priests process milk products (probably butter or cheese) on the left. (Photo courtesy of the British Museum; © The Trustees of the British Museum. All rights reserved.)

liters) to 14.2 gallons (54 liters). These records are also noteworthy because they reveal that other gods and goddesses in addition to Inanna received daily offerings of cheese and butter.

In addition to contracting out herding and cheese making to professional herders, some Sumerian temples also may have become directly engaged in producing and processing milk, as evidenced from a limestone mosaic frieze that was recovered from the temple dedicated to the goddess Ninkhursagin in the city of Al-'Ubaid and dated to around 2500 BC (Woolley and Moorey 1982). The frieze depicts cows being milked on one side of a doorway in a reed byre, through which two calves are seen entering (figure 2-2). On the other side are men whose dress appears to be that of priests, one of whom is seated and may be rocking a large narrow-necked jar while the other two seem to be pouring a liquid through a funnel, possibly a strainer, into a vessel set on the ground. Scholars have interpreted this scene as depicting either cheese making or the making of butter. According to the latter view, the large rocking vessel served as a churn to transform milk or cream into butter, and the strainer served to separate the churned butter granules from the liquid buttermilk. The large size of the "churn," however, raises questions as to whether a jar of such great size and weight (being partly filled with cream) could be rocked with enough force to induce churning.

If this scene indeed depicts butter making, it is more likely that the vessel was used to store a large volume of cow's milk for cream separation. The vessel was then tipped, as depicted, and the risen cream decanted into a smaller vessel that served as the churn. After churning, the butter granules were separated from the liquid buttermilk using the funnel/sieve as depicted. An alternate possibility is that the large vessel contained milk that was stored overnight and allowed to undergo acid coagulation. The vessel was then rocked to break up the fragile acid curd, and the curd/whey mixture then strained to separate the curds from the whey. Either way, the frieze indicates that the temple, spurred on by the deities' love of cheese and butter, had achieved an impressive level of sophistication in dairy technology.

What were the cheeses of Mesopotamia like? During the Ur III dynasty, around 2100 to 2000 BC, lexicons were written that listed Sumerian and Akkadian terms to assist scribes in the translation of Sumerian records and literature into Akkadian, which had become the common language regionwide. One lexicon included a food section that contained about eight hundred entries, including about eighteen or twenty different terms for cheese (Bottéro 1985). Terms that have been translated with reasonable certainty include cheese, fresh cheese, cheese seasoned with *gazi,* honey cheese, mustard-flavored cheese, rich cheese, sharp cheese, round cheese, small and large cheese, and white cheese (Bottéro 2004; Jacobsen 1983; Limet 1987; Owen and Young 1971). Some of the terms probably refer to a common fresh cheese that was flavored with various condiments such as herbs or honey.

The frequent reference in temple records to both butter and cheese produced in equal or nearly equal proportions (for example, a butter-to-cheese ratio of 2:3) suggests that the two products were usually produced simultaneously from the same batch of milk (Gelb 1967; Gomi 1980). For cow's milk, the simplest way to accomplish this is to allow the milk to separate into cream, which can then be churned into butter. The skimmed milk along with the buttermilk can then be fermented into an acid-coagulated fresh cheese, much as is done in Turkey today in the making of traditional Çökelek cheese (Kamber 2008a). The scene depicted in the Al-'Ubaid frieze fits well with this scenario. Alternately, the partly fermented skim milk remaining after cream separation can be heated to boiling to produce an acid/heat-coagulated (ricotta-type) cheese, similar to Eridik cheese, which is still produced by traditional methods in Turkey (Kamber and Terzi 2008).

Sheep's and goat's milk do not separate to form a cream layer the way cow's milk does; thus the above approach would not have been used in the making of sheep's- and goat's-milk cheese and butter. The most likely method in this case would be similar to that used in the making of Lor, Minzi, and other similar Near Eastern cheeses (Kamber 2008b; Kamber and Terzi 2008). Traditionally these cheeses are made from milk that has been allowed to ferment into yogurt. The yogurt is then churned to produce butter, which is removed by straining, and the remaining liquid (buttermilk) is transferred to a cauldron and heated to the boiling point. This causes the caseins and whey proteins in the buttermilk to undergo acid/heat coagulation to form a delicate ricotta-like curd.

All of these cheese-making technologies had likely been known since Neolithic times (see chapter 1) and probably passed down from Neolithic to Ubaid to Sumerian culture. Various funnels and perforated ceramic vessels that probably served as sieves, possibly for separating cheese curds from whey (as well as butter granules from buttermilk), have been recovered from a number of sites throughout Mesopotamia (Ellison 1984).

Most temple records quantified cheese and butter in units of *sila*, which corresponded to the volume of a ceramic bevel-rimmed bowl of about 1-liter capacity that was mass-produced throughout Mesopotamia from the Uruk period onward (Ellison 1981, 1984). It is possible that both cheese and butter were packed in sila bowls and then sealed with clay to preserve them until use. Other cuneiform tablets record temple deliveries of cheese in units of *nidu* containers, which were probably ceramic pots (Martin et al. 2001). As noted earlier, ceramic pots are still used in traditional practice to package acid-coagulated and acid/heat-coagulated cheeses in Turkey (Kamber 2008a).

It's important to note that Mesopotamian cheese was not only a sacred food for gods and goddesses, but also enjoyed by mere mortals. For example, religious and secular workers in Sumerian cities received food rations, which sometimes included rations of cheese (Ellison 1981). Cheese also was appreciated by the ruling elite, as evidenced by the inclusion among lists of the royal foods of a white cheese, as well as fruitcakes that contained butter and white cheese as ingredients (Limet 1987). According to Bottéro (2004), acid-coagulated cheeses that were dried and sometimes flavored with herbs were used in cooking applications. Interestingly, little evidence has been found of cheese in the cuneiform commercial records of Mesopotamian merchants, prompting some scholars to conclude that merchants did not deal in dairy products due to their perishability (Gelb 1967). Thus, the consumption of cheese and other dairy products may have been primarily restricted to the ruling elite and privileged temple workers in the cities, as well as to simple pastoralists in the countryside, while not available to the urban population in general.

Most Mesopotamian cuneiform references to cheese probably refer to acid-coagulated or acid/heat-coagulated fresh cheeses (Bottéro 1985; Gelb 1967). But the term *white cheese* in the Sumerian-Akkadian lexicon raises an important question: Does this refer to a rennet-coagulated cheese? In modern times *white cheese* is a common name for traditional rennet-coagulated brined cheeses that are produced throughout the Near East and Balkans, and derive their name from their white color. Feta is the most widely known of the traditional white cheeses. Unfortunately, it is impossible to determine whether Sumerian white cheeses were rennet-coagulated and similar to the traditional white brined cheese produced today. They may have been acid-coagulated or acid/heat-coagulated types, both of which also would have been white in color.

Another possible reference to rennet-coagulated cheese making occurs in a Sumerian poem lamenting the death of Dumuzi, Inanna's husband. In this lament, Dumuzi's mother memorializes the life of her son as a shepherd (Jacobsen 1983). She recalls how Dumuzi drove his flocks out of Uruk into the desert during the annual transhumant movement of sheep and goats to pasturelands around the desert margins, and she describes Dumuzi's experience making butter and cheese out in the desert following the spring lambing and kidding season. (You'll recall that it was Dumuzi's dairy-processing expertise that won him Inanna's hand in marriage.)

Interestingly, the poem indicates that Dumuzi produced two different cheeses, described as "small cheeses piled up high in heaps for him" and "large cheeses" that were "laid on the rod for him." The term *rod* evidently referred to a unit of length used to quantify the amount the cheese. "Large" and "small" cheeses also were mentioned in the Mesopotamian myth known as "The Marriage of Sud" (Bottéro 2004). The use of the term *large* implies that the cheese was firm enough and cohesive enough to hold together well, characteristics that are much more readily obtained through rennet coagulation than through acid or acid/heat coagulation. Under the right conditions rennet-coagulated cheeses can be made with great durability and longevity (not to mention great flavors and textures), and the development of rennet-coagulated cheese-making technology ranks as one of the most important milestones in cheese history.

Did the Sumerians perfect rennet-coagulated cheeses? It's impossible to say with certainty, though they certainly had access to lambs, kids, and calves, the traditional sources of animal rennet, as well as to fig trees (the source of fig sap rennet), which were widely raised in Mesopotamia (Ellison 1983). The first unequivocal evidence for rennet usage, however, did not emerge until somewhat later—in Hittite Anatolia to the north, where our journey will soon carry us. But before turning to the north, we shall briefly look west to Egypt and the Nile River and then east to the Indus River Valley that separates modern Pakistan from India, where two great civilizations arose soon after Uruk.

Egypt

The great dispersal of Levantine peoples that commenced toward the end of the Neolithic Age eventually progressed south across the forbidding Sinai desert and reached the Nile River Valley around 5500 BC (Bellwood 2005). Presumably, simple cheese-making technology arrived in Egypt at this time. There is also evidence that cattle herding and domestication in the northern Sahara may have preceded the arrival of domesticated livestock from the Levant by as much as three thousand years. During this period the northern Sahara enjoyed a much wetter climate than at present and was suitable for grazing (Barker 2006; Bellwood 2005). The nomadic herders eventually left behind evidence of their pastoral lifestyle in the Libyan desert in the form of rock art, dated to around 3000 BC. Some of the artwork includes depictions of cattle being milked, and what appears to be bags of milk products (cheese curd?) draining on racks (Barker 2006; Simoons 1971). Thus, we can speculate that nomadic milking and cheese making may already have been in practice in northern Africa at the time of the Neolithic arrival from the Levant.

Mesopotamia clearly influenced the culture, religion, and technology of Egypt (Chadwick 2005), but the extent to which Mesopotamia contributed to the rise of Egyptian civilization at the end of the fourth millennium BC is disputed among scholars (Najovits 2003). Whatever the cause for Egypt's rise, a turning point occurred around 3000 BC when Upper (southern) and Lower (northern) Egypt were united, probably under the reign of Narmer, to form the first true state (Chadwick 2005). In contrast with Mesopotamia, where the Sumerian kings were viewed as divinely sanctioned to rule but were not gods themselves, Egypt developed a mythology, probably borrowed to some extent from Mesopotamia, that elevated the pharaoh to the status of god.

Central to Egyptian mythology was the concept of the afterlife and resurrection, which inspired the building of great tombs and eventually pyramids to ensure the well-being of the Egyptian royalty in the afterlife, and of anyone else who could likewise afford to build and provision an appropriate tomb. An intriguing aspect of the early Egyptian tombs was the inclusion of vast quantities of foodstuffs that were meant to provide for the deceased in the afterlife. For most tombs, such foodstuffs were in scattered disarray and beyond analysis by the time of archaeological discovery due to looting and degradation over the centuries. However, two intact tombs dating from the first and second dynasties (circa 3000 BC) have yielded the earliest evidence of cheese in Egypt.

The Saqqara Tomb 3477 was not that of a king or queen but of a wealthy noblewoman. This particular tomb remained remarkably undisturbed until its archaeological discovery in 1937. Even the footprints of the burial party laid down some five thousand years earlier were still discernible in the dust that covered the floor (Emery 1962). Also completely intact was a multi-course precooked meal served in twenty-seven pottery vessels and twenty-one alabaster and diorite bowls and dishes, which were laid out on the floor in front of the sarcophagus. Among the food items were three small ceramic jars, the contents of which were subjected to a battery of chemical analyses and tentatively determined to be cheese. If in fact the jars contained cheese, it is likely that these were fresh cheeses (acid-coagulated or acid/heat-coagulated), similar to those such as Çökelek and Lor that are still produced traditionally in Turkey and stored in clay pots (Kamber 2008a). Unfortunately, very little is known about Egyptian cheeses from ancient written records because Egyptian scribes used papyrus, a fragile paper-like material, for their record keeping rather than the much more durable clay cuneiform tablets used in Mesopotamia, and few papyrus documents have survived intact in the archaeological record.

An even earlier tomb, that of King Hor-Aha of the First Dynasty, also yielded two pottery jars that were determined through chemical analyses to contain cheese (Zaky and Iskander 1942). Given the comparatively crude analytical methods available to these researchers in the 1940s, their results, like those from Saqqara Tomb 3477, must be considered tentative until confirmed using newer, more definitive methodologies such as those described by Evershed et al. (2008). Nevertheless, the evidence that these jars contained cheese is plausible and, indeed, made more so by hieroglyphic inscriptions on the jars from the Hor-Aha tomb, which seem to indicate that one jar contained cheese from Upper Egypt and the other, from Lower Egypt (Zaky and Iskander 1942). Whether the inscriptions had any political significance linked to Egypt's newly achieved unification of the Upper and Lower kingdoms around 3000 BC is anyone's guess (Dalby 2009).

Thus, it seems likely that by the start of the third millennium BC cheese making was firmly entrenched in Egypt, just as it was in the great Mesopotamian civilization at the opposite end of the Fertile Crescent. By this time, dairying and possibly cheese making also had penetrated far to the east, to the Indus River Valley that divides modern Pakistan and India, where another civilization was soon to form.

The Indian Subcontinent and China

The migration of Neolithic peoples and their agropastoral economy from the Fertile Crescent progressed rapidly eastward during the waning years of the Neolithic Age, reaching the Indus River Valley, the western gateway to the Indian subcontinent, by the seventh millennium BC (Bellwood 2005). Following this initial influx from the west, there apparently were no significant new migrations into the Indus region during the next few millennia, and the region underwent a gradual transition to pottery usage, the mastery of copper and later bronze, and a growing reliance on animal domestication and agriculture, much as occurred contemporaneously and independently back in southwest Asia (Singh 2008). However, toward the middle of the third millennium BC, numerous settlements sprang up over a vast area that shared a high degree of cultural uniformity (Sharma 2005). Many of the settlements rapidly grew into cities, the largest of which rivaled the cities of Mesopotamia in size and population (Singh 2008). This remarkable regionwide blossoming of urban growth and cultural unity over an area the size of Pakistan is known as the Indus civilization, or the Harappan civilization, named for Harappa, one of the largest cities.

A striking difference between the Mesopotamian and Harappan civilizations was the absence of monumental temples in the latter. Evidently, Harappan religious practice was much less institutionalized and less influential in government functions and the economic and agricultural systems of the region than was the case in Mesopotamia (Sharma 2005). Indeed, the basic structural principles of Indus civilization were completely different from those of Mesopotamia or Egypt, and Indus political and social organization remains shrouded in mystery (Bogucki 1999).

Cattle and buffalo, which were used for milk, meat, and traction, had become the most important domesticated animals by this time, but sheep and goats also were raised. Unfortunately, Harappan written script has never been deciphered; the nearly four thousand specimens of Harappan writing that have been recovered on stone seals and other objects have failed to yield up their secrets (Sharma 2005). It is known that the Harappan traded extensively, their reach extending to Mesopotamia and the Arabian peninsula (Sharma 2005), and it has been suggested that the Harappan may have shipped dried cheese to the Arabian peninsula in ceramic jars (Potts 1993). However, apart from perforated ceramic jars that have been recovered from the archaeological strata of this period (which may have been used to separate curds from whey or butter granules from buttermilk), little evidence has been recovered that speaks to the possibility of Harappan cheese making.

The first unequivocal evidence of cheese and other dairy products in the Indian subcontinent occurs in the sacred Hindu Vedic texts, written after the collapse of the Harappan civilization, which occurred suddenly around 1900 BC for reasons that are not well understood. The Vedas were compiled over many centuries, beginning perhaps around 1500 BC by a people who called themselves *arya* (Singh 2008). Various linguistic and other lines of evidence suggest that the Aryans migrated from Iran and south-central Asia to the Indus River Valley in multiple waves between 1500 and 1200 BC (Sharma 2005). The Vedic Aryans were a pastoral people who brought with them a strong emphasis on cattle rearing. Eventually the Aryans expanded eastward across northern India to the basin of the upper Ganges River, where the later Vedic texts were written. The Vedic texts reveal the pivotal role that the Aryans played in elevating the importance of dairy foods to a revered status in ancient India. Numerous references to milk, ghee, and curds (or fresh cheese) are found throughout the Vedas, highlighting both their importance in the diet and their role as offerings to the gods in religious observances (Prakash 1961).

The Vedas describe a process of curdling milk by mixing with it a portion of soured milk (Prakash 1961), which is the ancient equivalent of adding starter culture in the making of acid-coagulated fresh cheeses. The Vedas also speak of milk curdled through the addition of several plant substances, including the bark of the palash tree, the fruit of the kuvala (jujube), and putika, a plant that is usually identified as a creeper or jujube but could also be a mushroom (Achaya 1994; Kramrisch 1975; Prakash 1961). These plant substances may have contained rennet-like enzymes, in which case the Vedas may include some of the earliest known references to rennet-coagulated (enzymatic) cheeses. The Vedas mention two varieties of a food called *dadhanvat*, one with holes or pores, the other without, that are thought to be cheeses (Prakash 1961). Another passage describes the preparation of curds from boiled milk, possibly a reference to acid/heat coagulation, which is used in the making of paneer and related cheeses. Paneer is enormously popular in India today and is virtually the only cheese produced in India that is indigenous to the Indian subcontinent.

Buddhist and Jainist texts, written centuries after the Vedas, reiterate the importance of curds or fresh cheese in the Indian diet, and indeed medical and literary works written much later, up to AD 1200, continued to emphasize curds in the Indian diet (Prakash 1961). Yet despite India's long love affair with curds and fresh cheeses such as paneer, the development of ripened or aged (rennet-coagulated) cheese varieties seems to have been strikingly absent in India from ancient times to the present. Why did one of the largest milk-producing regions in the world with one of the longest histories in dairying and cheese making fail to develop aged cheeses? There is no single answer, but clearly the cultural environment of the Indian subcontinent did not encourage the type of trial-and-error experimentation that would have been necessary for the development of indigenous aged cheeses. For one thing, the revered status of the cow as an animal not to be killed, which was first mentioned in the Vedic literature and eventually became incorporated into Hinduism, discouraged the development of animal rennet. Furthermore, Buddhist and Jainist teachings, while upholding the value of curds or fresh cheese in the diet, expressed strong attitudes against the slaughter of animals and eventually made broad inroads in India toward vegetarianism (Prakash 1961), further discouraging the use of animal rennet as a curdling agent.

However, even plant-derived rennet-like coagulants apparently never gained a foothold in India as a starting point for aged cheese development. It seems that the very concept of cheese ripening, a process that essentially amounts to controlled rotting, violated the deeply ingrained Indian concepts of food purity that stretch back to the Vedas. The idea that purity of thought depends on purity of food gave rise to hygienic practices associated with food preparation and dining that became (and remain) central tenets of Indian culture (Prakash 1961). For example, perishable foods that were allowed to stand overnight, those that developed off-flavors, or those that were cooked twice were considered unfit for eating, according to the Vedas. So, too, was food that contained a hair or an insect, or had been touched by a foot, the hem of a garment, or a dog. It is hard to envision how many of the moldy, stinky, maggoty, mite-infected cheeses so beloved in Europe could have arisen within a cultural context where such emphasis was placed on food purity. Add to this the technical challenges of controlling the cheese "rotting" process (that is, the cheese ripening) in the subtropical heat that envelops much of India much of the year combined with the humid monsoon-soaked wet seasons, and the lack of aged cheeses in India is perhaps not surprising.

Farther to the east in China, cheese making in particular, and indeed dairying in general, never gained a lasting foothold. Agriculture developed early in China in the region between the Yangzi and Yellow Rivers, with cultivation of rice and millet occurring there by the seventh millennium BC (Bellwood 2005). This expansive, fertile, well-watered region was able to support vigorous population growth and a thriving Chinese food culture that was well established by the time that dairying spread from India to various parts of southeast Asia along with Hinduism and Buddhism during the first millennium BC. However, though there was apparently some acceptance of the ritual use of dairy products in China, milk and dairy products did not become a major element of Chinese cuisine, evidently because of a strong cultural conservatism that rejected foreign practices considered strange and unappealing (Simoons 1991). At various points in Chinese history, Tibet and especially Mongolia—neighbors with strong dairying traditions—also influenced China culturally in ways that encouraged dairy products, particularly during the Mongol conquest of the thirteenth century AD (Simoons 1991). However, acceptance of dairy foods was limited primarily to fermented milks and perhaps butter, cheese being all but absent. Thus, our attention must now return to the west, where the story of cheese would soon blossom and diversify.

CHAPTER THREE

Bronze, Rennet, and the Ascendancy of Trade

> Now Jesse said to his son David, "Take this ephah of roasted grain
> and these ten loaves of bread for your brothers and hurry to their
> camp. Take along these ten cheeses to the commander of their unit.
> See how your brothers are and bring back some assurance from
> them. They are with Saul and all the men of Israel in the Valley of
> Elah, fighting against the Philistines."
>
> 1 Samuel 17:17–19

According to the well-known biblical account of David and Goliath, the young shepherd David was sent by his anxious father Jesse to gather news about his three older brothers, who were serving in King Saul's army and facing a formidable adversary. The year was around 1025 BC. David's people, the Israelites, were descended from the patriarch Abraham and had settled in the interior hill country of Canaan about two hundred years earlier, about the same time that their archrivals, the Philistines, settled along the coastal plains. The Greeks called the latter people Palestines, a name that became synonymous with the region and continues in use to this day. The Philistines had abandoned their home in western Anatolia to the north around 1200 BC during a period of cataclysmic upheaval throughout the Mediterranean world that triggered the collapse of two great civilizations (Hittite and Mycenaean) and the crippling of a third (Egyptian); it also marked the end of the Bronze Age, which lasted from 3200 to 1200 BC.

David's father sent a care package to his sons consisting of roasted snacking grains and ten loaves of fresh bread, along with a cargo far more precious that was to be delivered to the commander of the battalion: ten cheeses, given as a gesture of respect and support. We know little about these ten cheeses except that they were most likely made from sheep's milk. David's home in Bethlehem was more than 10 miles (16 km) away from the Valley of Elah where Saul's army was camped, and David probably loaded his provisions onto a donkey fitted with carrying bags before heading out early that fateful morning. It would seem that the ten cheeses, which also can be translated as "ten cuts of cheese," must have been fairly firm and durable to withstand the rigors of transportation, which suggests that they were probably rennet-coagulated.

The use of rennet in cheese making was well established by this time in Anatolia to the north, where we will pick up the next leg of our journey through cheese history. The same was likely the case in Palestine itself, for long-distance trade in Levantine cheeses was occurring by this time, probably spurred on by the development of rugged, long-lived, rennet-coagulated cheeses during the Bronze Age. Indeed, the Bronze Age stands out as the time when rennet-coagulated cheese making came of age, and when trade, spurred on by the discovery and development of bronze technology, emerged as one of the great movers and shakers of both western civilization and cheese making.

The Rise of Anatolia

The Anatolian peninsula (modern Turkey) has long been shaped by trade, beginning in the seventh millennium BC when obsidian, a volcanic glass that is found in abundance in central Anatolia, became highly prized and traded throughout the Near East for the making of tools (Sagona and Zimansky 2009). Copper also occurs in abundance in Anatolia, and around 6000 BC copper began to be extracted from the mountainous terrain there, hammered into sheets, and then cut into strips and fabricated into small items such as beads, rings, and ornaments. This was the beginning of the Chalcolithic period, or Copper-Stone Age, which lasted until the latter part of the fourth millennium BC and led to the formation of a vast network of trade in copper that extended throughout Anatolia and beyond. Anatolian copper technology had advanced dramatically during the fifth millennium

BC with the discovery that this metal can be melted at high temperatures (above 1,981°F, or 1,083°C) and then cast in a variety of simple open molds to form tools such as axes and chisels.

In the fourth millennium BC Anatolian coppersmiths began to experiment with melting copper at even higher temperatures, which allowed metallic impurities such as arsenic or tin that were present at low levels in copper ore to fuse with elemental copper to create an alloy, through the process known as smelting. Alloys possessed new and sometimes desirable properties, as in the case of copper plus tin, which formed an alloy of enhanced hardness and resiliency that allowed the casting of much larger and more complex items (Sagona and Zimansky 2009). Toward the end of the fourth millennium BC Anatolian coppersmiths discovered that the deliberate addition of tin to copper at an optimum ratio of about 1:10 created a very strong and useful alloy, bronze, thereby ushering in the Bronze Age that would last for two thousand years. Around the same time Anatolian smiths were also perfecting metallurgy with gold and silver, both of which were also abundantly found in Anatolia.

These metallurgical advances in Anatolia were occurring during the period when the Mesopotamian city of Uruk to south was expanding rapidly and fervently seeking raw materials and other items from afar to fuel its increasingly sophisticated civilization. Among Uruk's most pressing import needs were gold, silver, copper, and eventually bronze, which were used for ceremonial artifacts and jewelry that adorned the temples, palaces, priests, and rulers (Sagona and Zimansky 2009). Copper and bronze tools and implements were also needed to support the intensive irrigation/plow-based agricultural system on which Uruk's large urban population depended. Metal weaponry was also coming of age and seeing rapid growth in demand. For these reasons and perhaps other more ideologically based motives, Uruk founded a far-flung network of trading colonies and enclaves that extended northward into southeastern Anatolia during the period known as the Uruk Expansion, which lasted from about 3800 to 3100 BC. For its part, resource-poor Uruk had few exportable goods, its most important being wool textiles. The ever-increasing demand for wool in Anatolia and beyond eventually prompted the building of the massive temple-administered textile factories that dominated the economies of southern Mesopotamia throughout the third millennium BC and later, as outlined in chapter 2.

Mesopotamian influence in Anatolia was enormous. The plow and wheeled transport quickly moved north from Mesopotamia into Anatolia and west to the Aegean coast during the fourth millennium BC, setting the stage for intensive agriculture and urban civilization there. Mesopotamia's highly centralized religious and administrative systems also were transferred to Anatolian culture and eventually shaped the Hittite civilization that dominated Anatolia for five hundred years. Among the many repercussions of this cultural transfer was the visible role that cheese played in Hittite religion as an offering to the gods.

Trade with Uruk also spurred the development of a much larger Anatolian trade network that extended west to the Aegean coast by the end of the fourth millennium BC (Şahoğlu 2005). Anatolia established close cultural and economic links to the islands of the Aegean Sea and the Greek mainland that lasted throughout the Bronze Age and eventually helped to shape classical Greek civilization. Maritime trade was still in its infancy, with small oared vessels plying their trade among the Aegean islands and the Anatolian coastline. However, to the south in Egypt, sailing vessels were already beginning to revolutionize sea trade, and by the end of the second millennium BC sailing vessels would prevail throughout the Mediterranean and Aegean, creating a massive trading block unlike any the world had seen. Anatolian metals were traded for textiles, wine, and scented olive oil, which were intensively developed as "cash crops" throughout the Aegean region for export. By the start of the second millennium BC flourishing trade and the accumulation of great wealth gave rise Anatolia's first empire, which ruled for nearly two hundred years before collapsing amid internal conflicts around 1800 BC. Waiting in the wings, however, was a new power based in the central Anatolian city of Hattusa, which would forge a great civilization that would last for five hundred years.

The Hittite Civilization

Though vast in area, the Hittite Empire was centrally ruled and administered from the capital city of Hattusa, a fortified metropolis encompassing some 408 acres (165 ha) at its peak, making it one of the largest and most impressive cities of the ancient world. The Hittite kings in Hattusa maintained order by delegating authority to governors who presided over regional centers throughout the empire, which in turn were subdivided into local districts (Bryce 2005). Hattusa also served as the religious center for the empire, with the reigning Hittite king acting as a high priest representing the Hittite people before all of the gods. The city, therefore, contained some thirty temples in addition to the royal palace and numerous administrative buildings (Beckman 1989). Much like their Mesopotamian counterparts, the largest temples housing the most important deities contained large storerooms for food and other items that were offered to the gods. In addition, extensive tracts of agricultural land outside the city supported temple activities; thus the temples were an important component of the Hittite economy (Beckman 1989). Various ceremonies and festivals were observed regularly, and the most important deities were fed daily with bread and wine. In addition, a wide variety of cultic rites were performed when circumstances called for divine intervention or the gods' special favor. The temple scribes routinely compiled detailed written instructions for the performance of such rites on cuneiform tablets, many of which have been recovered and translated.

From these cuneiform records it is evident that offerings or sacrifices of cheese were included among the ritual tasks that were to be performed during many of the rites (Beckman 2005). For example, when drought caused a spring to dry up, a ritual was performed at the spring to persuade the weather god (who had vanished into the spring hole) to return, along with life-giving rain. Cheese was one of the items sacrificed to appease the weather god (Bier 1976). Rites used to appease the storm god, sun god, and sun goddess also called for the offering of cheese (Goetze 1971; Hoffner 1998; Wright 1986). Similarly, Sandas, the god of the underworld who inflicted plague when angry, could be appeased through offerings that included cheese (Mastrocinque 2007; Schwartz 1938). Even spirits of the dead could be briefly lured out of the underworld through a special ritual involving the lowering of cheese and other foods into a sacred sacrificial pit as an offering. It is probably this same ritual, later brought to the Levant by Hittite immigrants, that is described in the biblical account of King Saul's visit to the witch of Endor (1 Samuel 28:13–14), where Saul calls the spirit of Samuel back from the dead in a desperate and misguided attempt to salvage his life and kingdom (Hoffner 1967).

The term used in Hittite cuneiform records for cheese often is coupled with various modifiers in order to designate cheeses that possessed particular characteristics. Examples of such terms include *small cheese, large cheese, crumbled cheese* (grated?), *scoured* or *finished* (by scraping or abrasive action) *cheese,* and *aged soldier cheese* (Carter 1985; Hoffner 1966). The latter two descriptors are particularly noteworthy because they suggest that rennet coagulation was now being used to create new and innovative cheeses. For example, an analysis of the context within which the term *scoured cheese* is used indicates that the surface of this cheese was probably cleaned or scoured through repeated abrasive action (Carter 1985). This very much sounds like traditional hard-rind cheeses that are subjected to repeated abrasion during aging to prevent excessive surface growth. If the Hittites did indeed develop hard-rind cheeses, they almost certainly used rennet coagulation in their production, and such cheeses represented a major step forward in the technology of Bronze Age cheese making. Similarly, the term *aged soldier cheese* implies a rugged, long-lived, probably hard-rind cheese that was valued for its use as a military ration. Again, such a cheese would almost certainly have required rennet coagulation and would have represented a major milestone in the history of cheese making. The biblical account of David and Goliath, it seems, was not the first example of cheese serving as a military ration, nor would it be the last. Armies and navies often would be provisioned with cheese throughout the history of western civilization, for hard-rind cheese was an ideal military ration, rugged and dense, providing soldiers with energy and vital nutrients.

Modifiers that appear with the term for cheese in Hittite texts, such as in the examples that we just examined, are often very difficult to translate, therefore the precise meanings of many modifiers remain uncertain. Translation is complicated by the fact that Hittite texts often borrowed cuneiform signs from other languages in the region at the time, including Hattic, Hurrian, Luwian, Sumerian, and Akkadian. For example, Brandeis University scholar Harry Hoffner described the tortuous process that he used to translate the modifier GA-PA-AN, which appeared in conjunction with the term GA.KIN.AG, the Hittite word for cheese, in a Hittite tablet that evidently describes a rite in which cheese is used as a burnt offering:

> he takes GA.KIN.AG GA-PA-AN and turns(?) it [onto . . . ?] for sepa-ration and puts it in/on the fire.
>
> (Hoffner 1966)

In the case of the modifier GA-PA-AN, the sign was not Hittite, there-fore Hoffner had to carry out a complicated process of elimination before concluding that GA-PA-AN is an Akkadian term. He then had to evalu-ate twelve Akkadian possibilities, which he eventually narrowed down to two prime candidates. The first likely possibility is that GA-PA-AN is a phonetic interpretation of the Akkadian noun *gapnu,* which can refer to any plant that bears figs, pomegranates, apples, or grapes. Thus, GA.KIN.AG GA-PA-AN could possibly be translated "cheese of the fig tree" or "cheese of the grapevine," which Hoffner rejected as nonsensical. The other possibil-ity is that GA-PA-AN should be read as the Akkadian *gaban* of *gabnu,* which probably refers to the shape of the cheese. Hoffner settled on this second rendering as the likely meaning. A cheese scientist would be less inclined to write off "cheese of the fig tree" so easily, because fig sap has been used as a coagulant for cheese making in the Mediterranean region since at least the first millennium BC. It's not unreasonable to postulate that the Hittites may have used the special term (GA.KIN.AG GA-PA-AN) to specify cheese that was made using fig sap. Even "cheese of the grapevine" is not beyond the range of possibility, given that wine must is a flavoring for traditional fresh cheeses made in Turkey and other regions of the Near East. Alas, we may never know with certainty the meaning of this or many other terms for cheese that are found among the Hittite tablets (or for that matter those contained in the Sumerian tablets of Mesopotamia).

Interestingly, not only cheese but also rennet (that is, the dried stomach lining material of ruminants used to coagulate milk) is mentioned in Hittite texts, and evidently was even offered to the gods alongside cheese and other foodstuffs (Güterbock 1968; Hoffner 1995, 1998). Hittite references to rennet dating to around 1400 BC arguably represent the first direct evidence for rennet-coagulated cheese making. The development of rennet technology and storable cheeses, in turn, was probably directly responsible for the growing maritime trade in cheese that began around this time, as evidenced from commercial records recovered from the Hittite vassal city of Ugarit on the Syrian coast. Ugarit was a strategic trading center at the crossroads of major land-based trade routes that extended south to the southern Levant, east to Mesopotamia, and north to Anatolia. It was also a strategic maritime trade center with extensive connections to the southern Levant and Egypt, the Aegean islands and Greece, and Anatolia (Sherratt and Sherratt 1991). During the period when the Hittites controlled Ugarit toward the end of the second millennium BC Hittite administrators maintained extensive cuneiform records of land-based and maritime trade passing through the city. Among the artifacts recovered from Ugarit are cuneiform tablets that record shipments of cheese received from the city of Ashdod in the southern Levant (modern Israel). These tablets, dated around 1200 BC, appear to be the first direct evidence of long-distance maritime trade in cheese (figure 3-1).

This represents another major milestone in the history of cheese because it means that by the late Bronze Age, not only had Canaanite cheesemakers perfected cheese(s) that could withstand the rigors of long-distance maritime travel, but the merchants and ports had also perfected shipping containers and storage facilities suitable for the transport of cheese by sea. Furthermore, the commercial markets of the Levantine coast had evidently developed a demand for "high-end" cheeses that was sufficiently compelling (that is, lucrative) to foster a trade in cheese. In other words, cheese had joined the ranks of wool textiles, wine, olive oil, bronze, and other precious metals as prized items of sufficient value to warrant their inclusion in the massive trade network that linked Mesopotamia, Anatolia, Greece and the Aegean islands, and Egypt during the late Bronze Age. And, in all probability, the Canaanite cheeses recorded in the Ugarit tablets were only the proverbial tip of iceberg with respect to Bronze Age cheese trading.

What were these cheeses like that were shipped by sea during the second millennium BC? First, they must have commanded a high price in the

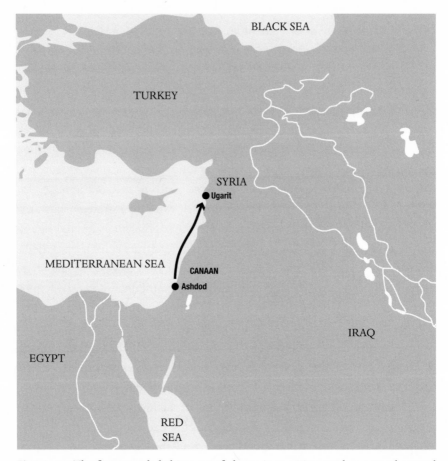

Figure 3-1. The first recorded shipment of cheese in maritime trade occurred around 1200 BC between Ashdod on the coast of Canaan (modern Israel) and Ugarit on the Syrian coast. The Canaanites were the first to develop clay jars specifically designed for maritime transport. It is possible that the Canaanite cheeses were brined feta-type cheeses packed in sealed Canaanite clay jars.

marketplace (presumably because of their unique character and high quality), because maritime transit was both costly and risky. Only high-value, low-bulk foodstuffs such as dried fruits (figs, pomegranates), wine and olive oil, or vital bulky foodstuffs such as grain could justify the expense and risk of sea trade. Like most articles of trade at the time, they were probably a luxury good for the elite. Furthermore, the cheeses must have been compatible with shipping containers used on Bronze Age ships. Archaeological evidence from shipwrecks and cuneiform records of trade transactions from maritime ports such as Ugarit indicate that ceramic jars became the universal shipping containers for the maritime transport of foodstuffs and other goods around this time (Monroe 2007).

The Canaanites were probably the first traders to develop a specialized, rugged, maritime-friendly ceramic jar for organic commodities, the Canaanite jar or amphora, which ranged from around 1.5 to 3 gallons (6 to 12 liters) in capacity and was used extensively in sea trade during the Bronze Age (Knapp 1991; Monroe 2007; Sherratt and Sherratt 1991). Food products that are believed to have been shipped by sea in clay-sealed ceramic jars during the second and first millennia BC, based on residue analyses of pottery shards, include high-value liquid foods such as olive oil, wine, and honey, as well as salted solid foods such as salted fish and olives in brine (Bass 1991; Faust and Weiss 2005; Knapp 1991; Monroe 2007; Vidal 2006). There is no direct evidence that cheese was shipped by sea in Bronze Age Canaanite jars, but much later during the Christian era brined white cheeses (that is, feta types) were commonly shipped throughout the Aegean in ceramic jars until the end of the nineteenth century (Blitzer 1990). Indeed, it wasn't until the twentieth century that wooden barrels and metal containers replaced the ubiquitous ceramic jar for storage and transport of brined Greek cheeses (Anifantakis 1991). Ceramic pots called *bournies* were (and probably still are) used to store cheese in brine in Greece during the latter half of the twentieth century (Birmingham 1967).

Thus, it is possible that the Canaanite cheeses shipped to the Bronze Age port of Ugarit were rennet-coagulated brined white cheeses of the same family as feta, packed in clay-sealed Canaanite jars. Brined white cheeses are produced traditionally almost everywhere throughout the Near East, eastern Mediterranean, and Aegean regions. They are very simple to make and can withstand the hot, dry Mediterranean summers without spoiling and drying out due to their high salt content, protective brine, and sealed packaging. It is likely that the use of brine for storing and preserving white cheese developed very early in the history of rennet-coagulated cheese making. The preservative value of brine must have become evident soon after the practice of dry-salting cheese became widespread because uncooked, unpressed, acidic, high-moisture white cheese (similar to feta) naturally releases large amounts of salty whey upon dry-salting. Thus, salted white cheeses form their own natural brine, especially when stored at warm temperatures. When such cheese is packed tightly in a skin bag or ceramic pot, the salty whey accumulates and forms a protective brine bath. Cheeses similar to this that naturally generate their own brine are still produced traditionally in the Near East (Kamber 2008b).

The Roman agriculturalist Marcus Porcius Cato was probably the first to write of the use of externally prepared brine to preserve cheese (along with meat and pickled fish) during the second century BC in his ground-breaking work *De agri cultura* (Brehaut 1933), but the practice likely originated much earlier. Another reference to the use of seawater or salt brine to preserve cheese occurred later in the *Geoponica,* a tenth century AD compilation of agricultural writings that draws from sources written much earlier, some of which ultimately may date back to the Hellenistic period (circa third century BC) and before (Owen 1805). The *Geoponica* notes that cheese remains white when stored in brine, almost certainly a reference to the storage of acidic white or feta-type cheese in brine.

All of this supports the possibility that the Canaanite cheeses exported to Ugarit may have included brined feta types packed in clay-sealed Canaanite jars. Within this context, it is perhaps noteworthy that the high salt and moisture contents of brined white cheeses stimulate the lipase enzymes present in crude animal rennet that break down milkfat to produce strong piquant flavors and aromas. The distinctive piquant flavors of feta-type cheeses were no doubt appreciated as much then (or more so) as they are today, and such cheeses may well have been considered worth the added cost of long-distance shipping in the eyes of the Bronze Age elite.

The woven sack may have been another common container used to ship bulky solid foodstuffs such as grain by sea (Monroe 2007). Thus, it is possible that Canaanite cheeses were shipped in sacks (or strong woven baskets), in which case they were probably small, rugged, dry-rind cheeses used for grating, roughly similar to traditional uncooked pecorino and caprino cheeses still produced in Italy such as Pecorino Bagnolese and Caprino d'Aspromonte. Though commonly produced in the northern Mediterranean, small rinded aged cheeses are difficult to make in the Near East because they tend to dry out excessively in the intense heat and low humidity of the region. It's possible that the cheeses shipped to Ugarit may have been the Canaanite counterpart to the contemporaneous Hittite "aged soldier cheese," though this is pure speculation. It is worth mentioning, however, that cheese graters make their appearance in the Mediterranean region and become very common in the Iron Age to follow, which seems to reflect the growing presence of small, hard, rennet-coagulated grating cheeses from the Bronze Age forward (Ridgway 1997).

The importance of rennet-coagulated cheeses in the Hittite world is further emphasized in a letter written by the Hittite king Arnuwanda to Madduwattaš, the ruler of a vassal state in western Anatolia, around 1400 BC (Bryce 2005). Madduwattaš and his people had recently been driven out of their homeland by an invading army led by Attaršiyaš. Arnuwanda had come to Madduwattaš's aid, providing refuge for his people and essential supplies needed to start a new life. In his letter Arnuwanda reminds Madduwattaš of all that he has done for him and his people:

> Just as the father of the Sun [a reference to the Hittite king Arnuwanda] had warded off Attaršiyaš from thee, then the father of the Sun received thee, Madduwattaš, together with thy women, thy children, thy troops and thy chariot-warriors and gave thee chariots—, corn and seed corn, everything in abundance, and he gave thee also beer and wine, malt and malt-bread, rennet and cheese, everything in abundance.
>
> (Wainwright 1959, pp.202, 203)

Note that Arnuwanda includes rennet and cheese among the essentials that he provided to Madduwattaš and his people to help them start anew. Clearly, rennet-coagulated cheese had become firmly entrenched in the Anatolian diet and culture, and ranked high in importance, on a par with bread, beer, and wine.

The account of Madduwattaš is intriguing because it speaks of the growing Mycenaean influence in the region. There seems to be a scholarly consensus that the kingdom of Ahhiyawa, the home of Attaršiyaš, was a Mycenaean colony on the Aegean coast of northwest Anatolia (Knapp 1991). This is one of the first indications of a growing tension between the Hittites and the great Aegean civilizations to the west. The stage was thus being set for a clash of civilizations, east and west, that centuries later would be immortalized in Homer's epic account of the Trojan War.

The Minoan and Mycenaean Civilizations

The Mesopotamian innovations of the plow and animal traction passed through Anatolia and reached the island of Crete and the Greek mainland during the third millennium BC (Halstead 1981). As in Mesopotamia and Anatolia, the plow opened up more area in the lowlands for the cultivated fields, which also provided greater opportunity for goat and sheep herding on the stubble and fallow fields. Here, as in Mesopotamia, transhumant practices developed to increase the herd-carrying capacity of lowland grazing by moving the animals to mountainous highlands during the growing season. Changes in faunal assemblages (that is, animal bone distributions) coupled with the appearance of perforated pottery shards in the archaeological stratum of this period point to an increased emphasis on milk production and cheese making (Barker 2006). Gradually these changes led to an intensification of cultivation and pastoralism that spurred population growth and began to foster new civilizations on Crete and the Greek mainland.

Cretan civilization, referred to as the Minoan civilization, was the first to blossom. By the start of the second millennium BC Crete was governed and administered by a network of large administrative and religious complexes that archaeologists refer to as "palaces," foremost of which was the palace at Knossos. In some ways Minoan regional palaces resembled the great Mesopotamian city-states and almost certainly reflect strong Mesopotamian and Anatolian cultural influences: They were dominated by monumental buildings with vast storerooms and workshops that served a massive redistributive economy administered by the palace and were apparently linked to temple worship (Neils 2008; Sansone 2009). They borrowed the technique of cuneiform writing on clay tablets from the Near East and developed their own written language, referred to as Linear A. And as in Mesopotamia, the Minoans institutionalized large-scale transhumant sheep herding for wool production and textile manufacture (Halstead 1996; Wallace 2003).

The archaeological record has yielded only limited evidence of cheese and butter production on Crete, however, which is limited to the context of the small-scale mixed farming model brought to Crete thousands of years earlier by Neolithic immigrants. Virtually no evidence for the use of cheese and butter in temple worship has been recovered, thus the Minoans apparently did not couple their wool industry with large-scale dairy processing to support temple activities, as in Mesopotamia. A cautionary note is in order, however, because the Minoan Linear A language has never been deciphered; therefore we know much less about the Minoans than the Sumerians and Akkaddians of Mesopotamia, or the Hittites of Anatolia (Neils 2008). A possible glimpse into the religious practices of Minoan culture was found on the neighboring island of Keos, where a Minoan-period fresco was excavated that portrays a religious procession of men carrying offerings. One of the men is carrying a pole from which hangs a sack that may have been filled with cheese according to Abramovitz (1980). Speculations such as this, however, must be considered tentative at best.

The Minoan civilization flowered briefly at the start of the second millennium BC but was soon subsumed by the rival and more militaristic Mycenaean civilization, known to Homer as the Achaeans, that arose on the Greek mainland. The Mycenaeans borrowed heavily from Minoan civilization, including the Minoan Linear A script, which they transformed into a new script, referred to as Linear B, from which classical Greek eventually evolved (Sansone 2009). They also established their own palace-centered economy on the mainland, and like the Minoans developed intensive sheep herding and wool production for textiles, as well as intensive olive oil and wine production, all of which were exported. Indeed, trade with Egypt, the Levant, and the west coast of Anatolia became a major driver of the Mycenaean economy and culture (Cline 2007).

We know more about the Mycenaeans than the Minoans because their Linear B script has been deciphered and several thousand cuneiform clay tablets containing palace administrative records have been recovered from this period and translated (Sansone 2009). From these records it is evident that the Mycenaeans worshipped many of the deities that would become the classical Greek pantheon. Furthermore, the records indicate that large quantities of foodstuffs, including cheese, were offered to the god Poseidon and other deities in the palace sanctuaries that served as the center of religious activities, and were consumed in sacred acts of religious feasting (Brown 1960; Lupack 2007; Palaima 2004), much along the lines of long-standing religious practice in Mesopotamia and in contemporaneous Hittite Anatolia.

Thus, from the temple of Inanna to the sanctuary of Poseidon, there appears to be a strong cultural continuity between east and west, Mesopotamia and Greece, which was manifested in many ways, including the use of cheese as a medium of spiritual expression. Indeed, cheese continued to serve dual needs in the Bronze Age Aegean, much as it had in the Near East for two millennia, as a basic staple of simple rural peoples and as a prestige food destined for temple worship and elite feasting (Palmer 1994). Though we know nothing about the nature of Mycenaean cheese, the close contact between the Mycenaeans and Hittites provided ample opportunity for rennet-coagulated cheese-making technology to pass from the latter to the former if the Mycenaeans didn't already possess the know-how. The first indirect evidence for aged rennet cheese in the Aegean does not occur until the tenth century BC in the form of bronze cheese graters (Ridgway 1997).

Mycenaean civilization collapsed catastrophically around 1200 BC, and the Greek mainland was plunged into a chaotic period that historians refer to as the Greek Dark Age, but the memory of the Mycenaean pantheon and their love of cheese would linger and become an important element of Hellenistic Greek culture that would arise a few centuries later.

Europe to the North

While the great civilizations of Mesopotamia, Anatolia, Egypt, and the Aegean rose in succession and eventually vied with one another for resources and territory, Europe to the north continued to be characterized by modest agrarian communities founded on the Neolithic Near East model of small-scale mixed farming. Nevertheless, important developments were occurring in Europe before and during the Anatolian Bronze Age that would have far-reaching implications for cheese making. Neolithic immigrants had introduced crop cultivation, herding, and dairying to Europe starting in the seventh millennium BC (Craig et al. 2005). However, Europe at this time was heavily forested; grazing lands were very limited and restricted primarily to clearings that Neolithic settlers had carved out of the forests with their stone tools. Pastoralism and dairying, therefore, were limited to very small scales. This would change, however, beginning in the fourth millennium BC.

The start of the fourth millennium BC marked the change from the climate period known as the Atlantic to the Sub-Boreal, the latter being characterized in Europe by a continent-wide onset of colder, drier winters and hotter summers (Barker 2006). Climatic fluctuations were especially large during the Atlantic/Sub-Boreal transition during the early fourth millennium BC, when central Europe experienced colder winter temperatures than at any time in the previous two thousand years (Anthony 2007). As a result, floods occurred more frequently in the settled floodplains of the river valleys where crops were grown, and harder frosts occurred later in the spring, which shortened the length of the growing season. This created enormous stress on Neolithic agricultural communities; hardship and hunger were on the rise, and the need to supplement crop cultivation with other sustainable food sources became increasingly urgent, reaching crisis proportions in some regions. In the lower Danube region of Romania, for example, many settlements were burned or abandoned and great cultural upheaval took place. Around the same time, the lower Danube experienced an influx of pastoral herders from the steppes north of the Black and Caspian Seas, who were also evidently in crisis because of the change in climate (Anthony 2007).

Nevertheless, the extremely cold winters of the early Sub-Boreal period did have a "silver lining," one that had a long-lasting impact. The dense forests that covered central Europe were not able to regenerate as readily in the colder environment, which quickly led to an opening of the forests in some locations (Barker 1985). Around this same time or shortly before, the plow and use of oxen for traction made their way from Mesopotamia to Europe, where they were widely adopted, even as far north as Scandinavia. The newly opened landscape, coupled with the eventual moderation of winter temperatures and the adoption of plowing, encouraged local clearing of forests to make way for new cultivated fields. In central Europe in particular, the resulting increase in fallow fields and access to field stubble after the harvest, in turn, encouraged a strong shift in animal husbandry in favor of dairying during the later centuries of the fourth millennium BC (Sherratt 1983). Europe north of the Alps was now moving in the direction of more intense dairying.

Of special interest was the effect that severe winter temperatures had on the alpine regions of Europe. The alpine timberline (the transition zone from closed forest stands to more or less isolated trees and finally alpine grassland) is in dynamic equilibrium with the local climate and is thus highly sensitive to climatic changes, even very rapid changes in climate (Tinner and Kaltenrieder 2005). The cooling that occurred as the Atlantic period transitioned to the Sub-Boreal resulted in significant lowering of the timberlines throughout alpine regions of Europe, by as much as 1,000 feet (300m), over the period from around 3500 to 2500 BC (Greenfield 1988; Tinner and Theurillat 2003). In other words, substantial increases occurred in the relatively open alpine and subalpine zones during this period, creating extended swaths of terrain that would prove suitable for grazing (Barker 1985; Greenfield 1988). This opening of the high-altitude landscape, in turn, encouraged striking changes in settlement patterns and agricultural subsistence strategies that shifted strongly in favor of pastoralism and dairying in mountainous environments.

In the Balkan peninsula, for example, a marked shift took place in domestic animal bone distributions, indicative of increased emphasis on goat and sheep herding and their secondary products, milk and wool. Furthermore, new transhumant herding strategies that took advantage of the more open highland pastures were put into practice at this time (Greenfield 1988), a development that would become a permanent fixture of Balkan agriculture, even to the present.

In Switzerland, although Neolithic agricultural communities had been established north of the Swiss border in the Danube River Valley since the sixth millennium BC, it wasn't until the fourth millennium that agriculture made its debut in the Swiss plateau and alpine regions (Wehrli et al. 2007). Whether agriculture was brought there by Neolithic farmers driven by the effects of climate change from the heavily populated Danube lowlands or, alternately, borrowed by the indigenous Paleolithic peoples from their Neolithic neighbors is a matter of scholarly debate (Barker 2006;

Sauter 1976). Either way, when farming began to be practiced in the lakeside communities and mountain valleys of Switzerland during the fourth millennium BC, seasonal pasturing of cattle, sheep, and goats, and transhumant herding of livestock up and down the lower valleys to take advantage of more open grazing in the higher country during the summer quickly followed (Barker 1985; Wehrli et al. 2007). The cultivation of fields in the plains and valleys, combined with a strong emphasis on transhumant pastoralism and dairying, proved to be a sustainable strategy for survival in the harsh mountainous environment.

Farmers in the highlands of central Europe quickly realized that they could lower the timberline even farther by clear-cutting, burning, and grazing, and beginning around 2500 BC evidence of significant human impacts on timberline altitude and composition can be observed in the pollen and plant fossil records of the Swiss highland plateau and Alps (Finsinger and Tinner 2007; Heiri et al. 2006).

This early form of alpine dairying relied on winter fodder that consisted almost exclusively of twigs and leaves gathered from the surrounding forests because accessible grasslands for haying were virtually nonexistent (Rasmussen 1990). It wasn't until around the end of the second millennium BC that extensive woodland clearance at lower altitudes opened up grasslands for hay cropping, which was used to supplement leaf foddering and eventually became the primary source of winter fodder. Leaf foddering, however, continued to be practiced in Switzerland as a supplement to haying even into the twentieth century (Rasmussen 1990). Thus, the transition from the fourth to the third millennium BC marked the beginning of the traditional alpine farming model based on transhumant dairying and winter stalling and foddering in byres that has continued into modern times (Barker 1985). Across the Alps in the subalpine regions of northern Italy a similar transformation was occurring, albeit more slowly. Alpine cattle and sheep dairying became firmly established there during the first half of the third millennium BC (Barker 1985; Wick and Tinner 1997).

Pottery assemblages from this period and organic residue analyses suggest that cheese making began in Switzerland and northern Italy about the same time that dairying was introduced (Barker 1985). This new alpine farming model proved successful and intensified in Switzerland and subalpine Italy during the second millennium BC (Sauter 1976). Farther to the south, in central Italy, transhumant pastoralism and cheese making were also being practiced along the Apennine Mountains by this time (Barker 1985). Indeed, alpine transhumant dairying and cheese making would ultimately become a nearly ubiquitous feature of mountainous regions throughout Europe, one that would foster the development of a diverse family of alpine cheeses that share a common technology tailored to the peculiarities of the mountain environment.

We know little about the early alpine cheeses of central Europe other than what can be gleaned from the repertoire of ceramic sieves and other cheese-making utensils that have been recovered from the archaeological strata of this period. By the time the Roman legions marched north across the Alps into central Europe near the end of the first millennium BC, however, cheese-making techniques throughout the transalpine region of central Europe had advanced impressively. Indeed, a strong dairying and cheese-making culture had taken root among the Celtic peoples of central Europe, which ultimately would be dispersed across the continent and would help to shape European cheese making.

The End of the Bronze Age

During the second millennium BC, changes were occurring back in the Near East and the Aegean that would contribute to a dramatic end to the Bronze Age around 1200 BC. In Anatolia metalsmiths were now smelting iron, and although the technology progressed slowly and iron could not yet compete with bronze because of its poor quality, experimentation would eventually lead to the discovery of quenched carburized iron or steel, which would render bronze all but obsolete (Muhly et al. 1985). The seeds were now sown for the coming age of iron, because iron ore was much more abundant than copper ore and tin in Anatolia and many other places; it would soon be possible to produce iron weapons and utensils that were not only superior to those of bronze but also much cheaper and more widely available (Muhly et al. 1985).

Also around this time (circa 1900 BC) the Near East witnessed the arrival of the premier military weapon, the domesticated horse and chariot, from the Pontic/Caspian steppes (Anthony 2007). Recent findings strongly suggest that horses were first domesticated, harnessed for riding and traction, and used for milk production around 3500 BC by the Botai people who lived in the steppes of Eurasia, north and west of the Caspian Sea in what is now Kazakhstan (Outram et al. 2009). The Botai culture ordered their lives and subsistence around the horse, from which they derived meat, milk, and a variety of animal by-products. Interestingly, bone assemblages recovered from this period indicate that the Botai kept no domesticated ruminants (goats, sheep, or cattle). Thus, they were latecomers to the practice of domestication, and they learned to exploit the horse for milk production independently of the Near Eastern cultures, whose experience with ruminant dairying stretched back some three thousand years.

Farther to the west, however, in the steppes north of the Black and Caspian Seas, lived pastoral peoples who had long ago migrated out of Neolithic Anatolia through the Balkan peninsula, the lower Danube, and on to Pontic/Caspian steppes, and who herded cattle, sheep, and goats. They soon followed the example of the Botai and domesticated the horse, then invented the chariot, which made them a force to be reckoned with (Anthony 2007).

The arrival of the horse and chariot from the Pontic/Caspian steppes to the civilizations of the Near East and Aegean around the beginning of the second millennium BC set into motion a new dynamic between the ruling elite and those whom they ruled. The fearsome power and elite status of the chariot gave rise to a warrior aristocracy that widened the gulf between the ruling elite and the common man, creating a new socioeconomic harshness accompanied by a rise in the dispossessed poor. The social fabric and the interconnected economic systems of the Near East and Aegean civilizations began to unravel (Liverani 2005; Schon 2007).

Added to these developments was a period of sharp climatic drying in the Mediterranean toward the end of the second millennium BC, which likely led to repeated years of drought, reduced harvests and famine, and ultimately mass movements of dispossessed and hungry peoples (Liverani 2005). Cuneiform records from Hittite Anatolia and its vassal city of Ugarit speak of famine and desperate pleas to Egypt for grain shipments to ease the crisis, along with ominous reports of social unrest and impending chaos (Wainwright 1959, 1961). In Greece, Mycenaean cuneiform records from the same period indicate that military assets were being mobilized to guard the coast, presumably from invasion by sea (Neils 2008). Invasions did occur around the beginning of the twelfth century BC, which resulted in the utter destruction of the Mycenaean palaces and civilization and evidently triggered the migration of Mycenaean peoples in various directions, which would have repercussions in Europe to the north and throughout the Mediterranean.

Migrations of Mycenaean peoples northward to the lower Danube River may have occurred, though the evidence is still inconclusive. And even as Mycenaean civilization collapsed, horse-riding pastoralists from the Pontic steppes were also on the move, expanding westward, perhaps under the same climatic stresses. They may have moved into the lower Danube around this time, though again the evidence is inconclusive. What is clear, however, is that a period of great upheaval and an infusion of new culture occurred in the lower Danube during this turbulent time, one that would soon help to shape a new social order farther to the west in the transalpine region of central Europe (Austria, Switzerland, eastern France). A new people, the Celts, were emerging out of the chaos; their language and identity were just beginning to take shape (Cunliffe 1997). The Celts would become great cheesemakers, and their eventual dispersal across Europe no doubt influenced the development of untold European cheeses.

Back in the Aegean, Mycenaean refugees evidently joined forces with dispossessed peoples from coastal Anatolia, who then went on a rampage of violence and pillaging in Anatolia and the Levant that would leave a path of destruction stretching from Troy in the north to southern Canaan. Centuries later Homer (*Iliad*) and Virgil (*Aeneid*) would recall of the turbulence of the times in their accounts of the Trojan War, which represented one episode in a series of wars, disasters, and migrations that lasted for two centuries (Wainwright 1959). Even Egypt was not spared the onslaught of invading hordes. Egyptian scribes recorded detailed accounts of invasions of the "sea peoples," first during the reign of Meneptah in 1219 BC and then again during the reign of Rameses III, in 1162 BC (Wainwright 1961).

These sea peoples were apparently a loose confederation of hungry and dispossessed peoples, primarily from coastal Anatolia, but also probably joined by marauding peoples from the Aegean islands and Greek mainland (Wainwright 1959, 1961). They swept through Anatolia to the gates of Hattusa, the capital of the Hittite empire, which like the Mycenaean civilization collapsed in utter destruction. They then turned southward through the Levant, destroying cities in their path, until they were repulsed, not once but twice, by the Egyptians (Wainwright 1959, 1961). Though the Egyptians prevailed, Egypt was seriously weakened, to the extent that it never recovered its status as the supreme regional superpower.

The failed attempts of the sea peoples to invade Egypt may have had a secondary repercussion on the history of cheese making. Among the various groups that constituted the sea peoples, the ones that the Egyptian scribes referred to as the Shekelesh, Teresh, and Sherden may have sailed west around this time and settled in Sicily, Italy, and Sardinia, respectively, after the failed Egyptian invasion (Wainwright 1959, 1961). However, evidence for the movement of sea peoples into the western Mediterranean derives mainly from ancient written records, whereas supporting archaeological evidence remains incomplete and controversial. Indeed, many scholars reject the notion of large-scale resettlement of sea peoples in the west.

What does seem to be well established is the arrival of a strong eastern or Aegean cultural influence in the western Mediterranean toward the end of the Bronze Age, which seems to coincide with at least some limited settlement activity from the east in Sicily, Italy, and Sardinia (Cunliffe 1997; Le Glay et al. 2009). Thus, it is possible that eastern expertise in rennet-coagulated cheese making may have found its way along with other eastern cultural elements to the west around the end of the second millennium BC, and in the process invigorated and reinvented the indigenous cheese making that had been practiced there since the Neolithic Age. Perhaps it was no coincidence, then, that Italy and Sicily became prolific producers of aged rennet-coagulated cheeses during the first millennium BC.

And finally, one of the groups of Anatolian origin who were numbered among the sea peoples were the Philistines. The Philistines settled in the coastal plains of the land of Canaan around 1185 BC just before the second unsuccessful attempt to invade Egypt (Barako 2000; Stone 1995). The Philistines prospered in Canaan for more than five hundred years using their strategically located ports on the Mediterranean, such as Ashkelon and Ashdod, to aggressively develop trade networks throughout the region. Philistine aspirations for territorial expansion were abruptly checked, however, by the arrival about the same time of a new people, the Israelites, who became the Philistines' nemesis under the leadership of King Saul and then King David and his son Solomon. This was the same David who, as a shepherd, had delivered cheeses to King Saul's armies and then slew the invincible Philistine warrior Goliath with a simple sling and stone, a feat that turned the tide of battle against the Philistines. David's victory over Goliath launched his meteoric rise to become Israel's greatest king. And from the lineage of David, a thousand years later, would come the son of a carpenter, whose influence on western civilization and cheese making was arguably greater than that of any other person, before or since.

CHAPTER FOUR

Greece, Cheese, and the Mediterranean Miracle

> Your hands shaped me and made me. Will you now turn and destroy
> me? Remember that you molded me like clay. Will you now turn
> me to dust again? Did you not pour me out like milk and curdle
> me like cheese, clothe me with skin and flesh and knit me together
> with bones and sinews? . . . Why then did you bring me out of the
> womb? I wish I had died before any eye saw me.
>
> Job 10: 8–11, 18

In the biblical account of Job, the main character confronts the universal
problem of human suffering in one of the most profound works of ancient
literature. Job had lived a blameless and upright life, yet he lost everything
including his health for no apparent reason. Thus, Job despairs of his life.
In the above passage Job uses the imagery of milk coagulation and cheese
making to eloquently express his confusion and frustration toward God for
creating him in the first place.

We do not know precisely when the Book of Job was written (most estimates range from around 2000 to 500 BC), but we do know that this was
not the last time that milk coagulation and cheese making were used as
imagery for human conception and the birth process. Aristotle, one of the
greatest among the many great Greek philosophers and an avid naturalist,
built his theory of human conception and embryonic development around
the metaphor of rennet coagulation and cheese making. Job's and Aristotle's
metaphorical imagery would surface again during the Roman era and play
a role in the development of the early Christian church. Later still, from
medieval times down to the present, cheesemakers and religious figures

alike have bundled the parallel mysteries of milk coagulation and human conception together through mysticism, folklore, and traditions. We can even hear echoes of the birthing analogy expressed among the new breed of artisan cheesemakers who have blossomed of late in America and other places where traditional cheese making had all but disappeared during the twentieth century.

But now we are getting way ahead of ourselves. In the end Job was restored to a position of even greater prosperity than he had enjoyed before his ordeal. From the writings of Homer it would seem that Greece of the ninth century BC felt a bit like Job, having lost all of its earlier Mycenaean glory. But like Job, Greece eventually experienced renewal, and by Aristotle's time in the fourth century BC it was restored to a position of even greater prosperity and grander civilization than it had enjoyed before the catastrophic collapse of the Bronze Age and the centuries of darkness that followed. By then extensive trade networks had been restored and Greece along with the Phoenicians were prospering through the establishment of far-flung colonies and trading outposts. Maritime trade in cheese would come of age in the Greek era. But the Greek renaissance was not merely economic in nature. A new vitality in Greek culture, with Greek religion at its center, spread infectiously around the Mediterranean, elevating civilization to new heights, and, some would argue, taking it to new depths. And once again cheese played an important role in Greek religious practice and expression, as it had in the religions of the great Near East civilizations that came before.

Greek Civilization Resurrected

The collapse of the Bronze Age around 1200 BC completely wiped out Mycenaean civilization on the Greek mainland and Aegean islands. Thus began the so-called Dark Age of Greece, which lasted several hundred years, during which centralized communities organized around the palaces disappeared; the art of Linear B cuneiform writing was lost; maritime trade all but ceased; population centers dispersed, populations declined precipitously, and those who remained resumed life in small, isolated settlements; and agriculture reverted from large-scale, trade-oriented cash crops (especially wool, olive oil, and wine) to the small-scale mixed farming that had been practiced in Neolithic times (Cherry 1988; Sansone 2009; Wallace 2003).

In the absence of written records our understanding of Greek life during the Dark Age is limited. Poverty evidently inspired significant movement of peoples from the Greek Aegean world eastward to coastal Anatolia and the island of Cyprus, where Greek communities were established during the twelfth and eleventh centuries BC (Sansone 2009). The existence of a Greek diaspora in Asia Minor probably encouraged the seafaring Greeks to gradually resume maritime trade.

Then, significantly, around 1000 BC the technology for smelting iron, which by then had spread beyond Anatolia to the Levant, was introduced to mainland Greece through contact with Cyprus. Because Greece was rich in iron ore, the production of iron tools and weapons there soon became a thriving industry and a stimulus for the expansion of trade, which in turn fueled broader economic recovery on the Greek mainland and Aegean islands (Sansone 2009). Over the next two hundred years, various Greek communities began to establish outposts throughout the Mediterranean to facilitate trade. Consequently Greek interaction with Asia Minor and the Near East increased, especially with the Phoenicians.

The Phoenicians were a Canaanite people who lived along the Levantine coast in what is now Lebanon. Soon after the widespread destruction of coastal Levantine cities by the "sea peoples" at the end of the Bronze Age, the Canaanite Phoenicians began rebuilding their major port cities. The Levantine coast had long served as the crossroads for trade between east and west, between the great civilizations of Mesopotamia and those of Egypt and later Hittite Anatolia and the Aegean. The collapse of Mediterranean trade and the weakening of Egypt at the end of the Bronze Age left a vacuum of power and mercantile potential that the Phoenicians and the Philistines to their south aggressively moved to fill at the start of the first millennium BC (Sommer 2007).

Initially, the Phoenicians faced stiff competition from their Philistine neighbors, but Israelite resistance under David's rule brought Philistine expansionism to a halt and opened the door for Phoenicia's ascendancy (Aubet 2001). The Phoenician city of Tyre eventually rose to preeminence and became a regionwide hegemonic power that established trading colonies throughout the Mediterranean, the most important of which was Carthage, founded in 814 BC on the coast of north Africa. Phoenicia became the intermediary for trade between the great Mesopotamian empire of Assyria and the Mediterranean, but by the early years of the sixth century BC a new power rose in southern Mesopotamia, the neo-Babylonian empire under Nebuchadnezzar, which overwhelmed Assyria and marched westward to the Levant. The Babylonians laid siege to Tyre for thirteen years, from 585 to 572 BC, resulting in its total destruction. Many, however, were able to flee from Tyre to the refuge of Carthage, which had been steadily increasing in prominence to become the new Phoenician capital in the west. Carthage and its Punic civilization would become Greece's and then Rome's major economic and military rival in the west.

Meanwhile, back in Greece, growing prosperity coincided with a vast increase in population by the eighth century BC, which put enormous strain on the limited agricultural resources of the mountainous Greek countryside. The need to ease population pressures, to establish new sources of grain for importation, and to counter growing competition with Phoenicia in Mediterranean trade prompted a period of unprecedented Greek expansion that continued for three centuries. This era was characterized by the establishment of a network of Greek colonies that stretched from the shores of the Black Sea in the east to north Africa, Sicily, southern Italy, France, and even Spain to the west. Hundreds of colonies were established, many of which became important cities, including Catania and Syracuse (Sicily), and Marseilles (France), which would all become important centers for a growing trade in cheese.

As the Greeks expanded their trade activities they constantly bumped up against the Phoenicians, from whom they borrowed and revised the Phoenician alphabet to represent their own language around the start of the eighth century BC, thereby creating the Greek written language. Through contact with the Phoenicians the Greeks also assimilated other elements of Near Eastern culture and religion into their own, to the extent that the period from the mid-eighth to the mid-seventh century BC is referred to as the Orientalizing Period of Greek civilization. It was during this period that the Semitic goddess of fertility and sex known variously as Ashtorith,

Astarte, and Ishtar, whose origins stretched back three thousand years to the Sumerian goddess Inanna, joined the Greek pantheon as Aphrodite (Sansone 2009). Certain elements of early Greek mythology also took on striking parallels with Near Eastern myths. But arguably the most significant Near Eastern contribution to Greek civilization was the *polis*, the characteristic unit of Greek social, political, and religious organization. The polis was a permutation of the Near Eastern city-state, a self-governing entity consisting of an urban center surrounded by an agricultural area that supported the city.

Central to the identity of the polis was its religious cult and patron deity, the worship of whom dominated both private and public life and bound the community together in shared ideology and ritual. The focal point of Greek religion was the cult sanctuary, an area of the polis set aside for the local deity in which were situated the temple—the physical structure that housed the image (statue) of the deity—as well as facilities for conducting sacrifices and other rites, and dining facilities for banquets and feasts (Kearns 2010). Though Greek religion borrowed much from the Near East, many elements of the Mycenaean past were also evident. For example, several of the Mycenaean deities named on the Linear B tablets took their places among the Greek pantheon and became prominent cultic figures. Also, Greek temples displayed clear similarities in design to the sanctuaries of the Mycenaean palaces (Neils 2008). But most important from the standpoint of cheese history is the significant role that cheese played in Greek religious practice.

Cheese in Greek Religion

Animal sacrifice served as the central act in Greek worship. Sacrifices were performed in the cult sanctuary at an open-air altar that stood in front of the deity's temple. Worshippers were expected to sacrifice to the gods according to their ability; thus, the frequency of sacrifice and type of animal slaughtered depended on the worshipper's prosperity. For most citizens of the polis, animal sacrifices probably took place only on special occasions rather than routinely. At other times, worshippers were expected to provide the gods with bloodless food offerings, preferably daily (in the morning and again in the evening), though it's unclear how diligently daily offerings were observed (Kearns 2010). Bloodless offerings consisted of common food items that the people would normally have for themselves, especially cakes, fruit, bread, and sometimes cheese. The offerings were placed on designated tables that were set off to the side of the altar used for animal sacrifices, or inside the temple itself (Gill 1974).

During the 1930s a fascinating set of marble inscriptions was excavated from the northwest slope of the Acropolis in Athens. The inscriptions apparently belonged to two monuments or altars that were erected around 500 BC, and they contained a detailed list of the amounts of cheese, barley meal, beans, sesame seeds, olive oil, and honey that were to be offered to the various gods associated with the Eleusinian cult. The inscriptions were a set of instructions that endeavored to standardize the rituals of the sanctuary as a permanent code (Jeffery 1948). The Acropolis is one of the oldest Greek sanctuaries and was already considered ancient by the fifth century BC. Therefore, it would seem that the Athenians of 500 BC were concerned about preserving their ancient religious traditions against changes that were probably creeping in as Athens grew in wealth and cultural stature. Within this context it is noteworthy that the Athenians endeavored to preserve the inclusion of cheese in worship as a bloodless offering, suggesting that cheese was an ancient and central article of worship.

Around the same time (circa 486 BC), the Greek comic poet Khionides described an Athenian public ritual that involved setting out meals on tables for the Dioskouroi (Castor and Pollux, the twin sons of Zeus). The meals were intentionally simple, consisting of cheese, a barley cake, ripe olives, and leeks, in order to remind the Athenians of their earlier and simpler way of life (Gill 1974). Thus, we see again an Athenian desire to remember the past, a simpler time when cheese played a central role in daily life and religious practice.

Bloodless offerings of cheese also were made to Demeter, the goddess of the harvest, as indicated from sacrificial inscriptions recovered from the sanctuary of Demeter near Sparta (Jeffery 1948). The Spartan temple of Artemis, goddess of the forests and hills, was particularly well known for its offerings of cheese, not because of Spartan piety but because of the sanctioned theft of cheeses from the temple. According to the fourth-century Greek writer Xenophon, Spartan schoolboys were intentionally fed very plain meals that didn't quite satisfy their youthful appetites. However, the boys were periodically allowed and even encouraged to raid the community in search of more savory fare as part of their training to become future soldiers. A boy caught stealing food was severely flogged, not for stealing but for getting caught, whereas successful raids were considered meritorious. The temple of Artemis, which was always well provisioned with bloodless sacrifices of food, became the premier target for such foraging raids, and a renowned competition developed among the boys to beat the record for stealing cheeses from the temple (Harley 1934).

Sometimes the gods required specific types of cheese for their offerings. In Hellenic Crete (the Hellenistic period extended from around 320 to 100 BC), for example, a special variety known as "female cheese" was used in bloodless offerings to Cybele, the Mother of the Gods (Halbherr 1897). Unfortunately, the answer to the intriguing question of how "female" cheese differed from other (male?) cheese was lost in antiquity, though the cheese may have been analogous to "female cake," which was made in the shape of the female breast. Strabo, the first-century BC Greek geographer, alluded to another divine preference for cheese. He reported that the priestess of Athena in Athens was not allowed to touch native green (fresh) cheese; only foreign cheese was set before her (Cooley 1899). Athena had evidently acquired a taste for imported cheese. As will soon become evident, Athena was not alone; Greece was known for its thriving market for imported cheese.

In addition to serving as an entrée in bloodless offerings, cheese often found its way into worship as an ingredient of sacrificial cakes. Cakes were a ubiquitous element of the Greek diet and Greek bloodless offerings, and different deities preferred different types of cake. A light flaky cake known as the *plakous* or *plakounta,* which consisted of honey and goat's- or sheep's-milk cheese alternating with thin layers of pastry dough inside a firm cake shell, was apparently a favorite of Demeter and Apollo (Brumfield 1997; Grandjouan et al. 1989). Another cake, the *phthois,* made from wheat flour, cheese, and honey, was customarily offered to Hestia, Zeus, Apollo, and Asklepios (Brumfield 1997). At the sanctuary of Demeter in Corinth, *plakous* and other cakes were offered to the goddess—as were clay representations of the cakes, arranged in miniature clay winnowing baskets. Hundreds of these baskets containing clay cakes dating from the sixth to second century BC have been recovered from the sanctuary in Corinth. Worshippers evidently purchased the clay replicas from a thriving community of potters that specialized in sacrificial paraphernalia outside the temple.

Asklepios, the god of healing, presents one of the most intriguing linkages of cheese to Greek religion. The offering of cakes, especially cheese-filled cakes, seemed to have been particularly prominent in the cult of Asklepios (Kearns 2010). Perhaps this was in deference to Asklepios's half brother Aristaious, who in Greek mythology was the god who taught humans the art of cheese making (Harrod 1981). Even more interesting is the possible role that milk coagulation and cheese making may have played in the healing rituals of the cult of Asklepios. Asklepios was not merely worshipped as the god of healing; his cult spread throughout the Greek and then the Roman world because his sanctuary, referred to as Asklepieion, served as a center of healing, the ancient equivalent of a hospital. For more than five hundred years the afflicted came from far and wide, seeking treatment and healing at sanctuaries of Asklepios scattered across the Mediterranean and Aegean (Kearns 2010). Sacred snakes with miraculous powers of healing were an important element of the sanctuaries, and cultic images of Asklepios invariably portray him with holding a staff around which the sacred snake is coiled (Bieber 1957). The image of the sacred healing snake coiled around Asklepios's staff has become a universal symbol of medicine and healing that is often included in medical-related logos, such as that of the American Medical Association.

What does all this have to do with milk coagulation and cheese making? Well, during the 1930s an archaeological team from the American School of Classical Studies at Athens led by Ferdinand Joseph de Waele systematically excavated the site of the Asklepieion at Corinth (de Waele 1933). The original sanctuary was built in the sixth century BC and then rebuilt in fourth century BC. Among the many artifacts found at the site were large flat terra-cotta basins that contained heavy spouts. Basins of this type were (and still are) typically interpreted to be mortars that were used to grind grain during sacred rituals. However, de Waele suggested that they also might have served as basins for coagulating milk, or perhaps even cheese vats, based on their striking similarity to milk basins/cheese vats used traditionally in Switzerland.

De Waele's hypothesis apparently attracted little attention for forty years. Then in the 1970s Rodger Edwards undertook a project to reconstruct the ceramic history of Corinth using the findings of the previous excavations (Edwards 1975). He, too, examined the terra-cotta basins that had been assumed to be mortars and pondered de Waele's hypothesis that they may have served as cheese vats. As Edwards examined the vessels more closely, he was impressed by the lack of evidence of abrasion or perceptible wear that you would expect to find on the inner surface of a mortar used for grinding. Furthermore, the peculiar design of the basin's handles and spout seemed better suited for liquid than dry contents. Edwards became doubtful that the basins had ever been used for grinding or pounding and favored the view that they had served as milk basins or cheese vats. He went on to suggest that some of the references to this type of vessel in the archaeological literature, where they are classified as *holmos,* the ancient Greek term for mortar, should be reconsidered (Edwards 1975). In other words, there may be other "cheese vats" among the inventories of Greek archaeological finds that have been misclassified as mortars.

If indeed these basins were cheese vats, what were they doing in the Corinthian sanctuary of Asklepios? Perhaps related to this question is a first-century BC inscription that was recovered from the site of the Asklepieion of Lebena on the island of Crete that mentions the use of milk in a medical recipe or treatment that was evidently used regularly at the Asklepieion "hospital" there (Chaniotis 1999). Homer's epic poem about the Trojan War, *The Iliad,* may help to explain the role of milk and milk basins/cheese vats in the Asklepieion. In *The Iliad* the gods of the Greek pantheon often took sides in the conflict and found themselves in battle with one another as they fought on behalf of the Achaeans or Trojans. So it was that Ares, the god of war, found himself in a deadly duel with the powerful warrior goddess Athena, who smote him with a mortal blow. Ares, being immortal and "not born to die," had to limp back to his Father Zeus and beg for healing. After lecturing his son, Zeus acquiesced and instructed his physician Paieon to heal Ares. Homer then used rennet coagulation (via fig sap) as a metaphor for Paieon's healing of Ares, stating that Ares' wound healed quickly the way that liquid milk curdles when wild fig sap is dripped in and stirred.(Fitzgerald 1989).

The Homeric connection between the mysterious phenomena of rennet coagulation and healing seems to be deeply entrenched in Greek language. One of the Greek words used to describe the healing of a wound also has strong connotations of milk clotting and curdling (Morgan 1991). Homer's Paieon was initially identified with the god Apollo, father of Asklepios, but by the fourth century BC Asklepios had replaced Apollo as the embodiment of Paieon and had become the healer god in Greek mythology; indeed Asklepios was often referred to by the name Paieon (Kearns 2010). Thus, it is conceivable that the linkage of rennet coagulation and healing that was embedded in Greek mythology and language may have also come together symbolically in the sanctuary of Asklepios (or Paieon) as a cultic rite of healing that incorporated milk coagulation and perhaps even cheese making. It would be interesting to determine whether similar basins that lack evidence of abrasion and wear were present at other sanctuaries of Asklepios, as might be expected if cultic rites involving milk coagulation were widely practiced throughout the Greek world. Analyses of organic residues from such basins perhaps might be able unlock the secret of whether milk coagulation played a role in the healing rites of the Asklepieion.

Cheese in Daily Life and Commerce

Religious expression permeated Greek life to the extent that even one of the premier forms of entertainment in the Greek world, the symposium or drinking party, included prayers and libations to the gods. The party began with a simple meal, the *deipnon,* during which food but not wine was served. After the food was cleared away and the guests' hands washed, the wine along with the "second tables" or dessert courses were brought in. Included among the latter were delicacies such as sweetmeats, eggs, nuts, fresh and dried fruit, cheeses, and cakes, among which the *plakounta* or *plakous* (the flaky cake made with goat's- or sheep's-milk cheese, honey, and dough) was held in especially high esteem (Grandjouan et al. 1989; Noussia 2001).

According to the fifth-century BC philosopher and poet Xenophanes, an honored or holy table with an altar at its center was also set up in the middle of the room and generously adorned with cakes, cheese, and honey in deference to the gods. Libations of wine were then poured and hymns and prayers offered to the gods. Thus, the role of cheese in the symposium straddled both the sacred and the secular because sacred and secular were inseparable, as was true in all of Greek life. According to Xenophanes's idealized account, the evening's main event then began, which consisted of responsible drinking, nibbling on the delicacies, virtuous conversation, and oration. However, other Greek writers as well as images depicting the symposium on Greek pottery reveal that the evening often became quite raucous and filled with sexual license.

Cheese was an integral element of the daily Greek diet, which consisted of two categories: *sitos* or simple food (staple) and *opson* or accompaniment (relish). *Sitos* was the main component of the meal and consisted primarily of porridge made from cereals such as barley meal and bread and cakes baked from wheat. Legumes including chickpeas and lentils were also regular additions. *Opson* was consumed in lesser quantities and consisted mainly of sheep's- or goat's-milk cheese, game, occasionally vegetables, and, above all, fish, usually pickled or salted. Meat was included only on rare occasions (Neils 2008; Wycherley 1956).

The urban dwellers of the polis procured their food from the daily markets that were held in an open, centrally located public space known as the agora. The agora marketplace in Athens had a section dedicated to the sale of fresh cheeses (Wycherley 1956), as undoubtedly was true for other Greek poleis, which were supplied by local farmers from the agricultural areas that surrounded the city. Writing perhaps in the third century BC, Aischylides, as later reported by Aelian, described cheese-producing farmsteads on the island of Ceos off the Attic coast of Greece that were probably also typical of the Greek mainland:

> In his work of agriculture Aeschylides says that in Ceos each of the farmers owns but few sheep, the reason being that the soil of Ceos is exceedingly poor and has no pasture-land. So they throw tree-medick and fig-leaves and the fallen leaves of the olive to the flocks, also the husks of various kinds

of pulse, and they even sow thistles among their crops, all of which afford
excellent feeding for the sheep. And from them they obtain milk which when
curdled produces the finest cheese. And the same writer says that it is called
Cythnian and that it is sold at the rate of 90 drachmas a talent.

(Aelian: Vol. 3, *On the Characteristics of Animals*)

This passage is of particular interest because it not only depicts the role of sheep rearing and cheese making within the small-scale mixed farming model that characterized Greek agriculture, but also indicates a strong commercial emphasis on cheese making for the market (Hodkinson, 1988)— and in this case the market was not simply local. Indeed, the Cythnian cheeses described by Aischylides were famous in the Greek world. Though they presumably were first produced on the Aegean island of Cythnos for which they were named, the style of cheese was evidently copied on the neighboring island of Ceos and perhaps elsewhere and marketed under the same name.

Cythnian cheeses became quite famous for their quality and were exported widely (Casson 1954; Migeotte 2009). Similarly, the Greek island of Rhenaea was known for its export of cheeses (Casson 1954), as was Chios off the coast of Anatolia. Chios was most famous for its wines, but its cheeses also must have been of world-class quality because they were exported along with Chian wines to a Greek colony in Syria, where Phoenician merchants then reshipped them to the lucrative Egyptian market. Egypt imposed a 33 percent and 25 percent import tax on Chian wines and cheeses, respectively, but that apparently did not deter upscale Egyptians from enjoying them, based on third-century BC Egyptian papyrus import records (Berlin 1997). Thus, Greek cheeses had moved beyond the simple fresh cheeses that served as the *opson* of daily life to include high-end gourmet varieties.

We know little about what these Chian export cheeses were like, but it is possible that Homer left us a glimpse of their method of production in his masterpiece *The Odyssey* (Fagles 1996). Although the place and date of the writing of the Homeric poems are not known for certain, several lines of evidence suggest an origin in coastal Anatolia, or on the island of Chios off the coast, around the ninth century BC. If so, Homer may have used local Chian cheese-making practices as a model for his description of Odysseus's encounter with the Cyclops on the island of Sicily. After landing there to the sound of its bleating sheep and goats, the hero Odysseus sets out with some of his crew members to find the cave of the reclusive Cyclops. Though the Cyclops was not home when they arrived, the adventurers were impressed with his well-ordered cheese-making operation where they found many cheeses drying on racks in the cave and the whey from cheese making carefully stored in various vessels.

Odysseus's crewmates, not keen to confront the monstrous Cyclops, suggested that they steal the cheeses, along with the kids and lambs that were penned in the cave, and hightail it back to their ship, but the ever curious and reckless Odysseus convinced them to hide in the cave and wait for the owner's return. As they waited they helped themselves to some of Cyclops' cheese and made an offering of cheese to the gods. It is interesting to note that even at this early stage of Greek cultural development (probably the ninth century BC), Homer had Odysseus and his crewmates present a bloodless offering of cheese to the gods.

Eventually the Cyclops returned to the cave and began his daily cheese-making routine in one of the oldest written accounts of the process in antiquity. The Cyclops coagulated the milk quickly, a clear reference to rennet coagulation, possibly with fig sap based on the nuances of the Greek text and the fact that Homer refers to the milk-coagulating properties of fig sap in *The Iliad* (Oldfather 1913). The fig is native to both Sicily and coastal Asia Minor and would have been available at either location as a source of rennet (Zohary and Hopf 2000). Alternately, the use of animal rennet was well established in Anatolia and beyond by this time, though it wasn't until Aristotle's *History of Animals,* written around 350 BC, that the use of animal rennet in cheese making made its appearance in the surviving Greek literature.

Homer makes no mention of a cooking step in Cyclops's cheese-making procedure, but he indicates that this was a pressed cheese, though only lightly pressed given the limitations of wicker draining baskets to withstand applied pressure. Homer also neglected to mention whether Cyclops applied salt to his cheeses. Assuming that this was an oversight and that salt was rubbed onto the surface, Cyclops's cheese-making procedure could have produced small rennet-coagulated cheeses with enough surface area relative to the volume of the cheese to permit extensive evaporative moisture loss and gradual rind formation, provided the cheeses were stored in an environment that was neither too humid nor too dry. It is quite easy to envision how the racks in Cyclops's open cave, filled with drying cheeses, could have provided suitable temperature and humidity conditions for gradual dehydration and rind formation, resulting in rinded pecorino and caprino cheeses that were low enough in moisture to be aged for extended periods. Such cheese would share much in common with some of the traditional pecorino and caprino cheeses still produced in Italy, such as Pecorino Bagnolese and Caprino d'Aspromonte. Alternately, Cyclops's cheeses could have been consumed fresh, similar to Pecorino Baccellon. Either way, this account in *The Odyssey* is arguably the first credible description of rennet-coagulated cheese making in ancient literature.

Whether Homer was describing cheese making in Chios, Sicily, or both in *The Odyssey* cannot be said for certain; more important is the fact that technology now existed to produce hard, rinded cheeses that were rugged, suitable for extended aging and for grating. In the centuries to follow, grated cheese would become an important element of Greek culture and cuisine, and Sicily would become famous for its grating cheeses. Initially these were probably small, uncooked rennet-coagulated cheeses of the sort described by Homer, and indeed Aristotle wrote of such cheeses that evidently weighed only around one pound or less (Thompson 1907). Eventually, probably many centuries after Homer, cheesemakers in Sicily and on the Italian peninsula added cooking steps to their cheese-making procedures, allowing them to produce curd of much lower moisture content that facilitated the production much larger aged, rinded cheeses like the traditional Maiorchino still made in Sicily today (Campo and Licitra 2006).

During the eighth century BC, probably not long after *The Odyssey* was composed, the Greeks began to colonize the eastern coast of Sicily. The Greek colonizers came to appreciate the native Sicilian cheeses. Cheese making seems to have been practiced in Sicily since at least the fourth millennium BC (De Angelis 2000), and waves of immigration from southern Italy and perhaps also from the Aegean and Anatolia around the end of the second millennium BC may have brought a new infusion of cheese technology to the island (Barker and Rasmussen 1998; Brea 1957; Holloway 1975; Procelli 1995; Trump 1965; Wainwright 1959, 1961).

Figure 4-1. Statuette of a woman grating cheese, from Greece, early fifth century BC. On the edge of the bowl is a pestle; on the base is depicted a cheese with a knife resting on it. (Photograph © 2012 Museum of Fine Arts, Boston)

By the fifth century BC the east coast colonies of Sicily were trading imported Greek pottery for cheeses and other pastoral products produced in the highlands of the Sicilian interior, some of which were then exported to Greece (Finley 1968). The pecorino and caprino cheeses that Homer attributed to Cyclops could conceivably have served as good candidates for export: rugged and able withstand the rigors of maritime transport, bursting with robust piquant flavor, versatile for use at the table as *opson* or for grating and as an ingredient in cooking (figure 4-1).

By the end of the fifth century BC, the reputation of Sicilian cheeses had grown to the extent that the comic poet Hermippus included cheese from Syracuse among a long list of luxury goods imported to Athens (which included books from Egypt, frankincense from Syria, cypress from Crete, and carpets and cushions of many colors from Carthage) in his satire of a utopian Athens flush with imported luxuries (Braund 1994). The reputation of Sicilian cheeses grew so great that they became known as "Sicily's Pride" and evidently were copied elsewhere, much like the Cythnian cheeses that were produced beyond the island of Cythnos (Ehrenberg 1951).

The comic poets Philemo and Antiphanes both wrote of the export of Sicilian cheese. Aristophanes clothed his political satire about the controversial Athenian general Laches Aixoneus, who was accused of mismanaging an expedition to Sicily during the Peloponnesian War, around the comical trial of a dog who was accused of eating too much Sicilian cheese during the night rather than sharing it (Braund 1999). Called to testify in defense of the accused dog was a cheese grater, which was a thinly veiled reference to the Sicilian colony of Catana (present day Cantania), because *katane* or *catana* was the word for grater in the local Sicilian dialect (Post 1932). Sicily had become closely identified with cheese, and specifically grated cheese, in the Greek world.

The blossoming Mediterranean cheese trade reflected a growing disparity in Greek society between the "haves" and the "have nots" that the comic poet Timocles acknowledged during the fourth century BC when he described the Athens market as a wonderful place for the upper class but miserable for the poor. To the former, the market furnished among other delicacies: fish from the Black Sea, wine from the northern Aegean island of Thasos, eels from Boeotia on the Gulf of Corinth, honey, olives, and fresh green vegetables from local Attic farms, local fresh-baked bread and cakes, and cheese from Sicily (Lever 1954). Sicily by this time was the preeminent supplier of imported cheeses to Greece and the epicenter of a Mediterranean blossoming of gastronomy (Rapp 1955).

Sicily of the fourth century BC had become extraordinarily wealthy and developed a sophisticated culture that was famous for the luxury of its cuisine. Two cookbooks written by the Sicilian authors Mithaikos and Herakleides during the fourth century BC helped to spread Sicilian cuisine throughout the Greek world. Both works featured cheese as an ingredient in cooking: Herakleides described a *kyboi* (literally dice in Greek) as a square loaf of bread, seasoned with aniseed, cheese, and olive oil, perhaps similar to today's focaccia; Mithaikos described the use of cheese and olive oil poured over fish as a sauce (Olson and Sens 2000). Evidently such cheese sauces were used extensively (and overused) by the late fourth century BC: The Sicilian gourmet Archestratos, who is considered "the father of western gastronomy," wrote derisively of the indiscriminate use of cheese sauces to smother fish (and certain meats). He considered such sauces appropriate only for tough, low-quality fish, whereas according to him other fish such as the electric ray are best served with only a little grated cheese, while the choicest fish, delicate and tender, should be prepared simply with no cheese at all, a little salt and olive oil being all that is needed (Rapp 1955).

Culinary enthusiasts apparently came from all over the Mediterranean to train under the Sicilian masters like Archestratos, and Sicilian chefs were in demand all over the Greek world (Rapp 1955). It was against this backdrop of culinary luxury and extravagance that Plato railed against the gastronomic excesses of Athens and pined for a return to the simple *opson* (barley and wheat loaves and cakes) and *sitos* (olives, cheese, roots and vegetables, figs, peas, and beans) of the past in his masterpiece *The Republic*.

Grated cheese seems to have occupied a special place in Greek culture. Homer alluded to this in his scene from *The Iliad* in which Nestor rescues the wounded Machaon from battle and brings him to his home. Nestor's slave Hekamede then prepares an elixir consisting of Pramnian wine on which she sprinkles goat's-milk cheese, grated with a bronze grater, and barley flour. The elixir soon exerts a restorative or healing effect on Machaon. This Homeric account coincided with a Greek practice that has been dated to at least the ninth century BC based on the archaeological discovery of bronze cheese graters in ninth-century graves of Greek warriors (Ridgway 1997; West 1988). Evidently the grating of cheese into wine was an important ritual associated with Greek warrior feasting (Sherratt 2004). The ritual spread to Italy during the seventh century BC through trade contacts and the establishment of Greek colonies in southern Italy, to the extent that numerous cheese graters have been found in graves of warrior princes along the western (Tyrrhenian) coast of Italy stretching from Tuscany in the north to Campania in the south (Ridgway 1997).

Eventually, in Athens and other Greek poleis, the ancient memory of the ritual seems to have found its way into religious festivals such as the footrace of ephebes, a race run in honor of the goddess Athena. The winner of the footrace was entitled to drink from a bowl containing a punch concocted of wine, honey, grated cheese, and a little barley meal and olive oil (Ferguson 1938). Thus, it is perhaps not surprising that Sicilian cheeses, which were likely aged pecorino and caprino types ideal for grating, became so popular with the Greeks.

Changing of the Guard

By the end of the fourth century BC Greece had passed its zenith. Greek culture had been carried all the way to India through the conquests of Alexander the Great, but the empire could not be sustained and it fractured almost immediately after Alexander's death. Moreover, Rome to the west was rapidly growing in stature and would soon surpass Greece.

Meanwhile in Persia the prophet Zoroaster had inspired a cadre of follow-ers, the magi, to carry on his teachings. According to the Roman writer Pliny, Zoroaster subsisted on cheese for twenty years in the Persian desert as he sought spiritual enlightenment. Following in the prophet's footsteps, Zoroaster's most dedicated disciples, the high magi, shunned the eating of meat and subsisted on only cheese, vegetables, and plain bread (Russell 1993). It was perhaps three of these elite Zoroastrian magi whom the Gospel According to Luke describes as the wise men from the east, laden with precious gifts of gold, frankincense, and myrrh (and also, perhaps, amply provisioned with cheese?), who followed an unusual star westward from Persia to the Levantine town of Bethlehem to honor a newborn child, one whose influence on western civilization and cheese history would soon be unleashed.

CHAPTER FIVE

Caesar, Christ, and Systematic Cheese Making

Therefore the Lord himself will give you a sign: The virgin will be
with child and will give birth to a son, and will call him Immanuel.
He will eat curds and honey when he knows enough to reject the
wrong and choose the right.

Isaiah 7:14–15

A round 600 BC the Hebrew prophet Isaiah spoke of a coming Messiah
who would be called Wonderful Counselor, Mighty God, Everlasting
Father, Prince of Peace. He would reign on David's throne with justice and
righteousness forever. Christians believe that this prophecy was fulfilled in
the person of Jesus Christ, the one whom Isaiah also said would be called
Immanuel and who, like the Hebrew patriarch Abraham nearly two millennia earlier, would eat curds or fresh cheese.

Around the same time that Isaiah was ministering to the fractured and
demoralized nation of Israel, the Mediterranean world was experiencing a
renaissance after having struggled for several hundred years through the
Dark Age that followed the collapse of the Bronze Age. Greece was prospering again through the establishment of far-flung colonies and soon
became the cultural and intellectual leader of the Mediterranean world. But
the glory of Greece would eventually wane, even as the power of Rome
waxed stronger. By the time of Christ, Rome was solidly in control of the
Mediterranean and well on the way to building an empire unparalleled in
size, longevity, and organization. The followers of Christ also sought to
build an empire, though one radically different from that of the Romans.
As fate or Providence would have it, Rome and the Christian church were

destined to become deeply entangled with each other. And both Rome and the church would profoundly shape western civilization and leave their indelible stamp on cheese making.

Etruscan Beginnings

According to Roman legend, Rome was founded around 750 BC by Romulus and Remus, the twin sons of the war god Mars (the Greek Ares), who were reared by a she-wolf. The actual story of Rome's meteoric rise began much earlier, however, and involved far-reaching events that transformed the cultural and economic landscape of the entire Italian peninsula. The story begins in the Neolithic, when cereal cultivation and animal husbandry arrived in Italy from the Near East around 5000 BC (Potter 1979). By the fourth millennium BC agricultural practices had shifted toward greater emphasis on animals for their secondary products. Perforated strainer shards from ceramic sieves, which almost certainly can be taken as indicators of cheese-making activity, make their appearance in the archaeological strata of this period, along with shifts in animal bone distributions that signaled the raising of sheep and goats for milk. The trend toward greater emphasis on cheese making and secondary animal products continued during the third millennium BC (Barker 1981). At this stage agricultural settlements were few in number and concentrated in the coastal lowlands and valley regions of the peninsula; the uplands of the Apennine Mountains were densely forested, and large-scale seasonal movement of animals to mountain pastures had not yet come into practice (Barker and Rasmussen 1998).

The Chalcolithic or Copper-Stone Age commenced in Italy toward the end of the third millennium BC. The west-central region of the peninsula known as Etruria (from which the name of modern Tuscany is derived) was rich in metal ores including copper, tin, and iron, and the Copper Age marked a blossoming of Etruscan metallurgy that would become the cornerstone of the region's economy and give rise to an impressive civilization. The Copper Age witnessed the rise of an Etruscan elite who distinguished themselves archaeologically through lavish burials that included prestige items of ceramic pottery and metal weaponry (Barker 1981). The Etruscan aristocracy's infatuation with prestige items would soon fuel a growing interest in trade.

Transhumance and Milk Boilers

Italy's Bronze Age, which lasted from about the beginning to the end of the second millennium BC, coincided with a series of striking developments. First, significant increases in population and number of settlement sites occurred in the lowlands; concomitantly, the systematic use of upland Apennine pastures for transhumant grazing came into widespread practice. Mixed farming continued to be practiced in the lowland settlements, but now shepherds herded their growing flocks of sheep and goats to summer camps high in the Apennines, returning to the lowland settlements in the autumn (Potter 1979).

The arrival of transhumance to the Apennines may have been associated with a decline in Italian woodlands that occurred during the second millennium BC. Though inconclusive, some evidence suggests that a change in climate toward drier conditions may have triggered an increase in open grasslands in the high Apennines (Barker and Rasmussen 1998). Whatever the cause, the adoption of transhumant shepherding was accompanied by the widespread appearance of pottery vessels dubbed "milk boilers," which seem to be unique to the Italian peninsula (Potter 1979; Trump 1965).

Milk boilers were ingenious ceramic vessels that were used to limit frothing and boiling over when heating milk to high temperatures during the making of acid/heat-coagulated (ricotta-type) cheeses. Most traditional ricotta-type cheeses today are produced from whey to which is added a small portion of milk (typically 10 to 15 percent of the volume of the whey). Ricotta-type cheeses can also be produced from whole milk or partly skimmed milk, but the process is more challenging because of milk's great capacity to froth and foam during high heating (think of cappuccino here), which renders it vulnerable to boiling over, and makes it difficult to collect the curds from the frothy mix (Kosikowski and Mistry 1997). The Bronze Age milk boilers were elegantly designed to limit this propensity, thus they

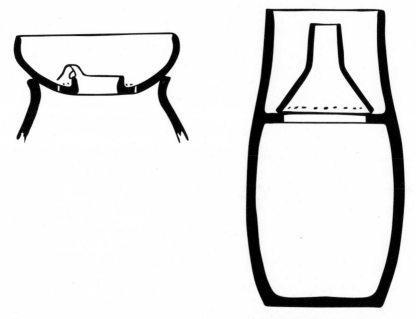

Figure 5-1. Milk boilers, which were used to limit the frothing and boiling over of milk during the making of acid/heat-coagulated (ricotta-type) cheeses, became common in Italy during the second millennium BC. A candlestick-shaped milk boiler (left) was used in southern Italy, whereas a cone-shaped milk boiler (right) was employed in the north. (After Trump 1965, figure 35, p. 111)

appear to have been tailor-made for producing acid/heat-coagulated cheese *from milk*. Two different vessel designs were widely employed: a candle-stick-shaped design that was used only in southern Italy, and an inverted funnel-shaped design used farther north (Trump 1965; figure 5-1). A third design, quite rare and apparently older in origin, dating back to the end of the third millennium BC, may have been the forerunner of the later two (Holloway 1975).

Thus, the evidence strongly indicates that ricotta-type cheese making became a major component of the agricultural economy throughout much of the Italian peninsula during the second millennium BC. These cheeses were probably initially made from whole milk, the technology being later adapted to whey/milk mixtures after rennet-coagulated cheese making became widespread (and the supply of rennet whey plentiful) on the Italian peninsula. Transhumant shepherding and ricotta cheese making ultimately became lasting features of the Italian countryside and culture; indeed, ceramic milk boilers were still being used by Apennine shepherd cheese-makers during the nineteenth century AD, and metal versions of the conical milk boilers are employed there today to make ricotta cheese using techniques that have changed little since ancient times (Barker and Rasmussen 1998; Barker et al. 1991; Frayn 1984).

It was probably also during the second millennium BC that the close synergy between cheese making and swine herding took root in Italy. Pigs were domesticated very early in the Neolithic Near East, and they accompanied the spread of agriculture throughout the Mediterranean and northern Europe during the Neolithic expansion. Pigs were a particularly valuable source of meat because their omnivorous feeding habits enabled them to eat almost anything, including a range of forest products such as acorns and beechnuts. They were prolific breeders as well. Thus, pigs were able to thrive in the vast forests that covered Europe (Barker 2006). Pigs also thrive on cheese whey. Even whey that has had its protein extracted, as in the making of ricotta, is rich in energy and nutrients and can serve as a valuable resource for fattening pigs. Swine herding has been practiced in Europe in conjunction with cheese making since ancient times.

The Roman writer Cato was the first to highlight and optimize this synergy during the second century BC in his agricultural manual *De agri cultura*, recommending that one pig be kept for every ten milking ewes to utilize the whey from cheese making (Brehaut 1933). However, the practice of feeding cheese whey to pigs likely began much earlier, which may help explain the remarkable consistency in the percentages of bone types (sheep, goats, pigs) recovered from Italian sites between the Bronze Age and Roman period, with sheep/goat fragments generally dominating and pig remains making up a minority (Holloway 1975; Potter 1976; Trump 1965). Pork was highly prized by the Romans, and Cato included a detailed recipe for salting and preserving hams in *De agri cultura*. In contrast with the Alps, where pigs eventually accompanied the dairy herd during the summer migration to the high mountain pastures and grew fat on the copious production of whey, the pigs evidently remained in the valley settlements year-round on the Italian peninsula (Potter 1976). This probably made sense given that, according to Cato, lambing occurred in November and December, and thus much of the cheese making was completed before the summer trek to the high Apennine pastures.

Etruscan Transformation

Another important development that took place during the latter half of the second millennium BC involved the infusion of new cultures into the Italian peninsula, which led to further cultural transformations, particularly in Etruria. This period was marked by the arrival of the so-called Urnfield culture, named for a new burial rite wherein the dead were cremated and the ashes interred in a cinerary urn. Along with changes in the burial customs of the Urnfield culture came new forms of metalworking and pottery, all of which had their origins in the blossoming Urnfield culture of central Europe. The Urnfield peoples lived north of the Alps in a broad swath that extended from eastern France to Hungary; they would soon give rise to the Celtic peoples (Cunliffe 1997). While most scholars now reject the idea of actual folk movements from central Europe across the Alps into Italy during this period, a clear infusion of northern culture did occur, becoming evident first in northern Italy around 1400 BC and then working its way south all the way to Sicily by the end of the second millennium BC (Potter 1979).

About the same time, another infusion of new culture, this time from the east, occurred in southern Italy and then worked its way northward up the peninsula. The adventurous Mycenaeans from Greece established trade contacts in the Italian south around 1500 BC, and by the fourteenth century BC had established trading posts and perhaps even colonies there (Barker 1981; Potter 1979). Trade contacts with Greece continued until the collapse of Mycenaean civilization during the twelfth century BC, resulting in a steady flow of prestige Greek imports that found their way to the elite of Etruria, whose appetite for status symbols was growing steadily. Also, the resettlement of sea peoples from the Aegean region to Italy and Sicily at the end of the Bronze Age may have reinforced this infusion of Aegean culture (Le Glay et al. 2009).

The Mycenaean and Urnfield cultural infusions catalyzed further social and cultural changes in Etruria that placed this specific region on a fast-track transformation from village to state society. Rapid development of mineral resources and bronze metallurgy took place during this period. Settlement sizes increased, followed by the rise of urbanized city-states ruled by an elite aristocracy during the first millennium BC. The amount of land in cultivation increased sharply, as did animal husbandry for secondary products, including milk and cheese. By the time iron production reached central Italy around 900 BC, a distinctly new culture had evolved in Etruria.

By the eighth century BC, the Etruscan countryside was dominated by fortified towns enclosed by walls with gates, which were loosely organized under a federation of twelve city-states (Le Glay et al. 2009). The urbanized culture of Etruria became progressively more sophisticated and accomplished: Mining and metallurgical practices became technically advanced; civil engineering flourished and the Etruscans became experts at road building, town planning, drainage and irrigation, and architecture; sophisticated artistic and religious expression blossomed, along with monumental architecture and the building of temples. It was also during the eighth century that the revitalized Greeks, having emerged from their Dark Age, began to colonize southern Italy and Sicily, and quickly established commercial interests with the iron- and copper-rich region of Etruria (Cunliffe 1997).

The Greeks had a strong "orientalizing" influence on Etruria as the Etruscans voraciously assimilated Greek culture. By the end of the eighth century BC, Etruria had borrowed the Greek written alphabet (which the Greeks had only recently borrowed from the Phoenicians) and adapted it to their language. Fueled by an ever-increasing aristocratic demand for imported luxury items, an Etruscan merchant class emerged during the seventh century BC and developed expanding maritime trade networks and connections with their Greek and Carthaginian counterparts. Etruscan wealth increased and Etruscan civilization blossomed.

Cheese Graters and Aged Pecorino

Even as Greek colonization of southern Italy was creating a "Magna Graecia" (Great Greece) and Etruria was crystallizing into a distinct and

Figure 5-2. Grave group from Campania, Italy, circa 440 to 420 BC. Items recovered from this tomb include a bronze grater (front right) and drinking equipment (bowl, wine strainer, and wine ladle, and Attic red figure bell-krater). (Ridgway 1997; photo courtesy of the British Museum; © The Trustees of the British Museum. All rights reserved.)

sophisticated Etruscan civilization, changes in cheese-making practices were occurring along almost the entire Tyrrhenian seaboard and in the Apennine Mountains to the east. Specifically, the use of milk boilers in cheese making declined precipitously throughout the entire Italian peninsula during the first millennium BC (Frayn 1984; Trump 1965). This shift away from acid/heat-coagulated (ricotta-type) cheese making was accompanied by the widespread appearance, beginning in the seventh century BC, of bronze (and occasionally silver) cheese graters in the tombs of the aristocratic elite, from Campania in the south to Etruria in the north (Ridgway 1997). That these graters were included in the princely tombs of the aristocratic elite along with other sophisticated feasting and drinking utensils made of precious metals and other imported luxury pottery strongly points to the elite status of hard grating cheese and its use in aristocratic feasting, a cultural practice inherited from the Greeks (Ridgway 1997; Sherratt 2004; figure 5-2).

Thus, during the first millennium BC cheese-making practices appear to have shifted decidedly toward rennet-coagulated aged pecorino and caprino types suitable for grating. Such cheeses soon became a Roman staple, and the bronze cheese grater became an essential tool of the Roman kitchen, but it seems that originally it was the emerging market demand of the aristocratic elite that catalyzed the shift in emphasis from fresh whole-milk ricotta to aged pecorino types. Emerging markets would continue to play a role in the development of many cheeses in many places from this point forward.

The Rise of Rome and the Celts

The sixth century BC was a watershed period that set into motion a series of developments that would ultimately transform Europe and shape western civilization. Experiencing the pressures of a population explosion, Etruria began to expand its territory south into Latium and in the process occupied the village of Rome. Rome was originally settled two or three centuries earlier but had remained a modest settlement (Le Glay et al. 2009). The Etruscans occupied Rome for about a century, during which time they transformed the primitive settlement to an urban civilization. They embarked on grand civil engineering projects to drain the swamps around Rome, pave public spaces, and build walled fortifications. They introduced advanced mining techniques, bronze and iron technology, and new construction techniques; they built temples and other monumental structures; and they brought advanced methods of administration, political and military organization, and forms of public worship and religious expression that served to unite the city and create a strong sense of identity. All the while, the Romans waited patiently and took good notes; they assimilated the best of Etruscan civilization, as well as vital elements of Greek civilization from their neighbors in Magna Graecia to the south. By the time they mustered the wherewithal to evict their Etruscan overlords at the end of sixth century BC, the Romans had acquired the tools necessary for future greatness.

Even as the Etruscans expanded southward during the sixth century BC, they also moved north and expanded into the Po River Valley by midcentury. There they encountered a growing trade across the mountain passes of the Alps with the Celtic peoples beyond. The origin of the Celtic peoples can be traced back to the Urnfield culture of central Europe, the same culture that was pivotal in the early development of Etruscan culture (Cunliffe 1997). During the turbulent period that marked the end of the Bronze Age in the Mediterranean, horse-riding pastoralists from the Pontic steppes north of the Black Sea penetrated the lower Danube River Valley to the Great Hungarian Plain, where they culturally infiltrated the Urnfield peoples, infusing into the region a new Indo-European dialect that would eventually evolve into the Celtic languages. They also brought horses with them, which their Urnfield neighbors to the west in Austria quickly put to use for warrior advantage and for trade.

A second and more sustained migration of horse-riding pastoralists from the east to the Great Hungarian Plain seems to have occurred around 1000 to 800 BC. These newcomers maintained a ready supply of superior horses and their breeding stock on the eastern border of the Urnfield peoples in Austria (Cunliffe 1997). The Austrian aristocracy acquired superior horses and horse-related military gear and riding techniques from their neighbors to the east, which elevated their military prowess and also gave them a sustained advantage in trading. By the eighth century BC the region around Hallstadt, Austria, had become the center of a flourishing Celtic warrior civilization that was prospering though trade in salt. Salt was mined extensively in the region and was a precious commodity in antiquity, highly prized for its use in food preservation and the treatment of animal hides. During the seventh and sixth centuries BC, the Hallstadt culture expanded westward into southern Germany and Switzerland to the border of France, and eventually to northern and eastern France, and even across the Pyrenees into Spain (Ó Hógáin 2002).

During this time the Celts were actively seeking to develop trade opportunities with their neighbors to the south (Maier 2003). The colony of Massalia (modern Marseilles), which the Greeks established near the mouth of the Rhône River around 600 BC, found enthusiastic trading partners in the Celts as they extended their activities northward up the Rhône to Lake Geneva during the sixth century BC. So, too, did the Etruscans as they moved into the Po Valley of northern Italy and established contact with the Celts across the alpine passes.

The goods that the Greeks and Etruscans had to offer for trade—elaborate bronze and iron weaponry and exotic dining vessels, exquisite pottery, wine (the new beverage of choice for the Celtic warrior elite), and the elite Greek cultural practices of the symposium and feasting—were immediate hits with the status-seeking Celtic warrior aristocracy (Cunliffe 1997). What the Celts traded in return is not well established, but probably included cheeses, along with metals, hides, rough wool, salted meat, and occasionally slaves and amber (Echols 1949; Sauter 1976). The Celts were an advanced agricultural people with a strong emphasis on dairy cattle, and they had already accumulated centuries of cheese-making experience in central Europe by this time. In Roman times the Celts were famous for their cheeses, and much cheese was imported to Rome via Massalia; however, the cheese trade through Massalia probably began much earlier.

Celtic infatuation with Greek culture, the lure of the warm Mediterranean climate, and the pressures of a population explosion in central Europe would soon draw the Celts southward and place them on a collision course with the growing city-state of Rome. Thus would commence a five-hundred-year struggle between the Romans and Celts that would ultimately Romanize most of the Celtic peoples except for an unbending remnant on the western fringes of the European continent.

The Ascendancy of Rome

Newly freed of her Etruscan overlords at the beginning of the fifth century BC, Rome embarked on a path of gradual expansion over the next three centuries that brought her into conflict with her Etruscan neighbors to the north, her neighbors in Latium to the south, and eventually with rivals throughout the entire Italian peninsula (Le Glay et al. 2009). Despite a few setbacks, Rome expanded relentlessly and ruthlessly. Once military victory was achieved, Rome expropriated a portion (typically around one-third) of the vanquished land to Roman colonists and established *coloniae* that were laid out as a miniature and standardized version of Rome itself (Barker and Rasmussen 1998). Thus, a permanent Roman presence was established after every military victory, a brilliant political and administrative model that eased population pressures and the plight of the landless poor back home, and ensured that Roman conquests remained under Roman rule and domination. By the middle of the third century BC virtually the entire Italian peninsula had either been annexed by Rome or was firmly under Rome's sway.

Even as Rome was rising, however, significant threats loomed. To the north, the Celts had grown in population and geographic area, and the center of Celtic civilization had shifted to northwest Switzerland, where a more organized and cohesive Celtic power emerged that possessed a greater sense of "national" identity and greater capacity to wage war. During the fourth century BC the Celts undertook three major invasions of Italy (Le Glay et al. 2009). The first, between 390 and 380 BC, resulted in the capture and sack of Rome around 381 BC. Ultimately, Rome would deal decisively with the "Celtic menace" under Julius Caesar, and in the process Romanize much of continental Europe. The Etruscans did not fare so well; already weakened by Rome's expansion, then trampled by successive Celtic invasions, Etruria faded and was soon annexed by Rome.

Rome faced a different threat as it expanded southward to the doorstep of the Greek colonies of Magna Graecia. Up until this time, the lucrative trade networks of the western Mediterranean had been divided up among the Greeks, Carthaginians, and Etruscans. However, the Roman annexation of Etruscan cities to the north and the direct threat that Rome posed to the Greek colonies of Magna Graecia to the south shifted the balance of power. Carthage held significant trading interests in Magna Graecia; thus Rome's conquest of the Greek colonies during the first half of the third century BC placed Rome in direct conflict with Carthaginian trade interests.

Situated between Carthage on the coast of north Africa and the Italian peninsula was the island of Sicily, the wealthy jewel of the western Mediterranean, which had long been colonized on the west coast by Carthage and on the east by Greece. Rome feared that Carthage might move to gain control of all Sicily and from there directly threaten the mainland. Carthage feared that a Roman invasion of Sicily would further encroach on its lucrative trade in the region. The stage was thus set for the first of three wars between Rome and Carthage, the Punic Wars, from which Rome would emerge as the undisputed leader of the western Mediterranean. The

Punic Wars would also dramatically transform Roman agriculture in ways that would influence cheese making for centuries to come.

The First Punic War was fought primarily on Sicilian soil and lasted for twenty-three years. In the end the Romans triumphed, a peace treaty was signed with Carthage in 241 BC, and Sicily became a Roman province. The two powers could not avoid bumping up against each other, however, as they both expanded their trading interests along coastal Spain. A second war broke out in 218 BC, this time on Italian soil as Carthaginian forces under Hannibal marched through southern France to the Alps, where they climbed the treacherous mountain passes and descended into northern Italy. For fifteen years Hannibal's army battled the length of the peninsula, living off the land and ravaging the Italian countryside. Carthage eventually capitulated after a devastating defeat in 201 BC. Half a century later, Rome put an end to Carthage in a Third Punic War: The city was destroyed, the population deported and many were sentenced to a life of slavery (Le Glay et al. 2009).

Roman Agriculture in Transition

The Punic Wars, especially the second war, had a devastating effect on agriculture in Italy and contributed to massive agricultural restructuring. However, agriculture had been changing along the west coast of Italy even before the wars. In the lowlands, areas dedicated to wheat cultivation expanded dramatically in response to large population increases during the first millennium BC. Grain fields were cultivated intensively year after year and probably soil fertility in some regions declined, resulting in reduced yields and greater vulnerability to crop diseases (Bowen 1928; Olson 1945). Meanwhile population pressures continued to increase, and farmers began clearing new fields on the wooded slopes of the surrounding hillsides and eventually even steeper slopes farther inland. This in turn triggered unprecedented hillside erosion that carried massive amounts of topsoil from the uplands to the river valleys below, where sediments soon clogged the waterways, creating poorly drained swamps in areas that had once been the site of fertile fields (Yeo 1948). Thus, small farmers who were the backbone of the Roman city-state and her *coloniae* found it increasingly difficult to continue their traditional farming practices, which were based heavily on wheat production, supplemented by sheep and goat raising.

The Punic Wars added enormously to the stress. Military service was mandatory for Roman citizens during times of war; adult males were forced to leave their farms in the hands of family members for years at a time. Furthermore, Hannibal's armies ravaged many farms from one end of the peninsula to the other, and farmers returned from military service only to find their farms in great disarray (Steiner 1955). To make matters worse, the deforestation of mountain slopes accelerated greatly during and after the Punic Wars due to massive shipbuilding in support of the new Roman navy, creating more erosion and misery for the small farmer. The shrinking availability of rich tillable land needed to raise wheat profitably forced farmers to shift their emphasis toward raising of the sheep and goats that could thrive on the deforested mountainsides (Yeo 1948).

The move away from wheat growing on the Italian peninsula was further accelerated by Rome's annexation of Sicily at the conclusion of the First Punic War. Sicily's rich agricultural lands and vast wheat production positioned the new Roman province to become Rome's granary. Rome immediately imposed a tributary tax on Sicily equaling 10 percent of grain production, or a staggering one million bushels of wheat annually (Bowen 1928; Yeo 1948). Furthermore, maritime transport of grain from Sicily to the Italian peninsula was far less costly than the ground transportation needed to bring domestically produced wheat to market (Yeo 1946). Much Sicilian wheat was thus also exported to Rome and sold on the open market. Faced with the flood of cheap imported grain, domestic production of wheat collapsed.

Not only was Roman agriculture shifting from wheat to livestock, but the nature and scale of the basic agricultural production unit also was changing radically. The Third Punic War resulted in the enslavement of fifty thousand Carthaginians. This was the beginning of a steady stream of slave laborers into the Roman countryside as Rome embarked on series of overseas military campaigns that created an ever-expanding empire and supply of foreign slaves. Furthermore, the successful completion of the Punic Wars concentrated great wealth in the hands of high-ranking Romans, who began to invest their newfound wealth in land, establishing country estates that they could manage from a distance while serving in Rome.

Land was plentiful and cheap because many small farmers were deeply in debt; labor was plentiful and cheap because enslaved "guest workers" flooded the labor market; and Rome and her provincial cities were becoming very wealthy, creating lucrative markets for elite, value-added agricultural products, such as fine olive oil and wines, meats, and cheeses, all of which could be produced on Italy's eroded hillsides much more profitably than grain. The confluence of all of these factors resulted in the rapid transformation of Roman agriculture from small mixed farms to *latifundia,* or landed estates that specialized primarily in olive oil, wine, and livestock production.

It was in response to these agricultural changes that a series of Roman writers, beginning with Cato around 170 BC and continuing to Columella in the first century AD, composed detailed agricultural manuals designed to systematize and optimize the management of large-scale profit-oriented agricultural estates. As time went on, the landed estates grew in size; Cato wrote of an estate mainly devoted to olive production that encompassed 160 acres (65 ha), which could support a flock of a hundred sheep. More than a century later Varro wrote of much larger olive plantations that supported up to a thousand sheep (Storr-Best 1912). A collateral consequence of the rise of *latifundia* was the displacement of innumerable small farmers and their families, who, with no means to support themselves, streamed into Rome to join the growing class of urban poor (Le Glay et al. 2009).

Cheese and Cheese Making in the Empire

Much of what we know about Roman cheese and cheese making comes from agricultural writers who were concerned with large landed estates, not the traditional small peasant farms that dominated the Italian countryside before the Punic Wars. Within this context, these writers provide a wealth of information concerning cheese-making practices of the time and the place of cheese in Roman life.

Cato

Marcus Porcius Cato (234–149 BC), the first of the great Roman agriculturalists, grew up on the family farm about 15 miles (24 km) southeast of
Rome, and even though he eventually rose to a high-ranking position in the
Roman Senate and achieved fame and fortune, he maintained close connections with the farm. Cato lived during the period of the Second Punic War
and witnessed with alarm the agricultural transformation that was taking
place around him. He was concerned about poor management practices and
careless environmental stewardship on the new landed estates headed by
absentee owners that were displacing the small family farms (Olson 1945).
Therefore, around 170 BC Cato wrote *De agri cultura,* an agricultural manual
for the moderately sized estates of his time. He focused on the production
of olive oil and wine as primary cash crops, and livestock (sheep and goats)
as secondary products. His management strategies assumed the use of slave
labor, which by this time had become the agricultural labor source of choice
(Brehaut 1933; Olson 1945).

Cato dealt only tangentially with cheese making. He recommended that
an olive plantation of 160 acres (65 ha) should maintain one flock of one
hundred sheep; that one shepherd was needed per flock; and that ten swine
were needed to consume the whey from the cheese making associated with
the flock. The lambing season took place from late November through
December; thus milk production and cheese making occurred mostly during
winter and early spring. For landed estates that did not maintain their own
flock of sheep, Cato recommended that they rent out their "winter pasture"
to tenant flocks from September to March, and that the terms of the rental
agreement include payment of 1.5 pounds (0.7 kg) of cheese per ewe. Thus
a tenant flock of one hundred milking ewes generated 150 pounds (68 kg) of
cheese in rental income by the end of the season. Cato also stipulated that
half of the cheese should be "dry," apparently referring to cheeses produced
early in the season that were dried and ripened for two or three months
(as is common in the making of traditional small pecorino cheeses) before
the flock vacated the estate at the end of March and payment was made
to the landowner. Thus, the tenant cheesemaker presumably had access to
an aging facility, probably a simple shed with wooden shelves as described
by the Roman writer Columella two centuries later (Forster and Heffner

1954). *Caseus aridus* (dry cheese) and *caseus mollis* (soft cheese) became the two standard categories for cheese in the Roman Empire, the former refer- ring to aged or preserved types, the latter to fresh varieties (Frayn 1984). Dry cheeses were much esteemed and in high demand in Rome and likely generated a handsome profit for the estate (Yeo 1946, 1948).

Interestingly, Cato also devoted considerable space in *De agri cultura* to cake recipes, all of which include cheese as an ingredient. Though at first glance it may seem odd to include such recipes in an agricultural manual, cakes were an important part of Roman life, as they were in Greek life. The Romans assimilated many Greek religious practices into their own religion, including the use of cakes, often made with cheese, as bloodless sacrifices. Cato's first cake recipe was for a sacrificial cheesecake that was offered to the gods during religious ceremonies held at critical stages of the agricultural cycle. According to his contemporaries, Cato was very socially conservative and deeply committed to upholding the religious traditions of the past. In *De agri cultura*, Cato described religious ceremonies in which cheesecakes were offered to the gods Jupiter, Janus, and Mars. He consid- ered religious activities to be important elements of the agricultural cycle, essential to securing the gods' favor for the harvest. The Roman poet Ovid around the beginning of the first century AD echoed this sentiment in his prayer to the god Pales, patron god of the shepherds, beseeching protection for the men and flocks, and for a goodly supply of water, food, cheese, and wool (Burriss 1930).

In addition to the sacrificial cake used specifically for religious func- tions, Cato included recipes for eight other cheesecakes, including six that were variations on *placenta*, an enormous pastry measuring around 1 foot wide by 2 feet long by 2 inches high (0.3 m by 0.6 m by 5 cm), and that included 14 pounds (6.4 kg) of cheese and 4.5 pounds (2 kg) of honey among its ingredients (Leon 1943). In preparation for use as an ingredient in *placenta*, the cheese was first soaked repeatedly in water. Recipes for cheese soufflés and puddings also were provided. All of these items were considered delicacies or luxury foods, which seems out of place in an agri- cultural manual. Nevertheless, Cato felt it important to emphasize luxury cheesecake recipes along with all his other instructions relating to agricul- tural best practices. The rationale behind this is uncertain; however, it is important to remember that Cato's agricultural manual was not intended for the peasant subsistence farmer of earlier times but for owners and senior managers (stewards) of landed estates. The landed Roman aristocracy had eagerly assimilated Greek culture, which included an appreciation for fine foods, among which cakes ranked highly. Moreover, Sicily, the epicenter of Mediterranean gastronomy, was now a Roman province, which likely helped to fuel Rome's increasingly sophisticated culinary tastes. Perhaps Cato's long years of service in Rome and his exposure to the blossoming food culture there instilled an appreciation for the useful role that good food can play in elevating worker morale, loyalty, and basic quality of life amid the boredom and toils of the agricultural cycle.

Varro

Around 130 years after Cato wrote *De agri cultura,* Marcus Terentius Varro (116–28 BC) compiled his masterpiece *Rerum Rusticarum,* a manual of farm management like Cato's, but much more detailed and systematic, and eminently practical. Varro was born on a landed estate and had accumulated a lifetime of agricultural experience by the time he wrote *Rerum Rusticarum* near the end of his long life. Unlike Cato, Varro wrote extensively of the rigors of the summer migration of the flocks to the high pastures of the Apennines. By this time landed estates commonly maintained multiple flocks of sheep, each flock comprising eighty to one hundred sheep tended by one shepherd, with a senior shepherd to coordinate the cadre of shepherds. Varro's own estate flocks consisted of seven hundred head, and he refers to other estates having up to a thousand sheep. Varro developed detailed management practices for coordinating the flocks, maintaining order among the shepherds, and providing for the shepherds' needs, which included, as Varro put it, for "the breeding of men" (Storr-Best 1912). Sturdy, "able-bodied but not uncomely" women were needed "who can follow the flocks, prepare the shepherds' victuals and keep the men from roving" (Storr-Best 1912).

Such large flocks must have supported considerable cheese-making activities, and in contrast with Cato, Varro described cheese-making practices in some detail. However, Varro cautioned that there was a trade-off between harvesting milk for cheese production and the amount wool that the ewe produced. He noted that some estates did not milk the ewes until the lambs had been weaned four months after lambing, and others elected not to milk the ewes at all in order to achieve a better yield of wool. Perhaps it was with this in mind that Varro described the cheese-making season as beginning in May and continuing into the summer. Thus, for Varro, cheese making was emphasized during the late-spring/summer season when the flocks migrated to the high mountain pastures. This seems to be a significant shift from the time of Cato, when much cheese making seems to have occurred on the estate in the lowlands during the winter and early spring.

Varro was the first to describe rennet coagulation in quantitative terms: He stated that 1.5 gallons (5.7 liters) of milk should be coagulated using an olive-sized piece of rennet that preferably originated from a kid or, interestingly, hare rather than a lamb. He also noted that milk could be coagulated using fig sap in combination with vinegar. (The vinegar likely serving as an acidulant that enhanced the coagulation process.) Varro included no details about the steps of cheese making that followed coagulation, except to say that salt was sprinkled over the final cheese, and that rock salt was preferable to sea salt. This very sound advice related to the coarseness of the salt: Rock salt is a coarser crystal that dissolves more slowly at the cheese surface, which allows for more gradual whey expulsion, better salt uptake, and better rind formation.

Although Varro distinguished between "soft and new cheese, and that which is old and dry," both were made by the same rennet-coagulated cheese-making procedure, the latter being the aged version of the former. Interestingly, Varro made no mention of milk boilers or acid/heat-coagulated (ricotta-type) cheeses. Either he was unaware of ricotta, which seems unlikely given the long history of ricotta making on the Italian peninsula, or he chose not to include the technology for ricotta cheese making in his manual because this cheese was generally not a good candidate for sale in the urban markets of Rome and other cities. The fragile nature of ricotta and its exceedingly short shelf life limited its distribution to very local markets. Ricotta by this time was probably made mostly from whey left over from rennet-coagulated cheese making and consumed by the shepherds themselves, though evidence from Roman paintings and literature indicates that ricotta was also certainly known and probably enjoyed by aristocrats (D'Arms 2004).

One of Varro's most enigmatic comments about cheese making had to do with *Ficus Ruminalis*, a famous fig tree in Rome that grew near the temple of Rumina, the ancient goddess of shepherds. According to Roman legend, Romulus and Remus, the founders of Rome, were suckled by a she-wolf under *Ficus Ruminalis*. Thus, the fig tree and adjacent temple became a revered Roman site, and the goddess Rumina eventually evolved into the patron goddess of nursing mothers. By Varro's time, however, the memory of Rumina as the goddess of the shepherds had evidently faded and the temple in Rome had fallen into obscurity (Hadzsits 1936).

Varro hadn't forgotten, however. He noted that sacrifices to Rumina consisted of milk rather than the more customary offerings of wine and suckling pigs, and he suggested that it was shepherds in the ancient past who had planted the fig tree near the temple to provide fig sap for coagulating milk. The precise point that Varro was trying to make is uncertain, but it seems to be either that the shepherds who supplied the temple with sacred milk were moonlighting as cheesemakers or, perhaps, that fig sap from *Ficus Ruminalis* was used to coagulate the sacred milk in sacrificial rites carried out in the temple. The latter possibility recalls to mind the Greek Asklepieion, where milk coagulation may have been practiced as a rite of healing.

Columella

Lucius Junis Moderatus Columella, the third great agricultural writer of the Roman period, was the most comprehensive, systematic, and arguably most impressive agriculturalist of antiquity. Columella was born in southern Spain around the start of the first century AD and wrote *Res Rustica* around AD 60 (Forster and Heffner 1954). This amazingly detailed farming manual consisted of twelve books, including book 7, which dedicates an entire section (section 8) to cheese-making practices. Columella was the first to describe the entire cheese-making process, and the first to stress quality control from start to finish. He warned that the milk used for cheese making should be "pure" and "as fresh as possible." Like Varro, he described rennet coagulation in quantitative terms, stating that the minimum amount of rennet needed to coagulate a pail of milk was equivalent in weight to a silver *denarius* (a common Roman coin). Columella recommended either lamb or kid rennet, but he warned against using more than the minimum amount needed for coagulation, which we now know was sound advice because overuse of traditional animal rennet can lead to excessive breakdown of protein and fat during aging, and bitter and rancid flavor defects. Columella understood the importance of controlling temperature during coagulation and provided advice on how to maintain the proper temperature during setting. He also described three alternate sources of rennet (the flower of the wild thistle, the seed of the safflower, and fig sap), all capable of producing good-quality cheese, provided that the minimum dosage needed for coagulation was employed.

Demonstrating great insight into cheese technology, Columella stressed the importance of promoting whey expulsion during cheese making, as well as controlling evaporative moisture losses during aging. He understood the critical importance of curd drainage, the use of pressure and the application of salt to promote whey expulsion, and the importance of controlling the surrounding environment (especially temperature and humidity) during aging. Columella correctly understood that the production of top-quality "dry" or aged cheeses represented a balancing act with respect to moisture control: Too much moisture retained in the cheese increased the risk of undesirable fermentations (gas production and off-flavors); too little moisture resulted in an excessively dry and lifeless cheese. Thus, Columella stressed the steps of curd drainage, pressing, and salting during cheese making, and the environmental conditions during aging—the goal being to produce a durable rinded cheese that was low enough in moisture content to resist unwanted fermentations, but high enough to allow the cheese to develop desirable qualities (flavor, texture) during aging. According to Columella, "This kind of cheese can even be exported beyond the sea" (Forster and Heffner 1954). Columella was clearly interested in producing cheeses for distant markets.

Like Varro before him, Columella also made no mention of milk boilers or ricotta cheese making. He was, however, concerned with tapping into local markets because he provided modified instructions for producing "Cheese which is to be eaten within a few days while still fresh . . ." (Forster and Heffner 1954). With respect to fresh cheese, Columella correctly recognized that "you can give the cheese any flavor you like by adding any seasoning you choose" (Forster and Heffner 1954), citing cheese flavored with pine kernels and thyme as examples. He also touted the use of apple-wood smoking to enhance flavor. Today we refer to this as product differentiation and market segmentation: using the same base cheese to produce a range of different-flavored products to appeal to a broader range of customers and increase sales.

Columella's uncooked, lightly pressed, surface-salted cheeses were not very different from the small Romano-type cheeses that Homer had described many centuries earlier. However, Columella also described another type of cheese called "hand-pressed" cheese, which he said was the "best known of all." During the making of "hand-pressed" cheese, hot water was added to the curds shortly after coagulation (Forster and Heffner 1954). The hot water may have served as an early form of cooking, as in the making of Pecorino Siciliano or Gouda cheese today, or it may have been used to plasticize the curd as in the making of pasta-filata cheeses such as mozzarella. Either way, the addition of hot water is significant because it indicates that Roman cheesemakers were experimenting with heating during cheese making. Therefore, it was only a matter of time before a whole new generation of cooked cheeses and pasta-filata cheeses were discovered and perfected.

By Columella's time, several cheese-making regions in Italy had established reputations for producing exceptional cheeses. The poet Marcus Valerius Martialis (Martial) compiled a list of his favorite cheeses in *Xenia,* the thirteenth in a series of books that he wrote during the first century AD. *Xenia* is a Greek word meaning hospitality, and Martial's book 13 provides a practical guide to the mandatory gift giving that took place during Saturnalia, a Roman agricultural festival held in December around the time of the winter solstice (Leary 2001). Saturnalia was the main Roman holiday of the year, lasting for several days, and private dinner parties that featured gift giving were a central feature of the celebration. It was customary for the host of the dinner party to present the guests with appropriate gifts of food. Evidently, finding the right gifts for Saturnalia was as challenging for some Romans as finding the right Christmas gift is today for some Americans; upper-class Romans were probably very anxious to have their dinner parties and gifts reflect positively on their privileged status. Martial's

Xenia was the ideal resource for Saturnalia planning, a witty and informative catalog of fine gift foods, sure to please.

Martial showcased four domestic cheeses in his catalog: Vestine, Trebula, smoked Velabrum, and Luna. Vestine cheese, produced in central Italy, was evidently popular as a breakfast cheese. Pliny the Elder, who lived about the same time as Martial, also noted the popularity of Vestine cheese in Rome in his work *Natural History* (Bostock and Riley 1855). Trebula cheeses were produced in the Sabine region south of Vestinum. Martial emphasized the desirability of Trebula when steeped in water and heated, which seems to indicate that it was especially well suited for cooking applications, as in the making of *placenta* cakes. Smoked cheeses were very popular in Rome; Martial considered the cheeses smoked at the Velabrum in Rome itself to be the best in its class. Pliny also commented on the popularity of smoked cheeses from Rome, noting that the flavor of goat's-milk cheese was enhanced by smoking.

Luna cheese, produced in northern Etruria, was the most intriguing of Martial's top four recommendations in *Xenia* because of its extraordinary size. According to Martial, Luna cheese was stamped with the impression of the Etruscan moon and was large enough to "afford your slaves a thousand lunches." Pliny agreed that Luna cheese was one of the most highly esteemed in Rome and noted its extraordinary size, which he claimed could weigh up to 1,000 pounds (454 kg). According to Pliny, Luna cheeses were produced on the frontiers of Etruria and in neighboring Liguria to the north and west.

Martial and Pliny no doubt exaggerated the size of Luna cheeses; hyperbole was very common among the writers of antiquity. However, it seems clear that these cheeses attracted attention because they were significantly larger than the smallish dry pecorino and caprino cheeses that typically graced Roman life. The uncooked, lightly pressed, surface-salted cheese-making technology described by Columella was well suited for the production of small aged and fresh cheeses, but was utterly incapable of producing large aged cheeses, which begs the question: How were the large Luna cheeses made?

The key technical issue relates to the moisture content of the cheese. Uncooked, lightly pressed, surface-salted cheeses (like those described by

Columella) characteristically have very high initial moisture contents; therefore, they must be either consumed fresh or small enough in size to dry out before spoilage sets in. Small cheeses possess large surface-area-to-volume ratios that cause them to lose moisture rapidly through surface evaporation; the entire body of a small cheese can be dried out quickly to prevent spoilage. Rubbing salt on the surface accelerates this initial drying while creating a dense impervious rind that will eventually slow the rate of evaporation during subsequent aging. The rind thus helps prevent excessive drying during aging, which is essential for desirable flavor and texture development. Small cheeses also have an advantage with respect to salt diffusion. Salt that is rubbed onto the surface must diffuse throughout the entire body of the cheese in order to exert a preservative effect and to promote desirable flavor and texture development. This occurs rapidly in small cheeses because the distance that the salt has to diffuse inward is small. For these reasons, the technology that Columella described in detail (uncooked, lightly pressed, surface-salted) resulted in cheese that "can even be exported beyond the sea."

In contrast, large cheeses possess much less surface area relative to their volumes than do small cheeses; in other words, the surface-area-to-volume ratio decreases steeply as cheese size increases. Therefore, large cheeses with high initial moisture contents cannot dry out sufficiently via surface evaporation before the rind forms and impedes further moisture loss. In addition, salt rubbed onto the surface cannot quickly diffuse throughout the voluminous body of a large cheese; the center may remain low in salt content for weeks. The resulting combination of persistent high moisture and low salt contents in the cheese interior renders such cheeses vulnerable to abnormal fermentations and rotting from the inside, especially in the warm Mediterranean climate.

The bottom line is that large cheeses must possess much lower moisture contents immediately after manufacture than small cheeses or they will retain too much moisture during aging. The larger the cheese, the lower the initial moisture content must be to prevent internal rotting. Lower initial moisture content, in turn, can be achieved only by squeezing more whey out of the curds during cheese making, through the use of either high-temperature cooking or high-pressure pressing, or a combination. The development of high-temperature cooking techniques and of high-pressure pressing methods were thus seminal events in cheese history because they opened the door to the creation of *much larger* dry or aged cheeses than it had previously been possible to produce.

So how did the cheesemakers of northern Etruria and Liguria manage to make such large cheeses? Presumably, they developed high-temperature cooking and high-pressure pressing technologies that were used in combination with large vats to process large volumes of milk into curd. For example, the large bronze vessels commonly used on Roman olive plantations and vineyards could have served as cheese vats capable of producing large quantities of curd necessary for large cheeses. Consistent with this, a large bronze vessel interpreted to be a cheese vat was recovered from a villa in Campania that allegedly operated a "cheese factory" along with a winery (Carrington 1931). The villa was destroyed in the volcanic eruption of Mount Vesuvius in AD 79. We know from Columella that Roman cheesemakers were experimenting with heating by the addition of hot water. It is also conceivable that a bronze cheese vat could have been fitted with a fire pit beneath to allow for direct heating during cheese making. Furthermore, the large sophisticated olive presses that were used on olive plantations could conceivably have been modified to press large wheels of cheese.

Indirect evidence also suggests that Celtic cheesemakers to the north may have been using cooking and pressing technologies by Roman times. The Celts were accomplished metalworkers, and iron and bronze cauldrons were used by the Celts from pre-Roman times. As various writers in antiquity pointed out, Rome became a major importer of Celtic cheese, much of it passing through the former Greek colony of Massalia (Charlesworth 1970; West 1935). This sizable trade in cheese almost certainly included hard-rind types that could withstand the rigors of transportation and may have included forerunners of the large, highly cooked cheeses that became common in alpine regions during the Middle Ages. Indeed, the Roman geographer Strabo (first century AD) wrote of widespread cheese production all along the northern slopes of the Alps (Jones and Sterrett 1917). He described these mountain cheeses as being brought down to settlements in the valleys and plains where the Celtic populations were concentrated. These cheeses must have been rugged and long-lived, and those that were exported to Rome were evidently quite exceptional in quality.

According to Pliny, a cheese from the Centronian Alps (the Savoie region of modern France where Beaufort and Reblochon are produced to this day) was very popular in Rome. Pliny called this cheese Vatusican (also rendered Vatusicum or Vatusicus), but unfortunately he did not describe its characteristics. Vatusican may have resembled the relatively large, highly cooked Beaufort cheese of today, as Rance (1989) has suggested, but we cannot say for certain based on the sketchy information available.

Galen, a prolific second-century writer of medical texts and second only to Hippocrates in his influence on medicine in antiquity, also noted that Vatusican cheese was the best and most popular cheese in Rome (Grant 2000). Writing from the perspective of digestive health, Galen divided cheeses into three categories. He considered very old, very dry cheeses (think of hard Pecorino Romano types) to be hardest to digest and most problematic for good health; less objectionable were the less old, less dry (intermediate) cheeses; best of all were the high-moisture fresh cheeses. Galen recommended a fresh cheese called Oxygalaktinos that was produced in his hometown of Pergamum on the Aegean coast of Turkey, which he considered ideal for digestive health.

Like Pliny, Galen did not specifically describe Vatusican, but he referred to Vatusican immediately after describing Oxygalaktinos. Because of this juxtaposition it is tempting, as Dalby (2009) pointed out, to conclude that Vatusican was somehow similar to the fresh cheese Oxygalaktinos and perhaps was a forerunner of Reblochon, an uncooked, hand-pressed, relatively high-moisture cheese. In view of the daunting challenges of transporting a relatively fragile cheese like Reblochon over great distances during Roman times, however, this seems very unlikely. Rance's view of Vatusican as a cooked, pressed Beaufort-like cheese (a cheese that fits reasonably well into Galen's intermediate category of less old, less dry cheeses) is easier to reconcile than a Reblochon forerunner.

In summary, it is conceivable that Vatusican and other Celtic alpine cheeses during Roman times may have been early forerunners of the large cooked cheeses whose production in the Alps can be clearly documented during the Middle Ages. If so, the large Celtic population that settled in Liguria and far northern Etruria after the Celtic invasions of Italy may have brought the technology of high-temperature cooking with them from the north, enabling them to develop their remarkably large signature cheese, the Luna.

Another possibility is that Luna cheesemakers did not employ a cooking step in the making of their large cheeses. There is another way to produce large cheeses with low initial moisture content that does not require cooking. The technique involves mixing generous amounts of salt into curd that has been "pre-pressed" and then broken up or milled into small particles. The salted curds are then pressed a second time to form the final cheese. This allows the salt to diffuse into the entire curd mass uniformly and in the process triggers the uniform release of large amounts of whey from the curd particles. The result is a mass of curd particles that are relatively low in moisture and high in salt. When such particles are pressed together to form a large cheese, the cheese interior is much lower in moisture and higher in salt content than in an uncooked cheese of similar size that is dry-salted or brine-salted at the surface. English cheesemakers eventually adopted this approach to produce a number of large pressed cheeses that did not require cooking, among which Cheshire is the best known.

However, the technique of salting milled curds before pressing had originated centuries earlier, perhaps many centuries earlier, in France. Although the supporting evidence is far from definitive, it is believed that this technique may have originated with Celtic cheesemakers in the Massif Central of Gaul where the forerunners of Laguiole, Cantal, and Salers (all large uncooked cheeses that are made by salting pre-pressed milled curds before pressing) may have been made as far back as Roman times. A well-known passage in Pliny's *Natural History* refers to cheeses made in the Gévaudan region of France (near the Cantal-Salers region of the Massif Central) that were very popular in Rome. The Roman system of roads in southern France was quite good, making possible the transport of salt, the vital ingredient of cheese making, from the salt works on the Mediterranean coast to the high pastures of Gévaudan, and the reverse transport of finished cheeses to Nimes near the coast for maritime shipment to Rome (Whittaker and Goody 2001). However, Pliny's description of this cheese—"its excellence is only very short-lived, and it must be eaten while it is fresh" (Bostock and Riley 1855)—seems at odds with the contention that this was the forerunner of Laguiole, Cantal, and Salers. Dalby (2009) attempted to reconcile this with the hypothesis that Pliny's cheese was made by the same basic Cantal technology (milled-curd salting before pressing) but was a lower-salt, shorter-lived forerunner. Though all of this is clearly speculative in nature, it is at least conceivable that the Celts in Liguria could have borrowed the pre-pressed, milled-curd salting technology from Gaul to develop their signature Luna cheese.

Whatever the details behind the development of Luna cheese, the fact remains that the cheesemakers had only two options for making very large aged cheeses: Either they employed high-temperature cooking combined with pressing and dry- or brine-salting, or they milled and salted the uncooked, pre-pressed curds before final pressing (or they combined the two technologies, as in the case of Cheddar cheese). The important point to stress is that cheesemakers were now using new technologies to push cheese diversity in new directions that would eventually give rise to the great families of cheese that we know today.

That it was Celtic cheesemakers who were the first (or among the first) to experiment with the making large cheeses is by no means surprising. The Celts were dairy farmers who brought their dairy cattle with them wherever they migrated. By Roman times they had accumulated the benefit of centuries of selective breeding, and their cows were known in antiquity for their rich milk-producing capacity (Churchill Semple 1922). Furthermore, the Celts brought with them centuries of transhumant cheese-making experience acquired in the mountainous regions of central Europe where they were originally concentrated. Alpine transhumance forced villagers in the valleys to combine their individual dairy cows into larger herds that could be led up to highland pastures. Thus, Celtic cheesemakers in the mountains of central Europe were regularly confronted with the challenges of producing cheese from large volumes of milk obtained from large herds of cows.

The logistical advantage of producing a smaller number of large cheeses rather than a larger number of small cheeses becomes greater as the volume of milk processed into cheese increases, and this likely provided an incentive for alpine Celtic cheesemakers to explore new technologies for producing large cheeses that could be stored for use during the long winters of central Europe. Large, highly cooked cheeses (such as Beaufort-type), as well as large, pre-pressed, milled-curd, pre-salted cheeses (Cantal-type), were well suited to the demands of Celtic transhumant dairying and Celtic life in general. In contrast, it wasn't until the creation of the great landed estates with large flocks in Varro's time that large volumes of sheep's milk for cheese making became the norm in Italy, only then creating a strong incentive to produce larger pecorino cheeses. Large cheeses eventually came to be produced on the Italian peninsula and in Sicily, perhaps soon after Italian cheesemakers began experimenting with heating techniques in Columella's time.

It seems likely that the Celts brought their technologies for producing durable, long-lived cheese wherever they migrated across Europe, which may account for the extraordinary geographic range of Celtic cheeses that were exported to Rome, extending from Toulouse in far southern France, to the Menapii region of Belgium and far northwest France, to the alpine regions of eastern France and the Massif Central, to Switzerland and Austria, to Dalmatia in the Balkan peninsula (Charlesworth 1970; Jones and Sterrett 1917). Thus, it would appear that Celtic cheese making, predominantly cow's-milk cheese making, was firmly established throughout large swaths of Europe by the time the Romans invaded Celtic lands and colonized the continent. Apart from the westernmost fringes of Europe (Scotland, Ireland, Wales), which remained largely untouched by the Romans, the Celts of western Europe quickly became Romanized, and new distinctive cultures emerged out of the Celtic-Roman fusions, but cheese making and the love of cheese continued.

The Merging of Empires

Even as Rome was Romanizing the "barbarian" peoples of its massive empire, another empire was forming in its wake: The followers of Jesus Christ were aggressively evangelizing almost every nook and cranny of the Roman Empire and beyond. Originally centered in Jerusalem, the leadership of the fledgling Christian church shifted west to Rome following the destruction of Jerusalem by the Romans in AD 70. From the start, the church faced enormous challenges in establishing and maintaining unity with respect to doctrines, practices, and canonic texts as Christianity spread explosively across vast expanses of geography and infiltrated diverse cultures.

Syncretism, the fusion of different religious traditions to form new hybrid belief systems, was deeply ingrained in the Greco-Roman world, and syncretism quickly began to creep into Christianity. It started with efforts described in the New Testament Book of Acts to graft Judaic practices onto Christian teachings, but quickly expanded to include Gnostic philosophies of Greek/Near East origin. At the core of Gnostic philosophies was the notion that transcendent truth is acquired through inner mysticism and then transmitted from person to person through secret teachings and writings. Gnostic Christianity, therefore, had no need for the historical Jesus, only his transcendent truths (Johnson 1976).

By the first half of the second century a powerful Gnostic sect known as the Docetists had taken root in the Christian church. Docetists rejected the incarnation of Jesus—the doctrine that Jesus was both fully God and fully man—denying that Jesus had ever been a man. Their teachings effectively severed Christianity from its Old Testament Judaic roots, a theological surgery that was very attractive in the Greek world, where there was great resistance to being spiritually yoked with the Hebrew scriptures, which were often viewed as barbaric, offensive, and incomprehensible (Johnson 1976). It was during this crisis of identity within the church that Quintus Septimius Florens Tertullianus rose to become one of the greatest defenders of the faith.

Tertullian was born in Carthage around the middle of the second century, became a well-educated Roman citizen. At some point he converted to Christianity, probably at a fairly young age because he had not yet married. He was the first Christian theologian to write in Latin (Greek had been the principal language of church writings up to this point) and had enormous influence, especially in the Latin west (Hill 2003). Like the apostle Paul, Tertullian was dedicated to preserving and transmitting the pure teachings that the apostles had received from Jesus himself and through the Holy Spirit; thus he worked tirelessly to codify church doctrines and to defend them against contamination with false teachings. Around AD 200 Tertullian distilled core church doctrines down to a manageable Rule of Faith that resembled the Apostles' Creed, still widely acknowledged in Christian churches today (Rist 1942).

Tertullian tirelessly defended vital Christian teachings that were (and still are) difficult to comprehend and accept, such as the concept of the Trinity (one God in three persons: Father, Son, and Holy Spirit), using common imagery to explain or illuminate deep spiritual mysteries (Hill 2003). This ability to communicate in common language was pivotal to countering the Gnostic Docetists who mocked the incarnation of Jesus. Tertullian correctly understood that the incarnation stood at the core of Christianity, and that the virgin birth was central to the incarnation. However, the virgin birth was (and is) difficult to comprehend and served as a great stumbling block for the rational-minded Greeks. Thus it was probably no accident that Tertullian marshaled the teachings of Aristotle, the foremost rationalist of the ancient western world, to defend the virgin birth.

Aristotle's description of embryology in his book *On the Generation of Animals* became the accepted "scientific" understanding of conception and embryology until the Renaissance. According to Aristotle, conception and gestation are similar to the action of rennet on milk during cheese making; Semen acts on the menstrual blood (like rennet acts on milk) to catalyze a reaction that fixes or coagulates the blood into the fetus. As curd then separates from the whey during cheese making, so also the fetus separates from the amniotic fluid (Needham and Hughes 1959).

In his treatise "On the Flesh of Christ," Tertullian used Aristotle's theory of embryology and imagery of rennet coagulation in his exegesis of the first chapter of the Gospel of Saint John, arguing that even though Christ's birth was not preceded by human sexual intercourse, conception occurred miraculously in Mary's womb and gestation and parturition took place in the usual manner. In other words, think of the incarnation as analogous to God coagulating milk and producing a perfect rennet-coagulated cheese in a normal cheese vat, but doing so miraculously, without the addition of rennet. Job's use of coagulation imagery in the Hebrew Scriptures (Job 10:8–11) to describe his formation in the womb provided Tertullian with a certain biblical justification for borrowing the Aristotelian imagery.

Tertullian's defense of the incarnation and virgin birth carried the day; the Docetists were eventually declared heretics and the church's core doctrines crystallized into a recognized orthodoxy. Church unity was preserved at the expense of heretical sects that were excommunicated, and the leadership in Rome eventually emerged as the church's central ecclesiastical governing body, entrusted with the daunting task of preserving and defending the faith throughout a vast organization that by now spanned three continents and encompassed many cultures and languages. It is easy to understand why the early Christian church was preoccupied with establishing and then preserving a definitive orthodoxy of doctrine and practice. Ironically, it was the growing rigidity of that orthodoxy that drove Tertullian to split with the church in his later years over a number of issues, including the Montanist controversy.

Montanus was a self-proclaimed Christian prophet in Asia Minor (modern Turkey) who started a prophetic movement that became known as the New Prophecy around the middle of the second century and quickly spread throughout Asia Minor and beyond (Tabbernee 2007). Prophecy and other miraculous works of the Holy Spirit had been central elements of the early apostolic church, but a tension existed from the beginning over the dangers of false prophets and the need to discern the genuine workings of the Holy Spirit. Montanus, along with Maximilla and Priscilla (two women who joined him as prophetesses), quickly raised concerns among church leaders in Asia Minor because of the manner in which they prophesied, which critics claimed involved ecstatic trances and *glossolalia,* that is, unintelligible speech or sounds akin to incoherent babbling (Butler 2006). Montanus claimed that this was the work of Holy Spirit moving in them and the voice of new prophetic knowledge from God. Church leaders were uneasy, unconvinced that the frenetic utterances of Montanus and his followers were genuine manifestations of the gifts of prophecy and "speaking in tongues" described so differently by the apostle Paul in First Corinthians, chapter 14, of the New Testament.

As time went on, Montanism spread far beyond Asia Minor, and splinter groups or subsects arose out of the movement that allegedly introduced novel worship practices. Church leaders grew increasingly hostile toward Montanists and the subsects that they had spawned, convinced that they were introducing false practices and doctrine under the guise of New Prophecy. One subsect, referred to as the Artotyrites, were accused of substituting cheese for bread during the celebration of the Eucharist, in direct defiance of Christ's instructions to the disciples during the Last Supper (Tabbernee 2007). The origin of this practice remains the topic of scholarly debate, but one train of evidence suggests that this was an infiltration of the bloodless sacrifice of cheese to the pagan deity Cybele into the Christian celebration of the Eucharist (Tabbernee 2007). Cybele, the Mother of the Gods, was widely worshipped in the region of Asia Minor where Montanism originated. Recall that a particular type of cheese referred to as "female cheese" was sacrificed to Cybele; thus, it may have been "female cheese" that infiltrated the Eucharistic practice of the Artotyrite Christians.

The issue eventually came to a head because of developments in north Africa that followed the martyrdom of Perpetua and Felicity, two Christian women who appeared to have strong Montanist leanings. Perpetua and Felicity were martyred in Carthage at the beginning of the third century during the persecutions under the Roman emperor Septimus Servus (Butler 2006). Servus ruthlessly attacked pagan magicians, astrologers, and prophets throughout the empire, especially the Celtic Druids because of their potential to incite political instability. The spread of the Montanist practices of ecstatic trances and prophecies of impending end times, which bore some resemblance to Celtic pagan practices, may have motivated Servus to initiate a more systematic and brutal persecution of the Christian church than had occurred previously (Wypustek 1997). Perpetua and Felicity, along with three male believers, were torn to pieces by wild animals in the arena of the amphitheater at Carthage in a spectacular public display designed to instill the fear of Rome in the Christian community.

Perpetua was a highly educated woman from the privileged ranks of Roman society in Carthage who kept a diary of her experiences with Felicity, her young slave, while they were in prison leading up to their martyrdom. The diary was preserved and incorporated into *The Passion of Perpetua and Felicity*, an eyewitness narrative written by an anonymous editor. Included in Perpetua's diary is an account of several visions that she and the others experienced while in prison, including Perpetua's first vision in which she climbed a bronze ladder to heaven. There she met a shepherd who was milking sheep and who gave her a mouthful of fresh cheese. As she ate, a multitude around her clad in shining white garments chanted "Amen," and then she awoke (Shaw 1993).

Perpetua was revered for her martyrdom and soon beatified to sainthood. However, her vision of Christ the shepherd in heaven was problematic for the church because it could be interpreted as a heavenly Eucharist in which cheese was administered, which was uncomfortably close to Artotyritic practice. The church subsequently redacted *The Passion of Perpetua and Felicity* into a shorter version, *The Acts of Perpetua and Felicity,* which incorporated a number of changes to minimize the Montanist leanings of the original work. Among the changes, the reference to cheese in Perpetua's vision was replaced with "the fruit of milk," a less threatening euphemism (Butler 2006).

Montanism eventually was declared a heresy and the infiltration of cheese into the Christian sacraments was routed out, never to return, but new charismatic prophetic movements continued to emerge periodically within the church throughout the centuries right down to the present. Indeed, charismatic movements constitute some of the fastest-growing segments within the Christian church of the twenty-first century. However, tensions within Christianity over the legitimacy of new prophecy and the practice of glossolalia (speaking in tongues) continue to this day.

Heightened persecution of Christians did not end with Servus; the third century witnessed a dramatic expansion of state-sponsored coercive and brutal policies aimed at suppressing Christianity under a succession of emperors culminating in the reign of Diocletian and the Tetrarchy at the end of that century. Diocletian is perhaps best known for his efforts to implement empire-wide monetary and economic reforms, including his Edict of 301, *De pretiis rerum venalium,* that fixed an upper limit on prices for salable commodities and wages (Le Glay et al. 2009). Under the Edict, no less than 759 categories of commodities and wages were regulated, including 2 categories of cheese: soft cheese and dry cheese. Dry cheese was included in a section devoted to fish, perhaps in recognition of the widespread use of grated cheese in fish sauces or because both were often eaten as relish with bread. Soft or fresh cheese was listed in a different section devoted to fresh farm produce (Frayn 1984).

Despite its naive impracticality, Diocletian's Edict remained in force during his reign, propped up by severe penalties that included death to both buyer and seller for exceeding the fixed price (Lacour-Gayet and Lacour-Gayet 1951). After Diocletian's abdication from the imperial throne in 305, price controls were eventually abandoned and the world of market forces restored. More important, the Christian church, which had been so viciously brutalized under Diocletian's rein, triumphed in its struggle with Rome when the emperor Constantine issued the Edict of Milan in 313.

Constantine's Edict reversed the Roman Empire's policy of hostility and granted Christianity full legal protection. Constantine subsequently enacted other friendly policies that favored Christianity and enabled the church to become very wealthy. As Christianity spread, it began to serve a unifying role in a Roman Empire, which by this time was under constant threat from Germanic peoples infiltrating from the north. By the end of the fourth century paganism was banned throughout the Roman Empire and Christianity became the state religion. As the Empire imploded under the weight of Germanic incursions and its governmental infrastructure crumbled in the provinces, the church increasingly assumed the role of the Empire's institutional memory and administrative and moral authority. Church and state were merging into a murky entity that would dominate western civilization for a thousand years and catalyze the development of new cheeses throughout Europe.

CHAPTER SIX

The Manor, the Monastery, and the Age of Cheese Diversification

Idleness is an enemy of the soul. Because this is so the brethren ought to be occupied at specified times in manual labor, and at other fixed hours in holy reading.

Saint Benedict (Gasquet 1966, p.84)

B enedict of Nursia was born around AD 480 amid the fall of the Roman Empire in the west. A deeply religious man, Benedict in his early years practiced an extreme form of asceticism that was characteristic of the eastern Christian monastic tradition. He eventually became disillusioned with the severe practices of the day and withdrew to Monte Cassino, a remote mountaintop haven situated between Rome and Naples, where he founded a new monastery based on a more moderate commonsense approach to ascetic ideals.

Followers of Benedict's Rule were to live as a community, separate from the world around them and as self-sufficient as possible, yet also dedicated to public service. They were to be the "instruments of good works" and committed to a strong social mission along with their spiritual calling. The Rule also elevated literacy and the reading (and by necessity the copying) of holy texts to the level of sacred service, and gave dignity to the mundane toils of life, which inspired the Benedictine motto: "To labor is to pray" (Gasquet 1966).

Benedict's Rule created an institution that was eminently suited for the times: a center of literacy and learning amid the ruins of an empire that had lost its educational and administrative infrastructure; a social safety net and source of community stability and moral courage in a turbulent and dangerous time; and a disciplined and innovative economic entity that complemented and served as a model for the medieval manor, the ubiquitous economic and social unit of Europe for centuries to come. Indeed, Benedictine monastic houses became a powerful engine for economic development in Europe for many centuries through their acquisition of vast manorial holdings. In the process, the monastery and the manor gave rise to new and diverse cheeses.

Roman Colonization and the Birth of the Manor

Following the decisive defeat of Carthage during the Second Punic War, Rome embarked on a relentless campaign of territorial expansion that created a vast empire extending southward from Britain and the western banks of the Rhine and Danube rivers to the shores of the Mediterranean Sea and beyond. By the first century AD the frontiers of the Roman Empire stretched for nearly 10,000 miles (16,000 km), bounded by a seemingly endless array of "barbarian" peoples who posed a constant threat. Thus, the Romans were faced with the monumental task of defending their empire, an effort that would eventually require upward of five hundred thousand soldiers permanently stationed along the frontiers.

The challenges of feeding, clothing, and otherwise provisioning the legions that made up this massive permanent military presence were daunting; therefore, the Roman military moved quickly to establish an agricultural infrastructure in the provinces. Each Roman fort included military lands—used for food production—that extended for a considerable distance around the fort. The soldiers themselves sometimes farmed this land; more often civilians leased the land and assumed the role of farmer (Davies 1971). Military lands north of the Alps often included extensive pasture for livestock production, especially for sheep, which supplied wool for cloth production and milk for cheese making.

The basic military diet consisted of cereals, bacon (pork), cheese, and probably vegetables (Bezeczky 1996; Davies 1971). Military logistical planners evidently brought cheese-making equipment and technology with them from Italy because ceramic molds of Roman design (cylindrical, perforated) for pressing cheese curd have been found at various military sites throughout Europe (Davies 1971; Niblett et al. 2006). Thus, cheese making was an important component of the Roman military machine, and in times of peace legionnaires even may have doubled as cheesemakers themselves. Cheese was not a new addition to Roman military life; according to Virgil (first century BC), the standard daily ration of the Roman soldier included 1 ounce (28 g) of pecorino (sheep's-milk) cheese.

In addition to raising their own food on military farmlands, the army also relied heavily on food supplies from local agricultural colonies, or *villas,* that the Romans established throughout Europe. Villas were large landed estates modeled after the *latifundia* of Italy. As in Italy, the aristocratic senatorial class acquired landed estates in the conquered lands north of the Alps. The Roman emperor and imperial family also maintained extensive estates and, indeed, the villa became the ubiquitous unit of Roman civilization in the provinces, along with the Roman town and city. The villas furnished vital agricultural productive capacity, whereas towns and cities were the administrative centers that established and reinforced political, ideological, and economic control over the provinces (Koebner 1966).

Like the military farms, provincial villas probably adopted Roman cheese-making techniques and equipment along the lines described by Columella, with sheep's-milk cheeses being common in many provincial regions (figure 6-1). The pastoral economies of northwest France, Flanders, and Britain, for example, were dominated by sheep raising for wool production and cloth weaving during the Roman occupation (Trow-Smith 1957; Wild 2002). The Roman aristocracy was well aware of the natural synergy between the wool industry and milk production and cheese making, as had been practiced on the *latifundia* of Italy since Cato's time.

At first the labor force of the provincial Roman villa consisted mostly of slaves, again similar to the *latifundia* in Italy. However, as Roman expansionism slowed and eventually ground to a halt, the supply of new slaves diminished. By the end of the first century AD, villas faced a growing labor shortage and needed to develop an alternate supply of workers. This was accomplished by dividing portions of the estate into small holdings that

Figure 6-1. Ceramic cheese mold of Roman design that was used in Britain during the period of Roman administration (AD 43 to 410). Note the perforations in the mold to facilitate whey drainage. (Photo courtesy of the British Museum; © The Trustees of the British Museum. All rights reserved.)

were made available to the local free population in the form of permanent leases. Thus, the large landed estates of the Roman Empire gradually became subdivided into small plots that were farmed by free tenant farmers, who in the northern provinces were usually drawn from the conquered barbarian (mostly Celtic) peoples. Slaves continued to work alongside these newcomers, but the proportion of slave labor on the villas decreased and that of free tenants increased as time went on (Doehaerd 1978; Gras 1940).

The provinces also continued to support many small independent farms operated by the native conquered peoples, but the balance between small native landholders and the great landed estates of the Roman aristocracy progressively shifted toward the latter. As time went on Imperial Rome levied increasingly burdensome land taxes on the small farmers, forcing many into bankruptcy and forfeiture of their land to the aristocratic estate holders, whose villas grew ever larger. Even the free tenants on the landed estates were taxed heavily on their leased holdings and languished under imperial exploitation.

By the beginning of the fourth century, the Roman agricultural system, like the empire itself, was in trouble. Heavy taxation had devastated independent small-scale farming, and the free tenants on the villas struggled to satisfy their tax burdens. Furthermore, the provinces were under constant threat of violence and destruction from incursions of Germanic peoples from the north. The vitality of both the provincial town centers and the country villas eroded as these complex changes spun out of control. Among many repercussions of this period was the abandonment of large tracts of formerly cultivated land and a dwindling of the villa labor force. To stem this hemorrhaging of agricultural productivity the Roman emperors Diocletian and Constantine enacted a series of reforms that legally bound the free tenants and their descendants to their villa in perpetuity, effectively creating a hereditary class of serfs (Pounds 1994).

By the end of the fourth century the Roman Empire in the west had descended into a state of siege under the pressure of perpetual Germanic incursions. Violence and chaos were on the rise, and the provincial towns and cities experienced population drain as members of the landed aristocracy either fled to more secure regions of the empire or withdrew from the very visible and vulnerable urban centers to the more secure and defendable confines of their country villas. The fortified villa became a common fixture of the countryside during this period (Koebner 1966).

As the empire's administrative and security infrastructure deteriorated, villas became more self-sufficient and self-governing. The aristocratic lords increasingly found it necessary to segregate a portion (usually quite sizable) of their estates as private farms or domains to support the lord's household. Much labor was needed to maintain these private farms, which prompted the lords to expand their tenants' obligations to include not only food rents but also manual labor services on the lord's farm. Around the same time, the status of the slaves who continued to make up a significant portion of the villa labor supply gradually began to change. Lords began to grant their slaves rights to small holdings, effectively elevating them to the status of unfree tenants, a step up from life as a slave, but a step below that of the free tenant. Thus, as the Roman Empire in the west came to an end at the close of the fifth century, the ingredients for the medieval manor, organized around the labor of free and unfree tenants, were beginning to take shape (Gras 1940).

The Germanic invasions of the late fifth century swept away the remaining vestiges of imperial Roman rule. However, the incoming barbarian kings inherited the Roman system of large landed estates, a system that had concentrated vast tracts of land and human resources in the hands of the aristocracy. The aristocratic rulers of the Germanic invaders, like all aristocracies, were very much concerned with wealth and status, and the ubiquitous Roman villa provided a very attractive infrastructure for perpetuating wealth and status among the incoming rulers. The medieval manor arose in part from the amalgamation of Germanic rule and social structure with the Roman villa infrastructure (Pounds 1994; Wood 1986).

The manor generally consisted of two components, a peasant side and a demesne side. The peasant side was made up of free and unfree tenants, or serfs, who lived together as a village community on the estate and who possessed hereditary rights to small parcels of the lord's land. Holdings were sometimes as small as an acre or two or as large as 40 acres (16 ha), but probably on average ranged from around 10 to 20 acres (4 to 8 ha) in England, slightly larger in northwestern France (Duby 1968; Pounds 1994). The peasant serfs typically shared rights to graze cattle on common lands, which enabled their families to raise a cow or two or a few sheep or goats, depending on which were better suited for the region. In return for these privileges, serfs were obliged to provide a portion of their agricultural output to the manor lord along with manual labor—for example, three days a week working in the fields of the lord's demesne, more during the harvest, and various other services.

The demesne was the lord's personal farm, which might occupy from one-quarter to as much as one-half of the estate's total cultivated acreage (Ganshof and Verhulst 1966). Depending on the nature of the land, the demesne might also include extensive woodlands, pasture, draft animals, and herds of cattle and/or flocks of sheep, along with other agricultural animals. The manor itself was the lord's dwelling place, a grand home along with a complex of outbuildings that were occupied by the lord's household, staff, and servants, and which served as the administrative center of the estate. As time went on aristocratic lords often acquired many manors, in which case the lord could make only occasional visits to the outlying manors; the day-to-day supervision of these manors was delegated to subordinates.

There were also some manors that did not possess a demesne but simply consisted of villages or groups of small tenant farmers who paid the manor lord a share of their agricultural production in return for their inherited right to their small landholdings. Manors without demesnes were often the product of the chaotic and dangerous times that followed the collapse of Roman rule. Free Romanized-Celtic villages that had managed to remain intact during the Roman occupation, as well as free villages of Germanic immigrants who had settled in the Roman provinces during the latter stages of the empire, now voluntarily surrendered their land to the new Germanic aristocratic lords and placed themselves under their authority in return for the lords' protection. This arrangement was more common in the remote and sparsely populated regions of central Europe, whereas manors with demesnes were more common in western France and England.

Initially the manors were solely in the hands of the aristocracy, but beginning in the seventh century monastic houses began to acquire manors as gifts from the aristocracy. The manors and the monasteries of Europe provided fertile ground for the development of new cheeses, and eventually monastic control over manorial lands was so extensive that the roles of the manor and monastery in medieval cheese making often became inseparable.

The Rise of the Monastery

The collapse of the Roman Empire left a much weakened Christian church in the west. The western church, still centered in Rome, was faced with the urgent task of winning the hearts and minds of the new Germanic conquerors, who were either pagans or adherents of a Christian heresy known as Arianism. A major breakthrough occurred toward the end of the fifth century when Frankish tribes that had settled in Gaul united under Clovis to become the Kingdom of the Franks, a regional power occupying most of what is now modern France. The conversion of the Frankish King Clovis to Roman Christianity at the end of the fifth century reenergized the Roman church by affording it a major foothold north of the Alps from which it could reassert its influence.

However, the sixth century brought a new threat (or perceived threat) to the Roman church, this time from within Christianity itself. The long reach of the Roman Empire had never extended to Ireland, and the Christian church there had developed independently of the Roman church, forging a vibrant and talented Celtic church culture of its own. In 575 Irish monastic missionaries under the leadership of Columbanus set out to evangelize the European continent, which, though nominally Christian, in some regions still remained largely pagan. Columbanus's missionary efforts were well received in northern Europe and resulted in the establishment of some forty Irish monasteries throughout France, northern Italy, and central Europe by the time of Columbanus's death in 615 (Johnson 1976).

In Rome, Pope Gregory I was alarmed by the reports of Irish evangelistic fervor because some of the practices of the Irish church were different from those of the Roman church. More important, Columbanus opposed the hierarchical structure of the Roman church and its entanglements with secular governments, and he refused to acknowledge the authority of the church in Rome and its bishops. Therefore, Gregory viewed Irish missionary zeal as a threat to papal authority and to the church itself, a rebellion that needed to be countered and brought into line with Rome.

By chance, Gregory had come across a copy of Benedict's Rule during the waning years of the sixth century, and he was impressed by the practicality of Benedict's approach to monasticism. Benedict's Rule was the perfect response to the Irish threat, an institution dedicated to education and learning, to public service and social responsibility, and one that acknowledged the authority of the Roman (Catholic) church. Gregory endorsed Benedictine monasticism around the start of the seventh century and energetically set out to establish monastic houses across Europe by encouraging aristocratic rulers to endow new monasteries with grants of land, often in the form of manors.

His efforts and those of his successors were stunningly successful: Benedictine monasticism expanded explosively throughout Europe during the seventh and eighth centuries. Germanic kings and aristocrats who controlled large tracts of land endowed new monastic houses enthusiastically, and hundreds of monasteries were established. At first there was considerable tension between the Irish monastic houses and the new houses of the Benedictine Order, but the Benedictine movement gradually overwhelmed the Irish influence and by the ninth century had become the official practice of the Holy Roman Empire.

Benedictine monasteries grew not only in number but also in wealth; by the tenth century many houses had become fabulously wealthy, possessing vast manorial holdings. The excesses of wealth and opulence that came to characterize the cathedrals, practices, and day-to-day life of the great monasteries triggered a backlash of reform movements that endeavored to return to the Rule of Saint Benedict in its original simplicity. The most important reform movement was that of the Cistercian Order, founded in 1098 in Burgundy, France, and championed by Saint Bernard during the twelfth century. Like the Benedictines of an earlier time, the Cistercians experienced explosive growth, establishing some five hundred abbeys in Europe by the beginning of the thirteenth century.

Following Benedict's original intent, the Cistercians sought to be self-sufficient and set apart from the entanglements of the world; therefore they refused endowments of manorial lands and serfs, accepting only gifts of land that generally consisted of wilderness or wasteland. To provide the labor force needed to tame the wilderness and support the abbey the Cistercians established an order of lay brothers (*conversi*) whose role was to serve the abbey with manual labor. As abbeys acquired more land over time they recruited lay brothers in large numbers to work the land and tend the monastic flocks and herds. The creation of a lay brotherhood essentially opened the door of the Cistercian monastery to men from every walk of life and extended the Benedictine ideal of "to labor is to pray" to a much broader segment of the population (Butler and Given-Wilson 1979). This created a powerful Cistercian work ethic, and many Cistercian abbeys eventually acquired vast tracts of land, became enormously successful agriculturalists, and grew very wealthy. The shrewd business sense and managerial savvy of both the Benedictines and the Cistercians profoundly shaped the economic development of medieval Europe and the course of European cheese history.

Manorial and Monastic Cheese Making

The manor and the monastery in their various forms played a central role in medieval cheese history, though one that is difficult to reconstruct and remains incompletely understood. The fragments of information that survive from the medieval period point to new cheeses that were born of the peasant side of the manor, others that developed from the demesne side, and still others that arose in manors without demesnes and within the monasteries themselves.

Soft-Ripened Cheeses

The typical manor of northwestern Europe—with its village of peasant tenant farmers, demesne, common lands, and temperate damp climate—created a peculiar environment for cheese making, which inspired the development of a group of cheeses on the peasant side that eventually evolved into the much-loved soft-ripened varieties that we know today. Manorial records from the early Middle Ages reveal that these peasant cheeses were often included in the food rents that tenant farmers paid to the manor lords and constituted an important part of the peasant diet (Pearson 1997). In times of surplus they were probably bartered in the manorial village for other necessities. Unfortunately, few accounts remain of these early medieval cheeses or the practices that were used in their production. It wasn't until the later Middle Ages and beyond that the soft-ripened peasant cow's-milk cheeses that we recognize today, such as Livarot, Pont-L'Evêque, Brie, and Neufchâtel, and the lactic goats'-milk cheeses, such as Crottin and Saint Maure, emerged as identifiable fixtures of the agricultural landscape of France. Although today's soft-ripened cheeses are the direct legacy of the small peasant farms that came into being after the breakup of the manors, it seems likely that their origins extend back to the murky centuries of the early Middle Ages.

It is possible to envision how the manor may have spawned forerunners of the soft-ripened cheeses by considering the conditions and constraints that the manorial environment placed on medieval tenant cheesemakers, keeping in mind the conjectural nature of such efforts. As a starting point, it is well established that the tenant households that made up the manorial labor force in northwest Europe often raised a cow or two for milk. Tenants were allowed to graze their cows on common lands during the growing season and on stubble left in the fields after the harvest, but the shared use of this land and the limited supply of fodder that each peasant household could stockpile for the winter months severely limited the number of livestock that could be raised, often to one or two cows per household. This meant that the volume of milk available for tenant cheese making was often very small indeed. Milk yields of cows during the early Middle Ages were only around 1 gallon (3.8 liters) per day (Trow-Smith 1957), which is equivalent to about 1 pound (454 g) of soft cheese; a single milking would thus have yielded the equivalent of only around 0.5 pound (227 g) of cheese.

The duties of milking the cows and making the cheese fell to the women of the households, who were also responsible for raising the chickens and swine, collecting the eggs, bringing the grain to the miller and returning with flour, baking the bread, brewing the beer, keeping the herb garden, feeding, clothing, and caring for the children, preparing the food and cooking the meals, carding, spinning, and weaving the wool and flax to produce clothing, blankets, and more, making a range of household necessities, and so on—a very demanding portfolio of duties (Williams 1967). From the perspective of the harried peasant wife and mother, the small amount of milk obtained from a single milking must at times have seemed hardly worth the effort needed to make cheese. Fortunately, in the cool temperate environment of northwest Europe it was possible to store milk overnight or longer, in contrast with the warm Mediterranean climate, where souring and acid coagulation occurred much more rapidly. Consequently, peasant cheesemakers in northern France had the option of combining two or more milkings before commencing the lengthy process of cheese making, an option that was probably quite attractive at times. Because these peasant women were multitasking domestic managers rather than full-time cheesemakers, it is likely that they also gravitated toward the simplest cheese-making practices that they could gracefully fit into their crowded daily routines.

One of the simplest ways to make cheese is the method that Columella had described centuries earlier for producing fresh cheese. Recall that Columella's approach involved adding rennet to fresh warm milk to induce coagulation, after which the curd was gently ladled into small draining forms that he described as wicker vessels or baskets. The curds were allowed to drain and mat together; a small stone or other weight might optionally be placed on top of the curd to hasten draining. Eventually a compact cheese, high in moisture content, was formed, ready to be rubbed with dry salt on the surface or submerged in a concentrated salt brine solution. It turns out that this basic technology, fine-tuned with a few simple modifications such as varying the coagulation time, breaking up the curd (more or less) before ladling into wicker vessels, and periodic turning of the curd during draining and matting, is quite similar to the traditional methods used to make the soft-ripened peasant cheeses of France.

Thus it appears that the peasant women of northern France adopted simple approaches to cheese making that resembled the fresh cheese method described by Columella, but in their hands this approach proved to be far more versatile than Columella could have ever imagined. In the warm Mediterranean climate of Columella's world high-moisture cheeses had to be eaten within a few days before they were rendered inedible by microbial spoilage; however, in the cooler, damper climate of northwestern Europe very different outcomes were possible when the right conditions were satisfied.

Columella's fresh cheese method produces small cheeses that are inevitably high in moisture content; still, the precise moisture content can vary considerably, as can the acidity and structural characteristics of the cheese, depending on three critical cheese-making parameters that French peasant cheesemakers learned to exploit. The first parameter was the length of time that the milk was stored before cheese making. In the world before refrigeration, use of milk from a single milking (fresh and warm from the udder) versus pooled milk from two or even three milkings dramatically affected the level of acidity in the resulting cheese. Fresh milk characteristically contains low populations of lactic acid bacteria that produce acid slowly during cheese making, resulting in cheese that is comparatively low in acidity. In contrast, pooled milk that is stored unrefrigerated between milkings becomes enriched with lactic acid bacteria, leading to rapid acidification during cheese making and cheese that is high in acidity.

Two other key parameters were the amount of rennet used to coagulate the milk and the temperature of the milk during coagulation, both of which affected the amount of time required for milk coagulation. Coagulation may require as little as thirty to sixty minutes when very active rennet is used and the milk is kept at a warm temperature (around 85 to 95°F, or 29° to 35°C). At the other extreme, the use of less rennet combined with cooler milk temperature (around 70°F, or 21°C) can increase coagulation times to as much as twenty-four hours. Long coagulation results in much more acidic cheeses that are structurally (and therefore texturally) different from cheeses produced by rapid rennet coagulation. Such cheeses are also different from acid-coagulated cheeses, both structurally and texturally, and are lower in moisture content because the resulting curd has better draining characteristics than that produced by acid coagulation.

The bottom line is that Columella's simple approach for making fresh cheese had the potential to diverge in a number of different, interesting directions when critical cheese-making parameters were varied. Such modifications gave rise to chemically diverse cheeses that varied considerably in acidity and moisture contents, and structure and texture. When such cheeses were stored under the right set of environmental conditions (including temperature, humidity, ventilation, and physical manipulations such as turning and rubbing) diverse microbiological changes were selectively favored that produce stunning outcomes. Through trial-and-error experience peasant cheesemakers in northwestern France learned to control critical manufacturing parameters, environmental conditions during storage, and physical manipulations that led to the development of three broad families of soft-ripened cheeses: bloomy-rind cheeses, acid/rennet-coagulated "lactic" cheeses, and washed-rind cheeses.

- **Bloomy-Rind Cheeses.** Peasant households that owned only one or two cows may have found it more practical to combine the milk from two or three milkings before making cheese. By rewarming the cooled pooled milk to around 85°F (29°C) and coagulating the warm milk rapidly (within around one hour) with active rennet, the peasant cheesemaker would have produced a high-moisture cheese that was relatively high in acidity. Storing this cheese in a cool and humid environment, such as in an underground root cellar, would have favored the growth of yeasts and molds present at the cheese surface as a result of environmental exposure. If the moisture content of the cheese and the humidity of the cellar were not too high, gray and white molds rather than black and blue molds would tend to be favored. Eventually, orange-pigmented coryneform bacteria might also colonize the cheese surface as late arrivals, made possible by the deacidifying action of the yeasts and molds. Peasant cheeses of this type would have borne some resemblance to traditional bloomy-rind varieties such as Brie de Meaux.

It is impossible to determine whether bloomy-rind cheeses were made on the manor, essentially as we know them today, or whether they evolved much later on the peasant farms that arose out of the breakup of the manors. Either way, it is easy to envision how the manorial environment might have nudged peasant women cheese-makers to adopt key practices that served as the forerunners of the bloomy-rind technology.

• **Acid/Rennet-Coagulated (Lactic) Cheeses.** A second way that Columella's fresh cheese procedure could have been modified by manorial peasant cheesemakers to produce a completely new cheese type was by using pooled milk from multiple milkings combined with extremely slow coagulation (twenty-four hours or longer), made possible by coagulating the milk at room temperature (around 70°F, or 21°C) with a smaller amount of rennet. This approach would have produced cheese that was very acidic, similar to acid-coagulated cheese, yet lower in moisture content than the latter because of its enhanced draining characteristics. Storing this cheese in a cool and humid environment would tend to favor the growth of a variety of yeasts and molds, particularly gray and white molds, as opposed to black and blue molds. In that sense these cheeses bear some resemblance to bloomy-rind types, but their structure and texture are quite different. This cheese-making approach was especially prevalent in western France south of the Loire River, where peasants traditionally raised goats rather than cows. Eventually the technology gave rise to a plethora of small acid/rennet-coagulated goat's-milk cheeses such as Crottin and Saint Maure.

• **Washed-Rind Cheeses.** Peasant households that were fortunate enough to own a few cows would have had sufficient volumes of milk available at times to make cheese immediately after milking. If these women cheesemakers employed Columella's fresh cheese method essentially without modification (by coagulating the warm fresh milk rapidly with very active rennet), the resulting cheese would have been characteristically high in moisture content but relatively low in acidity. Storing this cheese in a cool and very humid environment, such as an underground root cellar or cave, would selectively favor the growth of yeasts followed by orange-pigmented coryneform bacteria on the cheese surface. By inadvertently— or, later, deliberately—smearing the pinpoint surface colonies of orange coryneform bacteria across the entire cheese surface with their hands, preferably wetted with a weak salt brine, cheesemakers could then encourage a continuous orange-reddish bacterial lawn over the entire cheese surface.

This basic technology gave rise to a family of cheeses that are known as smear-ripened or washed-rind cheeses. Peasant cheesemakers of northwestern France used this approach to develop coryneform-dominated types such as Pont-L'Evêque. Washed-rind cheeses are also sometimes referred to as "monastery cheeses" in recognition of their long association with monastic cheese making in northern Europe. Several washed-rind cheeses, including Maroilles and Muenster, are believed to have originated in monasteries during the early Middle Ages (Rance 1989). Monastic cheesemakers were particularly well positioned to produce washed-rind cheeses because they had ready access to large volumes of fresh milk from their monastic herds or flocks, and to stone cellars within the monastic compound that provided uniformly cool and humid environments for aging cheese. The simple washed-rind technology also fit gracefully into the rigid daily schedule of monastic life, which allocated about four hours in the morning and again in the afternoon for manual labor. The self-contained nature of the monastery was also ideal for fragile washed-rind cheeses in that they were consumed on-site and thus did not have to risk damage and loss during transport to market (Kindstedt 2005). Whether the peasants who produced washed-rind cheeses such as Pont-L'Evêque developed their technology independently or learned from their neighboring monastic cheesemakers is not known for certain, but some cross-fertilization of knowledge is certainly possible. According to Rance (1989), some medieval monasteries taught their cheese-making secrets to the lay cheesemakers of their manorial holdings.

In summary, it seems that peasant cheesemakers in northwestern France gradually fine-tuned their simple practices and storage conditions in ways that rendered predictable, desirable outcomes. Their processes, which might best be described as controlled rotting, enabled the forerunners of our modern soft-ripened cheeses to emerge. Precisely when and how this occurred cannot be determined with any degree of certainty; however, medieval literature offers a few clues that suggest that soft-ripened cheeses were already being made in the early Middle Ages.

For example, a detailed compilation of monastic managerial directives from the year 822 known as the *Customs of Corbie* offers a glimpse into medieval monastic and manorial cheese making. According to the *Customs,* the Abbey of Corbie in northwestern France produced cheese "in-house" during the summer from its ten flocks of sheep. The abbey also possessed twenty-seven manors, or villas, that supplied food in the form of tithes (one-tenth of total production) on all agricultural products. The operations of each manor were managed by a monk, or "mayor," appointed by the abbey. Some of the manors raised sheep, others goats, in which case the tithes included either fresh milk to be delivered to the abbey if the manor was close by or cheese if the manor was too far away. Interestingly, tithes of cheese had to be delivered to the abbey on a monthly basis to prevent losses due to spoilage:

> In tithing and caring for goats, too, the same pattern that we have described for lambs is to be followed in every detail. If the milk of the she-goats is brought to the monastery, it should be tithed there; but if not, the agent and the mayor at each villa having goats should assume the responsibility for supervising in every detail the collection of the tithe in the form of cheeses. In this case, whatever tithe

accrues each month should be brought to the gate and should not be allowed to go bad from over-aging.

(Horn and Born, Vol. 3, 1979, p.115)

Clearly, these were not fresh cheeses that had to be consumed within a few days, nor were they dry aged cheeses that could last for many months. They had an intermediate shelf life that is characteristic of many soft-ripened cheeses from this region of northwest Europe. Thus, Corbie's handling of its manorial cheeses suggests that cheese making had started to diversify into soft-ripened varieties by the ninth century.

A ninth-century biography of Charlemagne (Charles the Great), the first emperor of the Holy Roman Empire, provides another glimpse into the emerging world of soft-ripened cheeses. According Charlemagne's biographer Notker, who was a monk from the monastery of Saint Gall in Switzerland, Charlemagne had an intriguing encounter with an unfamiliar cheese during one of his journeys:

> In the same journey too he came to a bishop who lived in a place through which he must needs pass. Now on that day, being the sixth day of the week, he was not willing to eat the flesh of beast or bird; and the bishop, being by reason of the nature of the place unable to procure fish upon the sudden, ordered some excellent cheese, rich and creamy, to be placed before him. And the most self-restrained Charles, with the readiness which he showed everywhere and on all occasions, spared the blushes of the bishop and required no better fare: but taking up his knife cut off the skin, which he thought unsavoury, and fell to on the white of the cheese. Thereupon the bishop, who was standing near like a servant, drew closer and said, "Why do you do that, lord emperor? You are throwing away the very best part." Then Charles, who deceived no one, and did not believe that anyone would deceive him, on the persuasion of the bishop put a piece of the skin in his mouth, and slowly ate it and swallowed it like butter. Then approving of the advice of the bishop, he said: "Very true, my good host," and he added: "Be sure to send me every year to Aix two cart-loads of just such cheeses." The bishop was alarmed at

the impossibility of the task and, fearful of losing both his rank and his office, he rejoined: "My lord, I can procure the cheeses, but I cannot tell which are of this quality and which of another. Much I fear lest I fall under your censure." Then Charles from whose penetration and skill nothing could escape, however new or strange it might be, spoke thus to the bishop, who from childhood had known such cheeses and yet could not test them. "Cut them in two," he said, "then fasten together with a skewer those that you find to be of the right quality and keep them in your cellar for a time and then send them to me."

(Grant 1966; pp. 79, 80)

If Notker's story is true, it would appear that Charlemagne was impressed by a soft surface-ripened variety of cheese, perhaps a bloomy-rind or washed-rind type with a creamy interior. It has been claimed that this text confirms the antiquity of Brie cheese (Rance 1989), but such claims go beyond Notker's text, which neither identifies the region where the event took place nor describes the cheese in enough detail to do more than speculate on its identity.

Dalby (2009) proposed that the cheese in question was a blue cheese, based in part on an alternate translation of the text concerning the portion of the cheese picked out by Charlemagne in which the phrase "picked out the mould" is substituted for "cut off the skin." This alternate translation, however, is at odds with at least three other English-language translations published over the last century, which render the phrase in question as either "cut off the skin" (Ganz 2008; Grant 1966), or "threw away the skin" (Thorpe 1969). Pourrat (1956) went a step farther, concluding that the cheese in question was specifically Roquefort. Such speculation clearly involves a leap of faith beyond what can be gleaned from the text; however, it is not uncommon to find unsupported statements and even outright myths concerning cheese history in popular works on cheese. Though entertaining, such myths sometimes take on very high stakes when they are used in marketing and promotional campaigns, or to justify the awarding of special legal status to specific groups of cheesemakers, as in the Protected Designation of Origin program of the European Union, a topic that we will return to in chapter 9.

Whatever the origins of the soft-ripened peasant cheeses, it is a marvel that they have persisted to the present. The early breakup of the manor demesnes in northern France, starting around the tenth century, seems to have been a pivotal factor. The great manor lords in this region found themselves bound by a web of feudal obligations to their armed vassals or knights, whom they relied on to maintain security and underpin their aristocratic authority. Grants of land were commonly awarded to vassals in return for military service, and as the manor lords' military forces grew ever larger during the turbulent tenth century of the Viking invasions, the breakup of manorial estates into feudal fiefdoms accelerated. This was happening at a time when the market economy of the region was still in its infancy, and the end result was the reallocation of demesne lands into fiefdoms that were then subdivided into the holdings of the manorial peasant tenants who previously had worked them as serfs, or into the holdings of new tenants who were added to the fiefdoms (Bloch 1966; Doehaerd 1978). In short, the demesnes disappeared along with tenant obligations of service and labor. In their place were established small peasant tenant farms that were often larger in size than the serfs' small holdings of the past, along with local peasant villages that grew out of the serf villages of the great manors. This landscape of small peasant farms and local villages and village markets remained remarkably resistant to change in northern France and positioned the region to become the bastion for soft-ripened peasant cheeses. On the other hand, the early breakup of the demesnes in northern France brought cheese making on the demesne side of the manor to an end there. The demesne cheeses either disappeared altogether or their secrets were passed on to peasant cheesemakers, who then made them their own.

England, in contrast, did not experience the large-scale breakup of aristocratic and monastic demesnes until end of the Middle Ages, by which time England had developed a strong market economy that spelled the end of peasant agriculture in favor of market-driven yeoman agriculture. The abrupt demise of peasant agriculture in England meant that English peasant cheeses quickly disappeared, and the memory of such cheese making soon faded. In contrast, the type of cheese making practiced on the manor demesnes continued in England long after the breakup of the manors and produced the forerunners of the English hard-pressed cheeses.

English Demesne Cheeses

Unlike peasant cheese making, which was organized around the family cow or a few goats, demesne cheese making in northwestern France and in England mainly involved large flocks of sheep, which dominated the pastoral economies of the region during the early Middle Ages. Sheep raising for wool production and textile manufacture was intensively developed during the Roman occupation, particularly around the coastal zones, where extensive salt marsh pastures provided ample grazing (Trow-Smith 1957). The high salt content of the grasses in these lush, marshy coastal pastures enabled sheep to resist the pernicious foot infections that commonly accompany the use of waterlogged grazing areas. Thus sheep raising flourished, and northwestern France and Flanders became famous for their textiles during the Roman period, providing a welcome supply of warm clothing and blankets for the legions facing the dreary, cold winters of the northern frontier (Nicholas 1991). England likewise became a major producer of woolen textiles under the Roman occupation (Wild 2002).

After the western Roman Empire fell and the long disruptive period of Germanic invasions had run its course, the new Frankish (French) and Anglo-Saxon (English) overlords quickly revived the pastoral economy based on wool textiles (Nicholas 1991; Wild 2002). By the ninth century large sheep ranges were again supplying wool to textile manufacturing centers in northern France and Flanders (Pounds 1994), and England also was producing wool and exporting wool textiles to France and Scandinavia (Trow-Smith 1957). Amid this burgeoning trade in wool, sheep's-milk cheese making became a natural complement to the business portfolios of the large manor demesnes that were engaged in sheep raising.

Much of what is known about demesne cheese making is specific to England, where the manor demesnes persisted right up until the end of the Middle Ages, in contrast with northern France where the demesnes broke up (and demesne cheese making ceased) much earlier. Throughout the Anglo-Saxon period, demesne cheeses in England were overwhelmingly made from sheep's milk, not cow's milk. Cows were raised primarily as breeding stock to maintain the teams of oxen needed to plow the fields, not as milking stock (Trow-Smith 1957). Sheep on the other hand often served the dual purpose of wool (primary) and milk (secondary) production. What were these early Anglo-Saxon demesne cheeses like? Most likely they were variants on the aged Pecorino Romano type described by Columella. According to the consummate Roman geographer Strabo, the Celtic Britons were less inclined to cheese making at the time of the Roman invasion compared with the Celts on the continent, where cheese making was well established:

> The men of Britain are taller than the Celti, and not so yellow-haired, although their bodies are of looser build . . . Their habits are in part like those of the Celti, but in part more simple and barbaric— so much so that, on account of their inexperience, some of them, although well supplied with milk, make no cheese . . .
>
> (Jones and Sterrett 1917, Vol. 2; p.255)

Under the Romans, wool and cheese production became high priorities in Britain in order to clothe and feed the roughly forty-five thousand Roman soldiers permanently stationed there; thus Roman cheese-making practices became firmly entrenched in the English countryside. The Angles and Saxons who succeeded the Romans inherited the Roman agricultural infrastructure. They likely assimilated the existing sheep's-milk cheese-making expertise from the Romanized Britons who had served as villa slaves and cheesemakers. Thus, although the Romans were not the first to introduce cheese making to England (recall that cheese making in England dates back to the Neolithic), their large-scale development of small (2- to 6-pound, or 0.9 kg to 2.7 kg), cylindrical, uncooked, lightly pressed, surface-salted sheep's-milk cheeses using Roman technology and equipment probably had an extraordinarily large influence on English cheese making for centuries to come.

The newly settled Anglo-Saxon kings rewarded their vassals with grants of land in the form of manors, which created an aristocratic class of manor lords who in turn were obliged to pay an annual tribute of food to the king from their manorial proceeds. Cheeses often were included in the lists of food that were due annually to the king. For example, the Anglo-Saxon law code issued by King Ine of Wessex at the end of the seventh century stipulated that for every ten hides of land (roughly 1,000 acres, or 405 ha) the manor lords were required annually to furnish ten cheeses along with various other food items (Hodges 1982). Annual tributes also were spelled out in the written charters that served as the nobleman's legal deeds for land granted by the king. For example, in the mid-eighth century King Aethelbald of Wessex granted to a nobleman named Eanwulf a manor with sixty hides of land in Gloucestershire, which was later inherited by Eanwulf's grandson Offa, king of Mercia. According to the manorial charter the annual tribute in this case called for forty cheeses rather than the sixty stipulated under Ine's law (Whitelock 1955).

The royal income from demesne cheese-making tributes became quite considerable in some regions by the ninth century. Around the year 858, for example, a large royal demesne in the marshy coastal region of Kent (east of London) rendered forty weys (almost 9,000 pounds, or 4,000 kg) of cheese in annual tribute to King Ethelbert of Kent (Trow-Smith 1957). North of Kent in Essex, Suffolk, and Norfolk (collectively referred to as East Anglia) sheep raising and cheese making were even more intensively developed. East Anglian sheep cheeses were well known by the eleventh century, especially those produced in coastal Essex and along the Blackwater and Thames estuaries (Faith 1994). Similar large-scale demesne cheese making was occurring contemporaneously on the continent side of the English Channel, along the maritime marsh pastures of northern France and Flanders. For example, the royal villa of Annapes, which encompassed more than 7,000 acres (2,800 ha), contained some 43 loads (over 2,800 pounds, or 1,200 kg) of cheese in its storehouses according to a survey that was conducted there at the end of the eighth century (Duby 1968; Pearson 1997).

Clearly, demesne cheese making was well developed on both sides of the English Channel in regions where sheep were raised intensively. On the continent side, however, cheeses of remarkably large size were sometimes produced. For example, the monastery of Fontenella on the lower Seine River received exceptionally large cheeses in payment of food rents from several of its manors in northern France and Flanders. Specifically, Fontenella's manorial holdings in Boulogne and Théouanne, Corialis, and Gregaria were obligated to supply the abbey annually with twenty-one, fifteen, and thirty cheeses, respectively, each cheese weighing 75 pounds (34 kg), according to early-ninth century abbey records (Horn and Born,

1979). Such large cheeses could not have been produced by the old Roman technology, which was geared toward making small cylindrical cheeses.

Monastic records from central Europe from around this same time period suggest that ancient Celtic cheese-making practices persisted in the mountainous regions of central Europe, which may hold a clue to the origin of the massive cheeses of Fontenella's manors. The Abbey of Saint Gall in western Switzerland, for example, received many large wheel-shaped cheeses from the abbey's manorial holdings during the ninth century. According to Bikel (1914) these cheeses were similar in size to the large alpine cheeses of Switzerland of his day (early twentieth century). The ninth-century technology used to produce alpine cheeses almost certainly was based on the cheese-making practices of the Celtic tribes who populated central Europe at the time of the Roman occupation. Such practices may have been carried to the northwest coastal region of France and Flanders by migrating Celtic tribes such as the Menappi who settled there, and who later exported durable, long-lasting Celtic cheeses to Rome during the Roman occupation. Thus, it is conceivable that native Celtic cheese-making practices persisted in northwest France and Flanders and continued to influence demesne cheese making in this region during the early Middle Ages. Unfortunately, the large demesne cheeses of Fontenella's manorial holdings disappeared without a trace, leaving behind no description of how they were made or what they were like.

As time went on the aristocratic nobility (and also the monasteries) often acquired manors that were geographically dispersed. In England it was common for the Anglo-Saxon noblemen to lease out the satellite manors to subordinates known as *firmarii,* or farmers who were given lifetime leases. The *firmarius* in turn was obligated to furnish the nobleman owner with an annual food rent, which often included cheese. Thus demesne cheeses served as a form of "in-kind" currency that was used to pay not only the royal tributes due to the king, but also rents owed to the manorial landlords of the upper aristocracy. Within the manor itself demesne cheeses also were used to feed and compensate the manorial staff and full-time workers (Hagan 2006). Whatever surplus of cheese remained after all the tributes, rents, and salaries had been paid was available to sell on the open market.

One of the few surviving descriptions relating to demesne cheese making from the Anglo-Saxon period is found in the *Rectitudines Singularum Personarum* or Rights and Ranks of Peoples, a document probably written in the half century preceding the Norman conquest in 1066 (Douglas and Greenaway 1953). The *Rectitudines* describes various aspects of Anglo-Saxon manorial organization, including the perquisites or "compensation packages" that were due to key "professional" positions within the manorial workforce, such as the shepherd, cowherd, goatherd, and cheesemaker. The cheesemaker's perquisites included one hundred cheeses over the course of a cheese-making season (Douglas and Greenaway 1953).

It is noteworthy that the cheesemaker in the *Rectitudines* was referred to as a woman. Women served as the professional cheesemakers on the demesne side of the Anglo-Saxon manor just as they did on the peasant side; the positions of dairywoman and dairymaid were already entrenched within the demesne economy of the early Middle Ages. The dairywomen became the developers and repositories of the "secret knowledge" of demesne cheese making that was handed down for many centuries. When the demesnes broke up at the end of the Middle Ages that knowledge passed to the dairywomen and dairymaids of the yeomanry, who brought forth the great family of English pressed cheeses.

The milking season for sheep in the Middle Ages lasted from around late April to late August, about one hundred days (Trow-Smith 1957). Therefore, according to the *Rectitudines,* the woman cheesemaker was basically entitled to one cheese per day for the entire season. The size of these cheeses is not known, but clearly they were not the 75-pound (34 kg) cheeses made on some of the manors across the English Channel. If the old Roman technology for uncooked, lightly pressed, surface-salted cylindrical cheeses of around 2 to 6 pounds (0.9 to 2.7 kg) was still being used, as seems likely, then the cheesemaker would have received one of approximately four to eight cylindrical cheeses produced each day from a flock of one hundred sheep. This estimate of cheese yield is based on the approximate daily milk yield of sheep during the Middle Ages, taking into account the high solids content of sheep's milk. Accordingly, the combined daily milk (that is, two milkings) from around twelve to twenty-five sheep was probably needed to produce a typical cheese.

The cheesemaker also was required to make butter for the manor lord, but it is important to realize that butter was produced from the whey that resulted from cheese making, not from cream collected from the milk (Douglas and Greenaway 1953). Unlike cow's milk, sheep's milk does not readily separate into a cream layer because it lacks a protein found in cow's milk known as cryoglobulin that causes the fat globules to cluster together and rise rapidly to the surface. Therefore, butter was not produced directly from sheep's milk due to its lack of creaming. During cheese making, however, about 10 percent of the fat in sheep's milk is lost to the whey. Much of this whey fat can be skimmed from the surface and recovered as "whey cream," which can be churned into butter and buttermilk. The butter so produced was reserved for the manor lord, while the buttermilk was divided between the shepherd and cheesemaker. The whey that remained after removal of the whey cream was divided between the shepherd and the women slaves (servants) of the manor; nothing was wasted. The amount of butter produced from whey was relatively small, about 2 pounds (0.9 kg) of butter for every 100 pounds (45 kg) of cheese (Trow-Smith 1957). Therefore, butter was something of a luxury in Anglo-Saxon times, and it wasn't until the later Middle Ages, when dairying shifted from sheep's milk to cow's milk (with its capacity to quickly separate into cream), that butter became more widely available.

The Norman Conquest of 1066 brought an end to Anglo-Saxon rule in England and signaled the beginning of a new era in market-oriented demesne cheese making. English trade with the continent increased dramatically under the new Norman rulers, and shipments of cheese soon began to cross the English Channel to Normandy. Monastic houses in Normandy such as the Abbey of Troarn pioneered the cheese export trade when they acquired gifts of English manorial lands from the new Norman aristocracy, along with the right to import agricultural products, including cheese, from their new English manorial holdings. English cheeses soon became highly esteemed on the continent (Farmer 1991; Gulley 1963).

North of Normandy, imports of English cheese also developed in conjunction with the rapidly growing trade in English wool with Flanders. Flanders's strategic location, with coastal ports on the North Sea and direct access to the Rhine River, gave Flemish maritime merchants a competitive advantage for exporting textiles to central Europe, England, Scandinavia, and coastal France. By the eleventh century Flanders emerged as the preeminent textile-manufacturing center north of the Alps and Pyrenees. The growing prosperity of the Flemish textile industry in turn encouraged rapid urban development and population growth, which soon exceeded the food-producing capacity of the region. The Flemish aristocracy responded by commencing large-scale land reclamation projects to drain and transform the marshy coastal lands, which previously had been suitable only for seasonal sheep grazing, into arable land (Nicholas 1991). The reclamation of new agricultural lands could not keep pace with the needs of the growing population, however, and food imports became increasingly necessary. Flanders looked to England for grain and cheese imports; the conversion of Flemish sheep ranges into arable land also made Flanders more dependent than ever on England for wool imports.

As time went on Flemish food imports increased sharply and the aristocratic nobility and growing merchant class responded by increasing textile production and cloth exports to finance their growing supply lines of imported foods, which in turn rendered Flemish weavers even more dependent on wool supplied by the English demesnes (Miller and Hatcher 1978). Wool prices inevitably rose in response to increased demand, and sheep raising in England became ever more profitable. Not surprisingly, demesnes in many regions throughout England, especially Essex and other regions in East Anglia, responded by raising more sheep and producing more wool during the twelfth and thirteenth centuries. Sheep's-milk cheese making also increased dramatically as major buyers of wool for export to Flanders began to purchase consignments of cheese along with wool to sell in Flemish cities (Farmer 1991; Trow-Smith 1957).

During the twelfth and thirteenth centuries the trend toward intensive commercial or market-driven agriculture accelerated in England. Whereas in northern France the great demesnes were breaking up into the small independent peasant farms and villages that would grace the countryside for centuries to come, in England the demesnes were rationalizing their operations to maximize profit. Dramatic growth in trade with the continent brought new inflationary pressures to England along with a steady flow of new luxury and prestige goods that were in high demand among the aristocracy. The old Anglo-Saxon system of farming out satellite manors based on lifetime leases and fixed food rents became untenable, unable to respond quickly enough to this new market economy. Therefore, by the thirteenth century manor lords began replacing fixed lifetime leases with direct management by professional managers (reeves and bailiffs), whom they hired to provide them with detailed accounting of their manor operations (Miller and Hatcher 1978).

The new emphasis on manorial efficiency and profitability is perhaps best reflected in three agricultural treatises on estate management that were written in England toward the end of the thirteenth century: *Seneschaucy, Walter of Henley,* and *Husbandry. Seneschaucy* goes into great detail about manorial administration and accounting, with emphasis on the responsibilities of the various officers who supervised and carried out the professional duties of the demesne. Concerning the Office of the Dairymaid, *Seneschaucy* instructs the following:

> The dairymaid ought to be loyal, of good repute, and clean; she ought to know her work and what relates to it. She ought not to allow under-dairymaids or anyone else to take or carry away milk, butter, or cream whereby the cheese will be less and the dairy will lose.
>
> She ought to know well how to make and salt cheese and how to preserve and look after the vessels of the dairy so that it is not necessary to buy new ones every year. She ought to know the day on which to begin making cheese and of what weight, when to begin making two cheeses and the days when number and weight ought to be changed.
>
> Bailiff and reeve ought to inspect frequently the dairy and the cheese, when they increase and decrease in number, what their weight is, and that no loss or theft occurs in the dairy whereby the weight might suffer. They ought to know, find out, and watch how many cows give a stone of cheese and butter and how many ewes yield a stone of the same, so that they can confidently answer in their *account*.

(Oschinsky (1971) *Walter Of Henley And Other*
Treatises On Estate Management And Accounting.
pp. 287, 289. By permission of Oxford University Press)

The head dairymaid evidently supervised a staff of under-dairymaids who milked the animals and assisted with cheese making. She was held accountable for maximizing the yield of cheese and butter and preventing product theft. She answered to the bailiff and reeve, who conducted frequent inspections and audits to determine whether appropriate targets for butter and cheese production were being met. Clearly, demesne cheese making was conducted as a business with an eye to profit. It is also important to note that both cow's and sheep's milk were being made into cheese. During the thirteenth century the production of cheese began to be uncoupled from the production of wool, with cows increasingly being raised exclusively for milk production and sheep raised exclusively for wool (Farmer 1991). This was the beginning of a progressive shift from sheep to cow's-milk cheese making on large demesnes, which resulted in the disappearance of most sheep's-milk cheeses in England by the end of the fifteenth century.

Finally, it is important to note that control over the size of cheeses was becoming an important management issue. A single large cheese was produced at the beginning of the season, but eventually was replaced by two or more cheeses during peak milk production, when a single cheese would have been too large. Monastic manorial records from the thirteenth and fourteenth centuries confirm that fewer (often only a single cheese) but larger cheeses were now being produced, on average perhaps 9 or 10 pounds (4 to 4.5 kg), but sometimes as large as 18 pounds (8 kg) (Finberg 1951; Page 1936). Controlling cheese size was becoming a preoccupation because larger cheeses presented new quality challenges associated with excessive moisture retention. Specifically, if the old Roman technology for small (2- to 6-pound, or 0.9 to 2.7 kg), cylindrical, uncooked, lightly pressed, surface-salted cheeses was scaled up to produce larger (perhaps 10- to 15-pound, or 4.5 to 6.8 kg) cylindrical cheeses, the resulting cheese would have too little surface area relative to its volume to provide for adequate evaporative moisture loss during aging (recall the discussion around Luna cheese in chapter 5). Too much moisture retention in turn would increase the risk of rotting from the inside. At some point therefore, probably around this time, demesne cheesemakers must have replaced cylindrical-shaped press molds with thinner wheel-shaped molds to increase the surface area and rate of evaporation. Wheel-shaped cheeses that were about 1.5 to 2 inches (4 to 5 cm) in depth and 15 inches (38 cm) in diameter but otherwise still made by the old Roman uncooked, light-pressed, surface-salted technology, were the norm during the early seventeenth century when the first detailed descriptions of cheese-making practices were written down and became available in the historical record (Foster 1998). However, the switch to thin wheel-shaped cheeses likely commenced centuries earlier when the larger cheeses began to be made on the demesnes.

Walter of Henley, written after *Seneschaucy,* was designed as a commentary on certain chapters of the latter. With respect to the dairy operation, *Walter* instructed the bailiff to make frequent inspections so that precise targets for cheese and butter yields could be formulated based on seasonal changes in pasture quality. Good-quality pasture was expected to render a yield increase of 50 percent relative to medium-quality pasture (Oschinsky 1971). *Walter* thus went a step farther than *Seneschaucy* in seeking to model the ever-changing cheese- and butter-yielding capacity of the milk supply (due to changes in pasture quality), so that the actual yields achieved by the dairymaids could be kept in line with the theoretical maximum.

Husbandry, the third agricultural treatise on estate management, also focuses heavily on yields in the dairy operation, but adds a new element to maximize profits when making cheese from cow's milk by optimizing the ratio of butter to cheese. According to *Husbandry* the dairymaid should produce one stone of butter (about 14 pounds, or 6.4 kg) for every seven stones (about 98 pounds, or 44 kg) of cheese. Furthermore, over the course of the cheese-making season, which lasted from the first day of May until Michaelmas (September 29), each cow ought to produce five and one-half stone of cheese, along with butter at the ratio of 1:7 (Oschinsky 1971).

The target butter-to-cheese ratio of 1:7 is much too high to be achieved by producing butter from whey; evidently the practice of skimming some of the cream from cow's milk to churn into butter had become commonplace by this time. The key to maximizing profits was to produce as much butter as possible (because butter commanded a higher price than cheese in the marketplace) without detrimentally affecting the quality of the cheese due to excessive reduction in the fat content of the remaining partly skimmed milk used to make the cheese. *Husbandry* set this ratio at 1:7, which left enough cream in the cheese milk to avoid severe quality problems associated with low-fat cheese. This would not always be the case; the ratio of butter to cheese would eventually shift heavily in favor of butter in some regions with grave consequences to cheese quality, as will soon become evident.

Records from monastic houses with large manorial holdings confirm that the approaches described in *Seneschaucy, Walter of Henley,* and *Husbandry* to systematize and rationalize manor operations were in fact being implemented during the thirteenth and fourteenth centuries. High butter-to-cheese ratios were becoming commonplace on some manor demesnes (Page 1936). Production targets based on complex assessments of the productive capacity of manor lands were also in use on some manors. At Saint Swithun's Priory in Winchester, for example, the total weight of cheese and butter produced over the season was expected to match a target average weight from each cow and ewe milked. A team of auditors, or lactage police, continually monitored the actual production of cheese and butter as compared with the targets; reeves who failed to meet their targets were liable to pay in cash the amount of the deficit (Drew 1947). The economics of cheese and butter production were becoming powerful driving forces for change and innovation in English cheese making.

The tide turned against the enormously profitable wool industry during the fourteenth century, which hastened the demise of sheep's-milk cheese making and its displacement by cow's-milk cheese. A series of disease outbreaks starting around 1270 devastated English flocks. The Hundred Years' War with France, which lasted from 1337 to 1453, also took a toll on the sheep industry by frequently interrupting wool exports to the continent and driving up costs. Also, the cash-strapped English government increased taxes on wool exports to finance the war effort, further driving up costs and reducing the profit margins of wool producers. Around the same time (circa 1386), the English military began to procure consignments of cheese from East Anglia to provision the English garrison at Calais in northern France (Trow-Smith 1957). East Anglia already had a long history of cheese exports to Flanders by this time and had shifted away from sheep's milk to cow's milk for cheese making. East Anglia was, therefore, preeminently positioned to take on the role of chief supplier of cheese to the military, a role that would increase dramatically over the next two centuries.

Finally, an entire decade of extremely wet weather during the 1430s and

1440s brought another wave of sheep disease that affected every county in England (Mate 1987). This further crippled the wool industry and essentially ended sheep's-milk cheese making. Regions that had already shifted to cow's-milk cheese making, which included not only East Anglia but also the western regions around Somerset, Gloucestershire, Wiltshire, and Cheshire, began to specialize in cow's-milk cheese for the market, outcompeting the dwindling number of demesnes that continued to produce sheep's-milk cheese.

Layered on top of these developments were dramatic social and demographic changes that accompanied the bubonic plague outbreak of 1348 through 1350, during which between 30 and 45 percent of the general population of England perished. The scarcity of labor that resulted dealt a fatal blow to the labor-intensive manor demesnes and catalyzed a progressive shift away from demesne agriculture in favor of capitalistic yeomanry. In the process, mass migrations of peasants who became dislocated from the rural countryside as the manors broke up streamed into London and other population centers in search of work, creating large urban centers for the first time in England and new markets for cheese. The London market would profoundly influence the next chapter in English cheese history, that of the yeoman cheeses.

Mountain Cheeses

Cheese making was already well developed in the mountains of central Europe before the Roman occupation. Recall that Strabo (first century AD) wrote of widespread cheese production all along the northern slopes of the Alps. He described these mountain cheeses as being brought down to settlements in the valleys and plains where the Celtic populations were concentrated. The cheeses must have been rugged and long-lived, and those that were exported to Rome were evidently quite exceptional in quality. Medieval monastic and manorial records from central Europe suggest that these early forms of mountain cheese making continued to be practiced and refined after the fall of the Roman Empire.

The Benedictine monasteries of Saint Gall in eastern Switzerland and Saint

Martin at Muri in central Switzerland provide instructive glimpses into the world of alpine cheese making during the early Middle Ages. St. Gall was founded around 612 by Gallus, an Irish monk who accompanied Columbanus on his missionary journeys throughout Europe. Gallus established a small hermitage in an undeveloped mountainous region about 8 miles (13 km) from the shores of Lake Constance, where he and around a dozen disciples followed the severe ascetic practices of Saint Columbanus's Rule. After Gallus's death the hermitage was nearly abandoned until around 700, when grants of land and serfs from local aristocratic lords were given to support and expand the hermitage. The first Abbot of St. Gall was appointed in 720, and the hermitage became a Benedictine monastery in 747 when the Rule of Saint Benedict was substituted for that of Saint Columbanus (Clark 1926).

During the eighth century the monks of Saint Gall, with the help of their serfs, cleared forest to make way for arable fields. They raised crops and tended flocks of sheep and herds of goats and cows (Clark 1926). The monks practiced pastoral transhumance, moving their herds and flocks to highland pastures in the adjacent Appenzell region during the summer; there, they evidently made cheese, but little is known about the methods they employed or the type of cheese they produced (Bikel 1914). It is sometimes claimed that the monks of Saint Gall taught the surrounding farmers how to make alpine cheeses, but it is far more plausible that the reverse occurred. The complex social arrangements, cultural attitudes, and sophisticated cheese-making practices and equipment that underpinned communal transhumance and alpine cheese making likely took centuries to evolve, stretching back to pre-Roman times.

Although Saint Gall was founded on the fringes of rugged wilderness, the town of Arbon on the shores of Lake Constance was only 8 miles (13 km) away. Arbon was an ancient Celtic Helvetic settlement that the Romans had transformed into a wealthy regional center, situated on a major Roman trade route. Celtic agriculture had been well established in this region for many centuries, and pastoral transhumance and mountain cheese making had almost certainly been practiced in the region since before the Roman occupation. Thus, the monks at Saint Gall probably acquired their cheese-making knowledge from the wealth of experience residing in the peasant tenant farmers, or serfs, who populated the monastic manors under their control.

The ninth century became a turning point for Saint Gall when the monastery received extensive new endowments of manorial lands and serfs in the surrounding area. Soon cheeses and other agricultural tithes from the newly acquired manors began to flow into the monastery in abundance. By the end of ninth century the monks no longer needed to be directly involved in the day-to-day work of agriculture; they became administrators of their manorial holdings and devoted themselves primarily to sacred, cultural, and intellectual pursuits. Indeed, Saint Gall became a renowned center of learning and culture starting around this time (Clark 1926).

The cheeses that Saint Gall received from its manorial holdings came in two sizes: *casei alpini,* Alp cheese, which Bikel (1914) described as large round cheeses having about the same diameter as the alpine cheeses made in this region in modern times; and much smaller hand cheese. As time went on Saint Gall acquired new landholdings and the income from manorial cheese tithes became quite considerable. During the tenth century the monastery acquired extensive gifts of land in the adjacent region of Appenzell, which had been wilderness and was only just beginning to be settled. Alpine cheese making quickly flourished in Appenzell under the watchful eye of Saint Gall and the region became a major supplier of the monastery, totaling more than two thousand cheeses in tithes annually by the eleventh century (Bikel 1914). Cheese making became a permanent feature of the Appenzell landscape, and wheel-shaped Appenzeller cheeses weighing about 15 pounds (6.8 kg) are still made in the region today.

Around the same time, the Abbey of St. Martin at Muri near Lake Lucerne began a targeted effort to bring transhumant pastoralism and alpine cheese making to the undeveloped frontier lands surrounding the monastery. The abbey was founded during the eleventh century by the aristocratic Hapsburgs and was generously endowed with landholdings, but the land was wilderness that needed to be cleared and settled if it was to support the abbey. The monks of Muri recruited new settlers by offering a "start-up" package of incentives that included "a plough, a wagon, four oxen, a sow, a cock and two hens, a scythe, an axe, and seeds of various sorts" (Simond 1822). In return, the tenants were required to render tithes from their farm production, plow 5 acres (2 ha) twice a year for the abbey, and perform other work services.

Presumably, settlers came from other areas of Switzerland that were experiencing population growth and shortages of cultivatable land, and they came eager to replicate their alpine way of life in the new frontier of Muri. The strategy apparently worked well, and soon villages of new settlers sprung up in the monastic wilderness. The villages organized themselves around cow and sheep transhumant pastoralism, and alpine cheese making and wool production (Coolidge 1889; Simond 1822). Transhumant dairying and cheese making were carried out by groups of twelve households who combined their family cows to form a single herd. The herd was led up to the mountain pastures during the summer under the care of a master cowman. The villagers constructed chalets in the mountains that were used for cheese making, and the chalets were inspected yearly by a monastic officer. The head cowman was obliged to deliver a fixed weight of cheese to the community tenants at the end of the season. As for the tenant farmers, their annual tithe of cheeses was due at the abbey on the Feast of Saint Andrew, November 30.

Transhumant dairying and alpine cheese making also flourished farther to the west of Switzerland near the French border, where two of the most well-known mountain cheeses originated: Gruyère and Emmental. Helvetic Celts settled in the lowlands of this area long before the Roman occupation and, as in other regions of Switzerland, they established agricultural communities that engaged in transhumant pastoralism and mountain cheese making to take advantage of grazing in the surrounding highlands. After the fall of the Roman Empire, Germanic immigrants moved into the area and settled among the Romanized Celtic inhabitants. By the ninth century the influx of new settlers created population pressures in the lowlands that also generated increased competition for summer grazing in the highlands, as well as increased cheese making (Birmingham 2000).

The growing trade in mountain cheeses caught the attention of the counts of Gruyère, who had been granted feudal authority over the highlands of the region in the eleventh century by the Holy Roman Emperor. The counts moved quickly to capitalize on the growing cheese trade by taking control of the highland grazing lands and the traditional summer migration routes to the highlands. Continued population growth and new settlement in the lowlands during the twelfth and thirteenth centuries created further pressure on highland grazing that led to the opening up of new, more remote grazing areas, and with it increased production of cheese. By the fourteenth century Gruyère's reputation for outstanding cheeses had traveled far and wide, and alpine cheese making there was becoming strongly market-oriented. Gruyère cheeses would continue to undergo refinements in the centuries to come, becoming much larger to facilitate their overland transport to markets. Eventually, they were specifically sized so that they could be packed in barrels and transported by boat from Lake Geneva to the Rhône River and on to the Mediterranean and even more distant markets (Birmingham 2000). According to Twamley (1816), Gruyère cheeses were packed ten to a barrel, each cheese weighing from 40 to 60 pounds (18 to 27 kg).

So lucrative did Gruyère's trade in cheese become that it attracted the attention of the canton of Bern, Gruyère's powerful neighbor to the north. Bern progressively wrested control of the Gruyère highlands from the counts of Gruyère during the fifteenth century in a bid to dominate the trade in highland cheese. Bern also recruited highland cheesemakers from Gruyère to settle in the Emme River Valley, or Emmental, region, which Bern controlled, in order to improve the cheeses there and increase the profitability of the dairy farms. The transplanted highland cheesemakers from Gruyère were instrumental in developing the large, firm cheeses that became the signature of the Emmental region (Birmingham 2000).

Aristocratic lords in Germany and Austria also came to appreciate the market potential of alpine cheeses and encouraged their development in the Bavarian and Tyrolean Alps, respectively, starting in the thirteenth century (Duby 1968). Similarly, in the French Alps alpine cheeses such as Beaufort flourished, as did Comte cheese making along the western slopes of the Jura Mountains, across the divide from Gruyère.

Thus, by the end of the Middle Ages an entire family of alpine cheeses that were moderate- to large-sized, wheel-shaped, firm-bodied, rugged, and long-lived were being produced throughout the Alps. The common thread that united the alpine cheese family was the ancient practice of pastoral transhumance, which gave rise to a unique set of cheese-making conditions and constraints. Small peasant farmers who lived in the lowland valleys or plains and who each raised perhaps two or three cows combined their stock with those of other farms in the village to create a larger herd. This enabled a communal herd to be led up to highland grazing areas during the summer by a small number of cowmen chosen by the community. The rest of the village remained in the lowlands to till the fields, harvest and store up hay and other winter fodder for the animals, and tend to the many chores of the small peasant farm. The cowmen were responsible for herding and milking the cows and making the cheese.

Cheese was produced in the highlands in simple open sheds or, later, more substantial cheese-making huts or chalets. Because of the large volume of milk produced by the communal herd and limited storage capacity, cheese sometimes had to be made twice a day, immediately after milking. In other cases the evening milk was allowed to cool overnight in the brisk mountain air until the next morning, when some of the cream was skimmed off and the rest of the milk combined with the new morning milk for making cheese. Either way, mountain milk typically contained relatively low populations of lactic acid bacteria, which in turn resulted in characteristically slow acidification during cheese making. The large volume of milk produced each day meant that the cheeses needed to be relatively large to facilitate their transport down the mountain. They also had to be durable and long-lived. Furthermore, the remoteness of the mountain sites meant that there was strong incentive to use salt sparingly because salt had to be packed up from the lowlands. It was expensive and logistically challenging to maintain adequate inventories of salt for use in cheese making and as a feed supplement for the cows (Birmingham 2000).

The above conditions posed a dilemma for the alpine cheesemaker. Slow acidification, large cheese size, and sparing use of salt made it exceptionally difficult to produce cheeses that were low enough in moisture to be durable and long lasting. Specifically, slow acidification reduced curd shrinkage and whey expulsion during cheese making; large cheese size reduced evaporative moisture loss from the surface during storage; and sparing use of salt reduced whey expulsion during salting. Consequently, alpine cheesemakers had to go to great lengths to produce cheeses of sufficient dryness, which inspired a number of technical innovations.

For example, elaborate cutting techniques and devices (knives or harps) were developed to produce very small curd particles with maximum surface area to promote whey expulsion. Also, elevated cooking temperatures, sometimes as high as 120° to 130° F (49 to 54°C), were applied to further encourage curd shrinkage and whey expulsion, using copper kettles that were suspended directly over a fire pit. The cooked curds were transferred to wheel-shaped (as opposed to cylindrical) forms to increase the surface-area-to-volume ratio of the final cheese and thus promote evaporative moisture loss during storage; and presses were devised to squeeze out whey and produce a very tight surface that facilitated the development of a resilient protective rind.

Although many variations on a theme developed around the technology just described, this basic technology was adopted by mountain cheesemakers of the Alps in Austria, Switzerland, Italy, and France, and beyond to the Pyrenees, where alpine sheep's-milk cheeses flourished. The result was a family of durable-rind cheeses with firm elastic bodies, sometimes with holes or eyes, and with flavor profiles often described as "nutty." The characteristic low acidity, high mineral content, and low moisture content of these cheeses gave rise to a firm, elastic structure that was capable of expanding under the pressure of accumulating carbon dioxide gas to form holes or "eyes." Their low acidity and salt content favored the growth of salt- and acid-sensitive bacteria called propionibacteria, which are naturally present in milk and cheese. Propionibacteria produce carbon dioxide as a fermentation by-product, and depending on the storage temperature they may produce enough gas to form many eyes, a few eyes, or no eyes at all. They also produce propionic acid, a powerful flavor compound that contributes to the nutty background flavor of alpine cheeses. The low acidity of alpine cheeses also predisposes them to surface growth of coryneform bacteria, which may be prolific or suppressed depending on the temperature and humidity conditions that prevail during storage and the physical manipulations (such as scraping or washing the surface) performed by the cheesemaker. Thus, the surface rind of alpine cheeses might remain very free of coryneform growth (as in Emmental cheese) or colonized extensively (as in Gruyère cheese).

Other mountain cheeses, quite different from those of the Alps or Pyrenees, blossomed in the Massif Central of south-central France during the Middle Ages. In the northern region of Auvergne, the seasonal movement of cows from the valleys to the highland pastures of the Cantal Mountains probably had been practiced since at least Roman times (Goldsmith 1973; Whittaker and Goody 2001). As noted in chapter 5, it is possible that early versions of Cantal cheese may have been exported to Rome. During the Middle Ages, peasants produced the large cylindrical Cantal cheeses in cheese-making huts or *burons* in the highlands, on manorial lands controlled by the aristocratic lords and the monasteries (Goldsmith 1973). The peasants of Cantal used a different strategy from that of their counterparts in the Alps to produce cheeses that were dry enough to be durable and long lasting. They did not heat the curds and whey during cheese making, yet the final cheese was rendered low enough in moisture by pressing the uncooked curd several times, and by breaking the curd up into particles and salting them generously before pressing for the last time. This "milled-curd" approach to salting, which was later adopted by Cheshire and eventually Cheddar cheesemakers in England, enabled whey to be pressed out more efficiently and the salt to be distributed uniformly throughout the cheese, which in turn helped to produce a longer-lasting and more durable cheese. By the end of the Middle Ages, Auvergne was exporting Cantal cheeses to distant markets, and the production of Cantal became increasingly commercialized (Goldsmith 1973).

Cantal required more salt than typical alpine cheeses, and cheesemakers in Auvergne were able to develop this technology because they had access to abundant supplies of salt. Salt had been transported from salt works along the Mediterranean coast to the Massif Central on Roman-built roads since the first century AD (Whittaker and Goody 2001). This vital pipeline of salt was instrumental in the development of not only Cantal cheese, but also Roquefort and other heavily salted blue-molded cheeses that arose in the southern Massif Central as a result of the many natural caves in that region. The area around the village of Roquefort is honeycombed with natural caves formed from horizontal and vertical geological faults in the surrounding mountain cliffs. The caves act as a near-constant temperature (43° to 50°F, or 6 to 10°C) and humidity (95 to 98 percent relative humidity) environment, and are endowed with natural ventilation by vertical fissures or *fleurines* that provide air exchange with the outside (Rance 1989). It turns out that the environmental conditions present in the caves are ideal for the growth of various molds, including the blue mold *Penicillium roqueforti.*

Evidence of cheese making in this region dates back to at least Roman times (Dausse 1993), but it is not known precisely when the Caves of Cambalou in Roquefort or other caves in the region began to be used for storing and ripening cheeses. A simple cheese-making technology that involved slow rennet coagulation of sheep's milk, no cooking, and heavy salting of the cheese surface with sea salt evolved in this region. The resulting cheeses, high in acidity and salt content, provided a chemical environment that was favorable to growth of *Penicillium roqueforti,* and when such cheeses were stored in the cool, humid environment of the caves, *P. roqueforti* growth was further enhanced. Cheesemakers came to appreciate the desirable effects of robust blue-mold growth on cheese flavor and texture, and they refined their cheese-making and aging practices to encourage blueing.

The first definite record of Roquefort cheeses dates from 1070, when an aristocratic lord donated a "cave" and a manor to the Benedictine Abbey of Conques. Cheese making was already well established in the area, and the monks worked with their tenant farmers to improve the cheese-making techniques. A number of other monastic houses in the area came to own "caves" in Roquefort, and the production of cheese expanded considerably under the management of the monks. The sheep that supplied the milk were grazed, and the cheeses were made, in the high pastures of the Larzac Plateau to the northeast of Roquefort. Salt was transported regularly up to the high pastures by muleteers, who then brought back salted cheeses to the Caves of Cambalou to be matured (Whittaker and Goody 2001).

The growing reputation and market success of the cheeses from Roquefort evidently attracted the attention of two religious orders that were founded in the eleventh century. The newly formed Templars and Cistercians expanded into the Massif Central and promptly gained control of grazing lands on the Larzac Plateau, where they exercised a near monopoly on the sheep's milk and the cheeses that were destined for aging in the Caves of Cambalou. The Templars also became part owners of a major salt works on the Mediterranean coast and had control over the vital salt route that led to Roquefort; thus, the Templars, along with the Benedictines and Cistercians, held enormous sway over the Roquefort cheese-making enterprise for a time. Indeed, the monastic influence on Roquefort cheese making probably helped to elevate Roquefort to a new level of notoriety and importance, such that the town of Roquefort was granted the first *appellation d'origine* (designation of origin) in 1411, which gave the town the sole right to market cheese with the name Roquefort (Whittaker and Goody 2001). The cheese became renowned in France and eventually achieved worldwide fame, which it retains to this day.

Before leaving the mountain cheeses of the Middle Ages, there is one family of cheeses that deserves consideration even though they originated in the lowlands. The hard Italian grana cheeses, among which Parmigiano-Reggiano (Parmesan) and Grana Padano are the most famous, originated in the upper Po River Valley of northern Italy during the Middle Ages. Though they were (and still are) cheeses of the valley their roots seem to lie with the alpine cheese-making tradition. The first recorded references to Parmesan or grana cheeses date from the fourteenth century, but their beginnings were somewhat earlier and coincided with a burst of monastic activity that resulted in large-scale land reclamation and development in the Po River Valley.

The Po Valley had been a swampy, poorly drained lowland until the tenth and eleventh centuries, when local Benedictine monasteries began to construct drainage ditches to convert wetlands into arable fields. Cistercian monastic houses joined the Benedictines in the Po Valley during the twelfth century, and the Cistercians elevated the management of land and water resources to a new level by constructing permanent irrigation works that serviced "water meadows" or irrigated fields (Jones 1966). Field irrigation dramatically increased the Po Valley's capacity for grazing and for hay and fodder production, which opened the door for the raising of dairy cattle during the twelfth and thirteenth centuries. Cattle raising and dairying steadily replaced traditional sheep raising in the Po Valley, and cow's-milk cheese making soon flourished. Written records and literature from the fourteenth century onward refer to grated Parmesan cheese, a cheese that was already in wide demand abroad by the fourteenth century. A large cylindrical aged cheese is depicted in a fourteenth-century illustration, suggesting that the medieval Parmesan was not unlike the Parmigiano-Reggiano or Grana Padano of today (Alberini 1998).

Precisely where and how the large grana cheeses originated is not known, but most likely they were of monastic origin. As noted, the Benedictine and Cistercian monasteries were instrumental in the reclamation and development of swampy Po lowlands that made large-scale dairying possible, and only the monasteries would have possessed sufficient resources to raise herds of dairy cattle large enough to support the making of large grana cheeses. Furthermore, the technology and equipment needed to make these cheeses was quite sophisticated, and very similar to that of the alpine cheeses. Specifically, grana cheeses require extensive cutting of the coagulum into very small particles and extensive cooking of the curds and whey to very high temperatures. It is unlikely that this technology developed independently in the Po Valley; it is far more likely that the monks there borrowed key cheese-making practices from contemporaneous alpine cheesemakers. By the twelfth and thirteenth centuries monasteries north of the Alps such as Saint Gall and Muri were managing large manorial holdings that specialized in alpine cheese making. Travel and communication took place regularly among monastic houses; thus there were probably ample opportunities for the transfer of alpine cheese-making technology from north of the Alps (or perhaps from Italy's alpine highlands) to the monastic houses of the Po Valley.

Even if the cheesemakers of the Po Valley borrowed elements of alpine technology, they nevertheless did create a new and different cheese. This was made possible by the abundance of salt in the valley. Venice, at the mouth of the Po, was a major center for salt production and distribution, and held a virtual monopoly on the salt trade to the Po Valley (Adshead 1992). Abundant salt supplies allowed grana cheeses to be salted more heavily than their alpine cousins, resulting in a higher-salt and lower-moisture cheese that did not require as much surface evaporation during storage to attain the necessary level of dryness for long life and durability. This in turn fostered the production of very large cheeses that were more cylindrical in dimensions as opposed to the thin, wheel-shaped alpine cheeses. Cylindrical cheese had the great advantage of occupying less shelf space during their long period of aging.

The higher salt content of grana cheeses suppressed the salt-sensitive propionibacteria and shifted the biochemical ripening pattern during storage, creating flavor profiles quite different from the alpine cheeses. The grana cheeses were destined for commercial success. Extremely large in size, almost indestructible, and wonderfully flavorful, Parmesan cheese had only to make a simple journey by river barge to Venice, one of the great medieval centers of maritime trade, and from there could be shipped anywhere in the Mediterranean region and beyond. It didn't take long for Parmesan to find its way into foreign markets, even as far away as England, where it was highly prized.

Many other noteworthy cheeses came of age during the Middle Ages. The great diversity of environmental, cultural, and economic conditions that existed across medieval Europe gave rise to many permutations of the cheese-making approaches already described. The result was myriad locally produced cheeses of great diversity. By the end of the Middle Ages, however, economic forces and social changes in northern Europe were giving rise to new forms of specialized commercial agriculture, which would profoundly affect cheese making and eventually undermine the very existence of diverse traditional cheeses.

CHAPTER SEVEN

England, Holland, and the Rise of Market-Driven Cheese Making

Whatever you do, work at it with all your heart, as working for the Lord, not for men, since you know that you will receive an inheritance from the Lord as a reward. It is the Lord Christ you are serving.

Colossians 3:23–24

The Benedictine work ethic, summed up in the motto "To labor is to pray," helped transform the monastery into the premier economic engine of Europe during the early Middle Ages. In the later Middle Ages the Cistercians extended the reach of that ethic beyond the monks themselves to men from all walks of life through its lay brotherhood. In the process the Cistercians created an even more powerful engine for economic development. Under both Benedictine and Cistercian influence the direction of cheese making inexorably became more commercially oriented as monastic landholdings accumulated and surplus agricultural production (including surplus cheese) grew. The monasteries in turn served as economic models for the landowning aristocratic lords, who increasingly adopted monastic strategies and administered their demesnes and their demesne cheese-making activities as commercial enterprises.

The monastic work ethic, which merged the daily labors of earthly life with spiritual service to God, found a new and more potent form of expression in the teachings of the Protestant reformer John Calvin, who elevated the New Testament exhortation to work as though you were working for the Lord to a universal doctrine. Calvin unleashed a powerful motivation for achievement in the workplace, accessible to all regardless of station in life, from the humblest to the greatest. Calvin's brand of Protestant Reformationist theology, which attracted strong followings in England and Holland, came at the end of the Middle Ages when much of Europe was already experiencing rapid growth in trade and commercial activity. The Calvinist reform movement accelerated the pace of economic development and brought unprecedented changes to the cultures and economies of England and Holland (Granto et al. 1996). In the process, agriculture in those countries became much more specialized and market-oriented, and cheesemakers came under the influence of powerful market forces that encouraged, or in some cases coerced, them to refine their age-old technologies in new ways.

English Cheese Making: From Manorial Demesne to Yeoman Farm

The bubonic plague of the mid-fourteenth century spelled the beginning of the end for the great manorial demesnes in England. Having lost upward of half of their labor force to the plague, many manor lords resorted to converting portions of their tilled acreage into grazing, which required less labor. Peasant tenants who survived the plague and had managed to become more prosperous than their tenant neighbors were now able to obtain leases for tenant lands that had been left vacant by the plague, and for demesne lands that the lords could no longer farm themselves. This encouraged the formation of a small class of entrepreneurial peasants on the manors who acquired control over larger parcels of land during the fifteenth century, enabling them to produce larger agricultural surpluses that could be sold in the local markets. As time went on, these enterprising peasants began enclosing their enlarged holdings to allow for better management of the land. They also began to compete for the labor of their less fortunate tenant neighbors, offering them better terms of employment than those provided by the manor lords (Kulikoff 2000).

The entire manorial system, therefore, began to unravel in the fifteenth century. The pace of disintegration accelerated in the sixteenth century when the lords began to enclose their common lands and rent them out to the enterprising peasants, who by then had emerged as a separate class of yeomen farmers. The yeomen were thus able to gain control over even larger tracts of manor lands, whereas the lords were now able to raise the rent to whatever the market would bear and thus maximize their financial returns from the enterprising yeomen. For their part, the yeoman farmers responded to the new economic pressures of capitalistic agriculture by specializing in those products that they could produce at lower cost and higher quality than farmers in other regions. As for the traditional peasant tenants who relied on the commons for their survival, the enclosure movement was devastating. Life for them on the manors became unsustainable, triggering mass dislocation from the countryside during the sixteenth and seventeenth centuries as the rural poor migrated to urban centers, especially London, in search of work. Consequently, the population of London grew explosively, from around fifty-five thousand in 1520, to two hundred thousand in 1600, to more than half a million in 1700 (Kulikoff 2000).

The progressive breakup of manorial demesnes during the fifteenth through seventeenth centuries also meant the steady demise of demesne cheese making. Even more abrupt was the end of demesne cheese making on the monastic manors when King Henry VIII commenced the dissolution of the English monasteries (eventually 578 in all) in 1536 and put the monastic manors up for sale in a bid to raise money for his cash-strapped government. The knowledge of demesne cheese making did not disappear, however. Many demesne cheesemakers (dairymaids) from the aristocratic and monastic manors probably found ready employment with the rising class of yeoman farmers who by then were prospering, accumulating land and animals, and eager to tap into the growing urban markets for cheese and butter. For centuries the demesne dairymaids had been drawn from the same manorial peasant communities that gave birth to the yeomen, and the dairymaids were revered for their expertise (Fussell 1966). Thus, the new yeomen farmers were probably keen to acquire the dairymaids' skills, and through the dairymaids the knowledge of demesne cheese making passed into the hands of yeomen farmers (Valenze 1991).

Around this same time another segment of commercial farming emerged in England as members of the new prosperous merchant class in London began to invest in country landholdings and join the growing ranks of the gentry class in the countryside. Among the new gentry was Adam Winthrop, a prominent London merchant and lawyer who took advantage of the monastic dissolution to purchase Groton manor in Suffolk, which had formerly belonged to the Abbey of Saint Edmund at Bury, in 1544. Like so many of their neighbors in the East Anglian countryside, the Winthrops maintained a dairy herd and produced cheese and butter at Groton manor. Adam Winthrop's grandson John eventually inherited Groton manor, and John's wife, Margaret, supervised the dairy operation, providing daily instructions to the dairymaid and her helpers. Besides their active involvement in commercial cheese and butter making, the Winthrops were deeply involved in the radical Calvinist Puritan movement that was sweeping England and threatening to plunge the land into civil war. John Winthrop would eventually lead a large-scale migration of Puritans to the Atlantic coast of North America, where they established a new colony on the Massachusetts Bay (Bremer 2003). The Massachusetts Bay Colony, led by its first governor John Winthrop, would profoundly shape both the course of American history in general and the history of cheese in America in particular, but that story will have to wait until chapter 8.

Back in England, the world of the yeomen and gentry commercial farmers was very different from that of the manorial demesnes, and soon all commercial cheesemakers would come under pressure to modify their cheese-making technology to meet the demands of the marketplace, especially the London market. Commercial cheesemakers would rise to the challenge and prosper. In contrast, peasant cheese making as had been practiced on the manors for a thousand years did not fare so well. Peasant cheeses all but disappeared in England—along with the peasants as they abandoned the countryside for London and other urban centers.

East Anglian Cheeses

London's burgeoning population became a mega-market that affected all of English agriculture. Regional specialization, which had already started in the later Middle Ages, accelerated during the sixteenth century with East Anglia leading the way. East Anglia's close proximity to London gave the

Figure 7-1. Map of nineteenth-century England showing the three major cheese-making regions (circles added) during the sixteenth through the nineteenth centuries: East Anglian cheeses (Essex, Suffolk, Norfolk); southern cheeses (Somersetshire, Wiltshire, Gloucestershire, Berkshire); northern cheeses (Cheshire, Lancashire, Staffordshire, Derbyshire, Leicestershire). (After Gray, circa 1824, *Gray's New Book of Roads*, Sherwood Jones, London)

region a competitive advantage; cheese and butter could be transported to London easily either by land or coastwise by ship. Thus, the region's long-standing emphasis on cheese and butter making now developed into highly specialized industries centered in Essex and especially Suffolk (Fisher 1935;

figure 7-1). The strong Puritan (Calvinist) movement in East Anglia further reinforced the culture of capitalistic entrepreneurialism there.

East Anglia established and maintained a virtual monopoly on the London market for cheese and butter during the sixteenth century. The region also continued to export much cheese and butter to Flanders and France, and military purchases of Suffolk cheese for the English army and England's growing navy increased as British strategic interests expanded. Likewise, England's fast-growing maritime trade also looked to East Anglian cheese to provision the many English merchant ships now plying the seas (Everitt 1967; Thirsk 1967). Other regions such as Cheshire and Somerset also specialized in dairy in the sixteenth century, but their markets were still local, their cheese-making techniques largely unchanged from those of the manorial demesnes.

According to Fussell (1966), the most general system of farmhouse cheese making in the sixteenth and seventeenth centuries was known as "new milk" cheese. Morning milk fresh from the cow was placed into a clean wooden tub and often a portion of cream from previous evenings' milk was added, along with some boiling water to prevent the milk from being overly rich. Upon cooling, the lukewarm milk was then coagulated rapidly with rennet, and cheese was made by a simple uncooked method that included moderate pressing and surface salting. This procedure (uncooked, moderately pressed, surface-salted cheese) was not much different from that described by Columella fifteen hundred years earlier for dry (aged) cheese, and was probably very similar to the technology used on the manorial demesnes for centuries. The most common sizes of cheese made in the sixteenth and early seventeenth centuries were 10- to 12-pound (4.5 to 5.4 kg) wheels, 12 to 18 inches (30 to 45 cm) in diameter and 1.5 to 3 inches (4 to 8 cm) thick (Foster 1998). In short, the evidence suggests that the yeoman dairymaids continued to practice the old demesne technology for making cheese.

By the start of the seventeenth century, however, market forces were beginning to influence East Anglian cheesemakers. England was becoming wealthy, and the demand for luxuries in London was growing. Butter, long considered a symbol of prosperity, was now in great demand and commanded a higher price than cheese. Essex and Suffolk were already famous for their outstanding butter at this time, and cheesemakers there recognized that it was now more profitable to skim more of the cream from their milk before making cheese so as to produce more butter along with cheese from the same milk (Blundel and Tregear 2006). Though such skimming had been practiced on the manor demesnes for centuries, the East Anglian yeomen extended the commercial logic of this practice to the extreme, heavily skimming the milk to produce much higher ratios of butter to cheese (Cheke 1959); however, they did so at the expense of the quality of the cheese, which became very low in fat content. In the long run, this turned out to be a devastating strategic error.

Initially, however, the strategy seemed to work well. The swelling ranks of the working-class poor of London provided a ready market for the low-quality but inexpensive "flett" or skim-milk cheese. The flett cheese also found a ready market in the growing maritime sector of the economy, where it was valued for its durability. Low-fat cheese is inherently durable and able to withstand abuse because low-fat curd expels whey more readily during cheese making, resulting in much drier cheese. Thus, flett cheese, despite its uninspiring quality, was well suited for the provisioning of ships, both commercial and naval (Fussell 1935). England's growing colonial empire, however, brought ever-greater prosperity, and the London market soon demanded not only butter but also fine-quality cheese. Imported cheeses were beginning to make inroads during the seventeenth century, with Parmesan from Italy and Edam from Holland being the most highly esteemed (Fussell 1966).

The London cheesemongers, a trade organization that received official government recognition in 1377, had built up monopolistic control of the London market for both cheese and butter by the seventeenth century (Stern 1979). The cheesemongers employed buying agents called "factors" who visited dairy farms, evaluated the quality and quantity of cheese on hand, and finalized purchase and sales agreements with the farmers for their cheese and their butter. The cheesemongers contracted with East Anglian ships to transport the cheeses coastwise from local ports on the brief two-day journey to London. During the first half of the seventeenth century the cheesemongers sourced almost all of their cheese and butter from East Anglia.

Things changed very quickly, however, starting in the late 1640s, when

Suffolk, by far the largest cheese supplier for London, experienced severe flooding and an outbreak of cattle disease, which in turn precipitated steep declines in cheese production. This prompted the cheesemongers to seek alternate supplies of cheese. Several regions in England in addition to East Anglia had become specialized in dairying and cheese making by the sixteenth century, notably Gloucester, Wiltshire, Berkeley, Somerset, and Cheshire (Thirsk 1967; figure 7-1). Indeed, Cheshire and Somerset had become renowned for their excellent cheeses by that time. However, cheeses from these regions were consumed locally, being too far from London to be marketed there. By the late 1640s, however, the spiraling price of cheese in London made other cheese-making regions more competitive, and the cheesemongers looked to Cheshire to meet the demand.

Northern English Cheeses

Although sporadic shipments of Cheshire cheese to London had occurred during the first half of the seventeenth century, the first regular shipment to London took place in 1650, where it was an immediate success. Though Cheshire was considerably more expensive than Suffolk cheese because of the longer transport (around fourteen days versus two days by ship) and because the cheese was made from whole milk rather than milk that had been skimmed, the market responded enthusiastically because the cheese was superior in quality and the growing class of prosperous Londoners were willing to bear the cost (Foster 1998). Consequently, cheese shipments from Cheshire immediately began to displace East Anglian cheese in the London marketplace. In 1664 around 874,000 pounds (440,000 kg) of Cheshire cheese were received at London docks; by the mid-1670s Cheshire shipments had increased to around 2.4 million pounds (1.1 million kg), by the 1680s to 4.8 million pounds (2.2 million kg), and by 1725 to around 13.8 million pounds (6.3 million kg). Thus, in less than a century Cheshire virtually displaced East Anglian cheese in the London marketplace, accounting for more than 90 percent of the cheese arriving coastwise to the city; Suffolk cheese retained only 5 percent of the market (Stern 1973). Even the navy stopped buying Suffolk cheese in favor of better-quality Cheshire (Foster 1998).

The cheesemongers' shift to Cheshire as their chief supplier of cheese had another, more insidious effect on East Anglian cheesemakers. For the cheesemongers it made increasing economic sense to segregate their butter suppliers from their cheese suppliers—that is, to have East Anglia (Suffolk and Essex) specialize in maximum butter production, while sourcing premium cheese solely from Cheshire. Thus the cheesemongers began to pressure East Anglian cheesemakers to increase their ratios of butter to cheese, refusing to contract for cheese unless it was coupled with larger shipments of butter. This had the effect of accelerating the downward cycle in cheese quality as the flett cheese became lower and lower in fat content. In desperation, Suffolk cheesemakers petitioned Parliament in 1690 for protection against the unscrupulous practices of the cheesemongers:

> The Cheesemongers in London have of late Years encouraged the Farmers to make Flett Cheese, whereby the Quantity of Butter sold with such Cheese is increased to Four Firkins in a Load; but the Cheese thereby becomes only fit for Slaves; from whence the Commodity is grown into Disrepute, and, if not prevented, will become a general Prejudice.
>
> (*Journal of the House of Commons*, vol. 10:1688–1693 (London, 1802), 475–6, Quoted in Blundel and Tregear 2006)

The "Slaves" in the petition were most likely slaves on the sugar plantations of the West Indies, which England had developed intensively by this time. However, even the West Indies market was falling beyond the reach of East Anglian cheesemakers. By the end of the seventeenth century Puritan cheesemakers of the New England colonies, whose grandparents had left East Anglia some sixty years earlier, were aggressively applying the same strategy to capture the West Indies market for cheese and butter that East Anglia had used to dominate the London market a century earlier. East Anglia never recovered as a cheese-producing region.

Although Cheshire cheesemakers flourished under the new system of agricultural capitalism, they, too, were pressured by the cheesemongers in other ways. The supply chain from Cheshire to London was longer and more complex than that from East Anglia, and carried greater risk for the cheesemongers. The farmers in Cheshire received payment for their cheese when delivery was accepted at the cheesemonger's warehouse. From that point on the cheesemongers and their factors financed the cheese and assumed the risk until the cheese was sold. The complexity of matching the warehouse inventory of cheese with the availability of shipping meant that cheeses were spending a longer time in warehouses and in transit before sale in London—perhaps up to four months, given that ships could make only three or four round trips from Cheshire to London in a year (Foster 1998). Cheese quality might deteriorate during this time and thereby reduce its value in the marketplace, and cheeses inexorably lost weight due to evaporative moisture loss. Therefore, significantly less cheese arrived in London than had been contracted for at the farm and paid for at the warehouse, and the cheese might be dried out (Stern 1979).

Consequently, the cheesemongers preferred to deal in larger cheeses, for which they paid a higher price, and eventually refused to handle smaller cheeses. Larger cheeses had the advantage of less surface area relative to their volume, enabling them to lose less weight during storage due to evaporation and remaining moist and more mellow in flavor in the interior. Larger cheeses also afforded more efficient handling and storage through the entire distribution chain. Unscrupulous cheesemongers also began to shift the cost of cheese weight losses during storage onto the cheesemaker by refusing to accept delivery of the farmers' cheese until well past the agreed-upon delivery date. They would use lack of warehousing and shipping space as a stalling pretext, forcing the farmer to hold on to cheeses longer (Stern 1979). Thus, the farmer was increasingly manipulated to bear the cost of storing the cheese until it suited the cheesemonger to accept it just prior to shipment by sea. For farmers, it became essential to minimize evaporative moisture loss while the cheeses remained in their possession.

Cheesemakers in Cheshire responded by producing cheeses of the same diameter (around 15 inches, or 38 cm) but thicker and heavier. The typical weight of Cheshire cheeses increased from around 10 to 12 pounds (4.5 to 5.4 kg) in the mid-1600s to around 20 to 24 pounds (9 to 11 kg) by the start of the eighteenth century. This was tricky business from the standpoint of cheese technology and quality, however, because larger, thicker cheeses had to be made lower in moisture right out of the press in order to avoid rotting from the inside due to excessive moisture retention (Foster 1998). Furthermore, the larger and thicker the cheese became, the longer it took for the salt rubbed on the surface to diffuse into and equilibrate throughout the cheese, further elevating the risk of rotting from the inside. Thus began an ongoing battle to control moisture and salt contents using new technologies, one that would preoccupy English cheesemakers for the next 150 years.

The first major technological breakthrough occurred early in the eighteenth century when cheesemakers in Cheshire developed heavy-duty cheese presses that used massive stone weights (up to 3,600 pounds, or 1,600 kg) to apply far more pressure than had been possible with traditional presses. In addition, the wooden press molds contained small holes into which wooden skewers were inserted and withdrawn from the cheese during pressing to facilitate the release of whey. This made it possible to produce larger cheeses that contained a lower moisture content right out of the press than had been possible previously.

The second breakthrough, which came around the middle of the eighteenth century, was achieved by mixing dry salt into the curd particles before pressing (Fussell 1966). This technique, used by cheesemakers in the Massif Central of France for centuries to make Cantal cheese, enabled Cheshire cheesemakers to expel more whey during pressing and distribute salt more uniformly throughout the cheese, effectively building into the large cheese greater resistance to internal rotting. At this point the cheeses were still salted on the surface after pressing to develop a rind, but—being lower in moisture and more uniform in salt content—they no longer required evaporative moisture loss to stave off internal rotting. Indeed, now the challenge was to limit evaporative moisture loss, or in other words to lock in the moisture to prevent the cheese from drying out too much. This inspired Cheshire cheesemakers to incorporate a third technological advance: rubbing the surface of the finished cheese repeatedly with butter, creating a thin film of lipids that slowed evaporation from the surface.

Though the cheesemakers of the Cheshire region led the way in cheese technology innovations, the surrounding counties followed in Cheshire's wake and a group of "northern cheeses," similar in technology to Cheshire, arose in Lancashire, Staffordshire, Leicestershire, and Derbyshire during the eighteenth century (Cheke 1959; figure 7-1). By the mid-eighteenth century Cheshire cheeses weighing 30 to 60 pounds (14 to 27 kg), still around 15 inches (38 cm) in diameter but now 5 to 8 inches (13 to 20 cm) thick, were commonplace (Foster 1998). Larger volumes of milk and herds of cows, in turn, were required to make the larger cheeses, a single cheese now requiring the milk from twenty to thirty cows. At first small farms combined their milks to make the "great" cheeses. Inevitably, however, the economic pressure of the times drove cheesemakers toward rationalization and larger farms, and so the merger of small farms into larger units began in earnest.

Southern English Cheeses

During the second half of the eighteenth century England engaged in large-scale projects improving its transportation network to support its increasingly sophisticated economy. New roads were built and existing roads improved, canal networks were built that linked navigable rivers, and improvements in river navigation were undertaken, all of which opened up access of new agricultural areas to the London market. Cheeses from Somerset and the adjoining regions of Gloucestershire, Berkshire, and Wiltshire began to flow into London on a regular basis, where they established stellar reputations for quality (Cheke 1959). Although the traditional wheel-shaped cheeses of around 10 pounds (4.5 kg) were made in this region, larger "Cheddar" cheeses from Somerset and "Double Gloucester" cheeses (around 20 to 25 pounds, or 9 to 11 kg) became common, no doubt in response to pressure from the London cheesemongers, who had built their distribution systems around the larger Cheshire cheeses.

The cheesemakers of the southern region used a different strategy than that of Cheshire to produce a drier cheese that resisted internal rotting. They developed a technique known as scalding, whereby the whey was drained from the curds, heated in a kettle, and poured back onto the mass of fused curd remaining in the vat to promote whey expulsion. Sometimes hot water or whey diluted with water was used in place of whey. The practice probably originated in Somerset, where cheesemakers in the Cheddar region were famous for producing large cheeses as early as the sixteenth century (Camden 1586). The use of scalding spread throughout the adjoining regions and became standard in the making of Double Gloucester cheese (Marshall 1796). Soon after, scalding was improved by heating the curd while it was still in particles—that is, before the whey was drained and the curd allowed to mat into a mass. This enabled each curd particle to be heated completely and uniformly, thereby enhancing curd contraction and whey expulsion.

At first, Cheddar, Gloucester, and similar southern cheeses were dry-salted at the surface after pressing, not pre-salted before pressing as was practiced in Cheshire (Fussell 1966). However, by the end of eighteenth century cheesemakers in Wiltshire evidently borrowed the practice of pre-salting before pressing from Cheshire to make the thick cheeses that were sold in London under the name Double Gloucester (Marshall 1796). The combination of scalding *plus* pre-salting was a landmark development in English pressed-cheese making. It allowed large cheeses to be produced that were low enough in moisture and high enough in salt throughout to preempt internal rotting, yet moist enough and low enough in salt to support the development of excellent flavor and texture during aging. Cheddar cheesemakers in Somerset embraced the combined technology by the early nineteenth century, as did cheesemakers in America around the same time. The Americans had been following the technological advances of their English counterparts, and cheese making in America closely mirrored that in England (Deane 1790; Hough 1793; Johnson 1801), a topic to be further explored in chapter 8. The name Cheddar eventually would be applied to any cheese made by this technology regardless of its place of origin, and so Cheddar cheese would become the most widely produced cheese on the planet.

By the early nineteenth century, most of the major cheeses in England fell into two categories: a northern group represented by Cheshire and other cheeses made by a similar uncooked, pre-salted, and highly pressed technology, and a southern group represented by Cheddar and sister cheeses, produced using a combination of scalding (cooking) and pre-salting before pressing at high pressure (Cheke 1959). Lacking the scalding step, the northern cheeses were somewhat higher in moisture than the southern cheeses and thus characteristically more acidic in nature.

Even more acidic were the much-acclaimed Stilton cheeses, which came to prominence in the mid-eighteenth century (Hickman 1995). Stilton cheesemakers shared the technique of pre-salting the curd before pressing with their Cheshire counterparts, from whom they perhaps borrowed the idea, but they did not press the cheese at high pressure as in Cheshire and, indeed, went to great extents to limit whey expulsion throughout manufacture. Likewise, during aging the large cylindrical size and shape of Stilton was designed to limit evaporative moisture loss. The result was an open-textured, high-moisture, acidic cheese that readily supported mold growth both internally and externally when aged in a cool, moist environment. The cheese was so moist and soft that it needed to be bound up in bandages to prevent the cylindrical form from slumping and becoming misshapen during aging.

Stilton was perhaps the first cheese to use bandaging as an outer protective wrap during aging, but it was the producers of Cheddar cheese who transformed bandaging into the first "packaging film" to enable the production of "semi-rindless" long-aged cheese. Up to this point cheesemakers had used surface salting to create a dense dehydrated rind to physically protect the cheese surface and act as a water vapor barrier against excessive drying during aging and storage. However, the incorporation of scalding (cooking) plus pre-salting in the Cheddar-making procedure obviated the need for surface salting. Technically speaking, it became possible to produce a "rindless" Cheddar cheese; however, the cheese still needed to be protected from physical damage and drying and cracking.

The need for surface protection was especially acute in America, where much warmer summers than in England caused extensive dehydration, cracking, and disfiguration of cheeses that were not adequately protected. Surface cracking was especially troublesome because it rendered the cheese very susceptible to maggots and decay (Deane 1790). By the end of the eighteenth century, and perhaps much earlier, American cheesemakers discovered that they could lessen the problem by "dressing" their cheeses; that is, by smearing the surface repeatedly with melted whey butter. The repeated applications of butter hardened into a thin, resilient coating that impeded evaporation and protected the surface from cracking and maggot infestation. It also increased the yield of cheese, because water that had formerly been lost from the cheese during rind formation now remained within. The thin films could be peeled off the cheese easily at the time of eating, minimizing wastage of cheese (Johnson 1801). Whether American cheese-makers borrowed this technology from their counterparts in Cheshire or developed it independently is not clear. Either way, this new way of dealing with the cheese surface was almost certainly the antecedent to the practice of dressing the cheeses with cloth bandages after pressing and then smear-ing the bandages repeatedly with melted butter, which developed during the early decades of the nineteenth century. The greased bandage hardened into a thicker and more resilient coating that furnished better protection for the large cylindrical cheeses. Thus, greased bandaged or clothbound "semi-rindless" cheese offered significant economic advantage over traditional rinded cheese, and both English and American cheesemakers embraced the technology.

Who came first? It's hard to say. We'll return to that question in chap-ter 8, but suffice it to say that greased bandaged technology may have first developed in America and then spread to England. Previously America had always looked to England for new cheese-making technologies, but now the transatlantic flow of new technology began to move in the reverse direc-tion. Bandaging technology improved over time: Lard replaced butter as a lower-cost and more effective lipid coating; dipping the finished cheese in scalding water helped to close up the surface to further improve durabil-ity. Bandaging was used widely in both America and England throughout the nineteenth century until wax coatings became available toward the end of the century, followed by new multilayer wraps and films in the twenti-eth century that afforded even greater physical protection and water vapor impermeability.

The Legacy of the Dairywomen

Although the rise of agricultural capitalism brought profound changes to the English countryside, dairywomen and dairymaids continued to domi-nate cheese making on the yeoman farms as they had for centuries on the manor demesnes. However, the influence of men began to infiltrate the women's world of cheese making in new ways. The Enlightenment of the eighteenth century brought a great blossoming of science and technology in England, which inspired efforts to systemize and rationalize many areas of the English economy, including agriculture. The drive to improve agricultural practices was championed by upper-class gentlemen and prosperous businessmen who were keen to apply scientific and empirical knowledge to improve the profitability of commercial farm enterprises (Valenze 1991).

Educated English gentlemen such as William Marshall, therefore, began to intrude into the women's realm of cheese making by studying practices on the yeomen farms and publishing technical discourses that highlighted best practices (Marshall 1796). Similarly, cheese factors began to study the women's practices on the farms from which they purchased cheese in an effort to promote best practices and consistent cheese quality. Josiah Twamley was one such cheese factor who published two comprehensive guides to cheese-making best practices at the end of the eighteenth and beginning of the nineteenth centuries (Twamley 1784; Twamley 1816). Marshall's and Twamley's discourses, along with various technical tracts and scientific articles published around the same time by other male writers, began to demystify the cheese-making process and unseat the position of the dairywomen as the caretakers of "secret knowledge" that they alone possessed and handed down from mother to daughter and mistress to servant.

The migration of technical cheese-making knowledge into the male-dominated public domain culminated during the mid-nineteenth century with Joseph Harding's landmark work to develop scientific principles for cheese making. Harding and his contemporaries applied rapidly progressing knowledge in the natural sciences to systemize cheese making along scientific principles, creating for the first time standardized instructions or "recipes" for specific cheese varieties that could be reproduced anywhere (Blundel and Tregear 2006). The snowballing accumulation of public knowledge in cheese science and technology led to the establishment of technical dairy schools during the latter half of the nineteenth century, further eroding the unique status of the dairywoman and dairymaid as guardians of the cheese-making arts.

Equally threatening and even more disturbing to traditional women cheesemakers were the attitudes that male writers often expressed toward them; female cheesemakers often were portrayed as backward, narrow-minded, and having a natural aversion to learning new techniques (Valenze 1991). Thus, the demise of women cheesemakers in England seemed imminent by the mid-nineteenth century. The dairywoman and dairymaid did not disappear, however, nor did farmhouse cheese making. Both persisted and even made a comeback during the opening decades of the twentieth century. In an odd twist of history the rise of the cheese factory in America helped to preserve the special status of women in cheese making along with their traditional cheese-making venue, the farmhouse dairy, for a while longer in England.

In America factory cheese making grew phenomenally during the second half of the nineteenth century following the successful launch of the first cheese factory in 1851. This growth came at a time when the population of England was rising steeply and England was lowering its tariffs on food to encourage imports. Thus, around the time of the American Civil War, American "Cheddar" cheese began to trickle into England; soon, this trickle grew to a torrent. The influx of inexpensive factory-made American cheese drove down prices in England, and English cheesemakers responded in one of three ways. Some turned to producing milk for the growing liquid milk markets of the great urban centers like London, which became possible with the development of the English railroad by the mid-nineteenth century. The price of liquid milk provided better returns for many dairy farms than the highly competitive cheese market. Thus, a number of farmhouse cheesemakers stopped making cheese altogether (Blundel and Tregear 2006).

Other cheesemakers banded together and established factories of their own, the first of which commenced operation in 1870. The English factories, however, proved unable to compete with the Americans, who were twenty years ahead in their experience with factory cheese. Furthermore, there was great resistance in the dairying regions to establishing new cheese factories, based on the continued perception that the best cheese was made in the farmhouse by a skillful dairywoman. Factory cheeses made in both America and England were seen as mediocre in quality compared with the best farmhouse cheese, and this brought into focus a renewed appreciation for the dairywoman's skill and her importance to the economy and culture of rural England (McMurry 1992). Ultimately, the influx of lower-cost and increasingly uniform-quality factory cheese from America and later Canada and New Zealand devastated English cheese making. By the mid-1920s around 75 percent of the cheese consumed in England was imported, primarily from New Zealand and Canada. However, of the cheese still produced in England, farmhouse cheese accounted for an impressive 75 percent of total domestic production. After experiencing steep declines during the later decades of the nineteenth century, farmhouse cheese making rebounded significantly during the first three decades of the twentieth century (Blundel and Tregear 2006). Progressive artisan cheesemakers now cultivated a growing niche market for premium cheeses, and farmhouse cheese making managed to survive through the skill of the dairywomen.

Ultimately, however, farmhouse cheese making was driven to near extinction during the crisis years of the Great Depression and World War II. Wartime policy in particular mandated the replacement of farmhouse cheese making with factory production of a few high-priority hard cheeses. Though wartime controls were lifted in the early 1950s farm-based cheese making failed to recover, and by the late 1950s factory cheese making had risen to around 95 percent of total domestic production (Blundel and Tregear 2006). Still, the memory of fine farmhouse cheeses lingered and would eventually give birth to a movement to restore traditional cheese making to England.

Holland: Cheese Provisioner of All Europe

In many respects the development of market-driven cheese making in Holland mirrored that in England, with the important exception that Holland's transformation got off to a later start and occurred more explosively over a shorter span of time. Indeed, much of Holland was an uninhabited or sparsely populated wasteland before the tenth century, consisting of vast waterlogged peat bogs and maritime salt pastures that were too wet to cultivate in the summer and flooded by North Sea storms during the winter. It wasn't until the fifteenth century that commercial dairying began to emerge in Holland as a significant element of the economy.

Coastal Holland nevertheless had a long history of primitive dairying and cheese making stretching back to the late Neolithic, when small settlements were established on dune ridges that were situated amid the expansive coastal salt marshes. These early inhabitants raised a few crops on the well-drained crests of the ridges and were heavily dependent on cattle raising and dairying. They practiced a form of transhumance whereby the cattle were grazed on the coastal maritime pastures below the settlements in the summer and returned to higher ground during the winter. Dairying and dairy products were important to these early inhabitants of Holland, as evidenced by the large proportion of cattle bones in the faunal remains at pre-Roman settlement sites, and the discovery of butter churns and cheese molds (TeBrake 1985).

When the Romans occupied Holland they established military garrisons along the Rhine River, which of course needed to be provisioned. The Romans extracted livestock, dairy products, and other agricultural goods from the native population through tribute, taxation, and trade to support the military installations (TeBrake 1985). However, the Romans did little to colonize Holland, evidently dissuaded by the inhospitable environment. Instead, they concentrated their colonizing efforts to the south in Flanders and Brabant, where they established an extensive infrastructure of roads, cities and agricultural villas. Because of this, Flanders and Brabant developed into strong manorial economies after the fall of the Roman Empire, whereas Holland remained largely wilderness (de Vries 1974). Indeed, apart from the long-standing dune ridge settlements and a few other settlements along the river estuaries, much of the landmass of western Holland remained empty through the early Middle Ages. Thus, Holland was a soggy backwater frontier economy, in stark contrast with Flanders, which emerged as the preeminent textile-manufacturing center of northern Europe by the eleventh century.

Over the next few centuries, however, the Dutch landscape was dramatically transformed. Perhaps inspired by the booming economy and extensive land reclamation projects under way in Flanders, the aristocratic counts of Holland and the bishops of Utrecht, who jointly controlled much of Holland's wastelands, initiated large-scale land reclamations from the eleventh through the fourteenth centuries (van Bavel and van Zanden 2004). The work of reclaiming soggy peat bogs was painstaking and very labor-intensive. Each new field required the construction of a network of drainage ditches about a yard deep to lower the water table sufficiently to allow the surface to dry. Low dikes also needed to be constructed to divert runoff from surrounding undrained areas (TeBrake 1981). The daunting task of large-scale land reclamation was rendered even more challenging because of chronic labor shortages. Holland's sparse population and paucity of large aristocratic and ecclesiastical manorial estates afforded few sources of surplus labor. The counts and bishops were thus compelled to take extreme measures to recruit the necessary labor force, offering local peasants their freedom and almost absolute, exclusive property rights to the land that they reclaimed in return for their labor. Such liberal peasant land-use policy, in turn, gave rise to a reclaimed countryside that was characterized by relatively large family farms worked by free peasant owners (van Bavel and van Zanden 2004).

Initially the reclaimed lands were turned into arable fields that were planted with bread cereals, resulting in a dramatic rise in grain production between 1000 and 1300; dairying in contrast continued to be practiced on a small scale in the salt-marsh regions as it had been in the past. The new peasant farms on reclaimed lands prospered, and the population of Holland grew steadily. Grain surpluses produced on the small farms supported the growth of new urban settlements including Leiden, Haarlem, Amsterdam, the Hague, Delft, Rotterdam, and Gouda. At the same time, Holland's strategic location on the North Sea and near the mouth of the Rhine River encouraged the development of maritime trade that brought new prosperity to the rising coastal towns and cities. The reclaimed Dutch countryside of the fourteenth century, oriented around cereal production to feed the growing domestic urban population, appeared to be poised for steady growth and prosperity.

During the next two centuries, however, the production of bread cereals collapsed, brought on by an ecological crisis of largely human making that catalyzed dramatic changes in Dutch agriculture, including a sharp increase in dairying and cheese making. By the mid-fourteenth century the accumulated centuries of peat bog draining and land reclamation began to take their toll on great expanses of the Dutch landscape through contraction of the landmass and gradual sinking of the surface. Peat bogs can be thought of as massive biological sponges that expand in volume as they absorb large amounts of water, creating a concave rise in the land surface that continues to expand upward as the peat grows and absorbs even more water. Conversely, when peat bogs are drained, growth is halted and the peat "sponge" contracts as it loses water, eventually creating a convex, bowl-shaped depression in place of the raised concave bog surface. Consequently, large areas of reclaimed land in western Holland that stood on peat bogs experienced a gradual sinking, from as much as several yards (meters) above sea level before draining and reclamation to several yards below sea level thereafter (TeBrake 1985).

To make matter worse, the middle of the fourteenth century saw a modest rise in sea level. The contraction of peat lands and rise in sea level, in turn, raised the water table in the reclaimed lands and rendered them more vulnerable to coastal flooding. As their reclaimed lands grew progressively wetter, Dutch peasant farmers found it increasingly difficult to grow wheat and other cereals that require well-drained soils, and they were soon faced with a crisis: They had to either cease farming altogether or adopt new agricultural practices compatible with the new wetter soil conditions and develop measures to protect against flooding. In an amazing example of human determination and ingenuity, many Dutch peasants chose to adapt their agriculture and fight the North Sea.

To combat flooding, the Dutch developed the *polder* system, whereby they enclosed their fields with dikes and then pumped out surface water to create permanent dry lands. In 1408 the windmill, which had been in use since the thirteenth century for grinding cereal grains, was coupled for the first time with the pump to remove water from a polder. By the mid-fifteenth century windmill pumps were a common feature of the Dutch countryside, once again reclaiming lands that had been first reclaimed centuries before. The higher water table, however, still meant that many polders could not support wheat production and had to be used differently. Some peasants switched to raising barley and hops, which tolerate wetter soils, and so stimulated the rise of artisan brewing. Many others abandoned arable farming altogether and converted to dairying and artisan cheese and butter making. Thus, between 1350 and 1500 the production of cheese and butter rose steadily, finding strong markets in the nearby urban centers that were growing rapidly and prospering through maritime trade.

Faced with shortages of domestically grown grain, Holland now needed to import large amounts of grain from France and the Baltic region to feed its growing urban population. To pay for food imports, Holland in turn needed to develop new high-value exports. Prosperity and trade were on the rise throughout Europe by this time, creating new opportunities for Dutch exports, which began to include beer and cheese, now produced in greater surpluses as farmers transitioned away from wheat to barley and dairy. By the fifteenth century Holland was shipping modest exports of cheese to the Rhine region of Germany and to Flanders, where Dutch cheeses began to compete with imported English cheeses that had long commanded a strong market presence there (van Bavel and van Zanden 2004).

The end of the fifteenth century witnessed the rise of Calvinism in Holland, further underpinning the entrepreneurial spirit that had developed so strongly over the past several centuries. The confluence of Holland's strong maritime and urban infrastructure, her independent peasantry and entrepreneurial culture, and her increasingly specialized, value-added agricultural products (beer and especially cheese) now propelled this small patch of former wasteland to become one of Europe's richest and most powerful empires. Between 1500 and 1700 Holland's economy expanded, probably more rapidly than any other in Europe; closely connected to this expansion was a transformation in the rural economy. Peasant farm households, led by dairy farms, became highly specialized and grew in size. The typical dairy herd increased from around five or six head at the start of the sixteenth century, to around fifteen head by midcentury, to around twenty-five in the seventeenth century. These larger, more specialized farms, having moved away from relative self-sufficiency, in turn became major consumers of goods and services, and villages sprang up across the countryside to satisfy the new rural demand (de Vries 1974).

Large increases in cheese production created the need for regional markets to handle the increasingly complex marketing and distribution functions, especially those that serviced the growing international markets. Alkmaar in the north of Holland was one the earliest cheese markets, first mentioned in 1408. The Alkmaar market underwent repeated expansions during the sixteenth century and again in the seventeenth. By the early 1700s Alkmaar was handling 6 to 7 million pounds (2.7 to 3.2 million kg) of cheese annually, and during the period from 1758 to 1830 the weigh scales at Alkmaar recorded an amazing total of 536,834,830 pounds (243,504,183 kg) of cheese that passed through the city (Flint 1862). Gouda was the largest cheese market in the south of Holland, handling between around 4 to 6 million pounds (1.8 to 2.7 million kg) of cheese annually during the seventeenth century, with Hoorn to the north, near the market town of Edam, close behind, handling around 4 to 5.5 million pounds (1.8 to 2.5 million kg) per year. There were also many smaller markets across Holland (de Vries 1974).

Alkmaar, Rotterdam, Amsterdam, and Hoorn specialized in international exports, with Rotterdam and Amsterdam typically exporting around 3 to 5 million pounds (1.4 to 2.3 million kg) of cheese per year during the eighteenth century. The city of Hoorn, described as the "cheese provisioner of all of Europe," was considered the main export center for cheese, but reliable figures are not available (de Vries 1974). In 1803, the first year for which reliable countrywide records exist, cheese exports totaled 18.7 million pounds (8.5 million kg), a remarkable output for the time for so small a landmass. Italy and the Iberian peninsula had become the major destinations for Dutch cheese, along with Germany, England, France, the West Indies, and North America, and wherever else Holland's mighty merchant fleet traveled, for cheese was a regular provision on its maritime vessels.

Detailed descriptions of Dutch cheese-making methods, first published in German (Ellerbrock 1853) and later translated into English (Flint 1862), offer insight into how Dutch cheesemakers were able to achieve such meteoric success in the marketplace. The Dutch became highly specialized: They developed new equipment that allowed for larger scales of production; they concentrated their efforts on a few cheese varieties that were distinctive in quality; they differentiated their cheeses from others through innovative "packaging;" and they purposefully designed their cheeses for durability and convenience during shipping and handling. Whereas English cheesemakers *responded* to the market by adapting to the demands of the cheesemongers, Dutch cheesemakers *created* new markets for their cheeses through entrepreneurial innovation.

For example, cheesemakers in East Anglia responded to the growing demand for butter by skimming their cheese milk and producing increasingly lower-fat and lower-quality flett cheeses. As pressure from the London cheesemongers for more butter mounted, this strategy progressively eroded the quality, reputation, and competitiveness of East Anglian cheeses and ultimately crippled the once mighty East Anglian cheese empire. Holland, too, became a major producer of butter at the same time that its cheese production was expanding rapidly. Dutch cheesemakers, however, did not allow butter production to interfere with their two stunningly successful export cheeses, Edam and Gouda. Instead, the Dutch developed a novel product made from skim milk known as "spice cheese," which transformed bland skim-milk curd into a flavored cheese that could be consumed fresh, before the cheese became rock-hard through evaporative moisture loss.

Spice Cheese

Spice cheese was a rennet-coagulated cheese made by a simple uncooked, pressed, and surface-salted technology. Flavor was added by layering caraway seeds and pounded cloves in with the curd before pressing during the filling of the cheese molds. The cheeses were pressed into 20-pound (9 kg) wheels, surface-salted to develop a rind, and then "packaged" in a distinctive red coating that was applied by painting annatto coloring on the surface and then rubbing with *beistings* or colostrum, the first milk of a cow newly calved, which turned the normally yellow-orange annatto to bright red. The red coating not only improved visual appeal but also promoted a firm, smooth rind (Flint 1862). Clearly, Dutch spice cheese was a far cry from the rock-hard, insipid East Anglian skim-milk flett cheese derisively referred to as "Suffolk bang." The production of spice cheese provided both a source of cream for the lucrative butter market and a profitable value-added market for the skim milk, while freeing up other milk to be made into Edam and Gouda—two high-value whole-milk cheeses—for export.

Edam Cheese

The name Edam was first used by merchants in the German Rhineland, who called imported Dutch cheeses "Edamer" after the market city of Edam, which served as the major trade connection with the region. The name spread and came to designate all "sweet-milk" cheeses made in the north of Holland. Edam was a simple rennet-coagulated, uncooked, moderately pressed, and surface-salted cheese, not very different from Columella's aged pecorino cheese, apart from a couple of key innovations. The cheese was made from whole sweet milk (fresh from the cow), but instead of pressing the curd in cylindrical molds as in Roman times, the Dutch developed a rounded wooden press mold that enabled the curd to be pressed into 4-pound (1.8 kg) ball-shaped cheeses. Thus, Edam was free of troublesome edges and corners that might crack and chip during rough handling and thereby expose the interior to rotting. Edam's round shape was an innovation that gave these cheeses exceptional durability, enabling them to withstand physical abuse during shipping. The round shape also made it easier to pack and unload the shipping barrels used in maritime transport. Finally, the round shape minimized the surface area of the cheese relative to other geometric shapes such as cylinders or wheels, enabling these small cheeses to retain moisture longer on long hot ocean voyages and to support full flavor development. By combining a small, spherical geometry and a high salt content achieved through extended (nine- to twelve-day) brine-salting, Dutch cheesemakers struck the perfect balance between leaving too much moisture in the cheese, which increases the risk of internal rotting, and too little moisture, which prevents full ripening and flavor development.

The durability of Edam was further enhanced by scalding the pressed and salted cheese in hot whey, enabling any unevenness and roughness to be etched off to create a very smooth and compact outer rind. English cheesemakers around the end of the eighteenth century also practiced scalding in hot whey, particularly for cheese to be shipped long distances by sea (Twamley 1816). English agriculture was heavily influenced by Dutch practices by this time (Fussell 1959), and it is possible that English cheesemakers borrowed the technology for scalding from the Dutch. On the other hand, the Dutch studied the English market for cheese and indeed were producing English-style cheeses specifically for sale in England (Flint 1862); the possibility that the Dutch acquired scalding technology from the English can't be ruled out. The former seems more likely, however, because cheese production in north Holland for export increased dramatically between 1500 and 1700, and presumably the basic method for making Edam cheese, including the scalding step, was already developed by 1700, long before scalding was mentioned by English writers.

The smooth outer rind of Edam was further enhanced by the application of turnsole, a dye that had been in use since medieval times to illustrate manuscripts (Thompson and Hamilton 1933). Seeds from the plant named turnsole (*Chrozophora tinctoria*) were ground up and pressed to extract the juice. Linen cloths were then soaked in the juice, dried, and hung over a basin filled with urine, from which ammonia vapors were absorbed into the linen. The alkaline ammonia converted the turnsole dye to a violet color. Edam cheeses were rubbed with the turnsole rags impregnated with the violet dye, which imparted a dark violet color to the surface that changed to glowing red when the surface dried. The turnsole treatment was not only visually stunning but also acted as an insect repellent, protecting the rind from maggots and other pests that were so troublesome for aged cheeses. Thus, the Dutch transformed the age-old small, cylindrical, dry cheese of Roman times into a stunning, eye-catching, round, nearly indestructible whole-milk cheese that retained moisture long enough to develop outstanding aged flavor.

Gouda Cheese

Larger sweet-milk cheeses (15 to 16 pounds, or 6.8 to 7.3 kg), called Gouda, after the major market city of the same name, were made in south Holland using a different technology from Edam. Being larger in size, Gouda cheeses needed to have a lower moisture content right out of the press and greater surface area to allow for evaporation than Edam to avoid the risk of internal rotting. To accomplish this the cheesemakers in south Holland employed a process of removing the whey after cutting and stirring and scalding the curds in hot water before molding and pressing, similar to the scalding process used by Gloucester and Cheddar cheesemakers in England at the end of the eighteenth century. Again, it's not certain whether the English borrowed scalding technology from Dutch or vice versa. However, as in the north, the production of cheese for export in south Holland increased dramatically between 1500 and 1700; the basic method for making Gouda cheese, including the scalding step, was probably already in practice by 1700, long before scalding was mentioned by English writers. Gouda was made into a wheel-shaped cheese, providing greater surface area, but was pressed in rounded wooden molds to eliminate troublesome edges and corners, thus creating a more durable rind similar to Edam.

Like Edam and spice cheese, Gouda was "packaged" in a bright colorful coating. The dye was prepared by extracting color from saffron threads with vinegar, which when painted on the cheese surface dried to a very distinctive yellow color. The coating also provided protection from flies and maggots—a huge advantage for a cheese with ample surface area. Gouda cheese, made from milk fresh from the cow and scalded or washed with hot water, produced a very sweet or low-acid cheese. English cheeses also used a scalding step, but scalding in England evolved into a process of directly heating the whey without the addition of water, which altered the chemistry and ripening of the cheese. Thus, Gouda came to be characterized by a very different flavor profile from Gloucester and Cheddar. Ultimately, Gouda was so successful in the marketplace that Edam cheesemakers borrowed the washing technology from their colleagues to the south and transformed Edam cheese into a smaller version of Gouda.

Exports of Edam and Gouda continued to make essential contributions to the Dutch economy long after the "Golden Age" of the Dutch Empire had drawn to a close (de Vries 1976). During the second half of the nineteenth century the Dutch government invested heavily in improvements in dairy production and processing, including in the development of the new factory system of cheese making. In contrast with England, where the cheese factory languished, annual factory cheese production in the Netherlands by 1910 was 42.1 million pounds (19.1 million kg), exceeding farmhouse production (41.8 million pounds, or 18.9 million kg); most of this factory-made cheese was for export (Blundel and Tregear 2006). Holland went on to become arguably the most industrialized, technology-intensive, specialized, and successful (as measured by market penetration) cheese-producing country on the planet. Farmhouse cheese making, in contrast, largely disappeared from Holland until the end of the twentieth century, when a new appreciation for traditional cheeses emerged there as in so many other countries.

CHAPTER EIGHT

The Puritans, the Factory, and the Demise of Traditional Cheese Making

. . . for wee must Consider that wee shall be as a Citty upon a Hill, the eies of all people are upon us . . .

John Winthrop (1630)

John Winthrop, first governor of the Massachusetts Bay Colony and arguably one of America's founding fathers, described the new Puritan colony in Massachusetts as a City upon a Hill, a great experiment that would change the world for the better. In many respects he was right. The egalitarian notion that all men are created equal, born of Puritan Calvinist theology that all are indeed equal before an Almighty God, profoundly shaped the moral character, democratic institutions, and governing philosophy of the New England colonies and eventually the new American Republic.

The Puritans also profoundly shaped cheese making in America for centuries to come. Winthrop himself knew of cheese making firsthand: His wife, Margaret, had supervised the dairymaids at Groton manor, the Winthrops' farm in Suffolk, England. More important, the demographic makeup of the Puritan immigrants provided the foundation for vibrant commercial cheese making in the New World from the outset. The majority of the early immigrants to Massachusetts Bay came from the dairying regions of Suffolk, Essex, and Norfolk in East Anglia, and to a lesser extent from the West Country, another region in which dairying was concentrated. Also numbered among the immigrants was a strong representation from the London merchant class, who were as keen to sell cheese and butter in the New World as the London cheesemongers were to sell Puritan cheese and butter back in England, provided that suitable markets could be found. Almost immediately, the merchants and cheesemakers of the Bay Colony found the markets that they needed, and commercial cheese making took off.

There was a dark side to all of this, however. The City upon a Hill did not shine and provide refuge for all peoples. Puritan interpretation of the Bible and Calvinist theology allowed for exceptions to the universal rule that all men are created equal; the native peoples, the Indians, were not considered equal, nor were black Africans. Puritan farmers were among the first to clash with the Indians over grazing rights for their cows and pigs, conflicts that quickly escalated to large-scale hostility and efforts to dislocate and annihilate native tribes. Puritan farmers also quickly became entangled in the rapidly expanding system of human trafficking and slave labor that was centered in the West Indies and soon spread to the southern colonies of America and even to New England. Commercial butter and cheese making in New England flourished through their assimilation into the massive Atlantic economic system that bound together in mutual dependency the slave plantations of the West Indies and the southern colonies, the merchants and rum distillers of New England, and the New England farmers. This insidious synergy drove the New England economy and created enormous wealth for a privileged class of Puritans and their descendants for nearly two centuries; it also imposed unspeakable suffering on the African slaves and their descendants.

The stamp of Puritan English hard-pressed cheese making is still evident in America today in the more than 3 billion pounds (1.4 billion kg) of Cheddar cheese produced each year. Indeed, the story of cheese making in America and the legacy of the Puritans are intertwined, and it wasn't until the second half of the nineteenth century that other cheese-making traditions began to make major inroads in America. By that time the cheese factory had arrived on the scene, and American cheese making would never be same.

The Great Migration

The New England colonies were born of the turbulent sixteenth century, during which England witnessed widespread religious dissatisfaction in the form of a powerful Calvinist reform movement that swept the country. Although East Anglia was the epicenter of the reform movement, the Puritans also had strong followings in London and other port cities, particularly among the rising merchant class. Because the reformers aggressively sought to purify the Church of England of objectionable practices and theology that it had inherited from Roman Catholicism, the movement came to be known as Puritanism. Staunch opposition to the Church of England brought the Puritans into increasingly bitter conflict with the English Crown, which in turn responded with growing persecution (Kulikoff 2000).

By the start of the seventeenth century, some within the Puritan community abandoned the effort to purify the Church of England and instead endeavored to form a separate church. The English Crown, viewing this as a direct challenge to royal authority and a dangerous threat that could lead to civil war, increased the level of persecution and drove some Separatists out of England. One Separatist group eventually obtained a charter to form a colony in North America, which led to the founding of the Plymouth Colony in Massachusetts in 1620. The Pilgrims of Plymouth were poorly financed and ill prepared for life in the New World; they were not dairy farmers, or even farmers in general, and it wasn't until 1624 that dairy cows were brought to the colony from England. Nevertheless, the colony managed to survive, and in doing so fueled new aspirations among the Puritans in England for a separate church and new life (McManis 1975).

Back in England social unrest was growing, brought on by the breakup of the medieval manorial system and massive dislocation of peasants from the countryside to the urban slums. Poverty, hunger, alcoholism, crime, and moral breakdown were all on the rise in the early seventeenth century, which the Puritans viewed in apocalyptic terms. As religious persecution intensified, Puritan leaders increasingly came to view England as beyond redemption and destined to experience God's judgment and wrath, and Puritan aspirations for a New England in the New World began to take shape. Those aspirations came to fruition in 1629 when a group of influential Puritan merchants in London obtained a royal charter to create the Massachusetts Bay Colony. That spring five well-provisioned ships carrying settlers, along with thirty cows, set sail for Massachusetts and settled in Salem (Pirtle 1926). The following spring a fleet of eleven ships carrying 240 cows and 840 passengers, including John Winthrop and other leading Puritans, embarked for the Massachusetts Bay (Hurt 1994). By year's end a total of seventeen ships carrying more than a thousand settlers had arrived in Massachusetts Bay.

This was the beginning the Great Migration, the period between 1630 and 1640 when some twenty thousand Puritans immigrated to the new colony. During the years 1630 through 1633 dairy cows and other livestock arrived on almost every ship, establishing a solid foundation for dairying in the Bay Colony (Bidwell and Falconer 1941). These early imports became the breeding stock that supplied later immigrants with cattle on their arrival so that they could establish their own farms. From the outset, Puritan farms were organized around the sale of agricultural surpluses in the marketplace. Initially, the newly established farms had a captive market in the steady influx of new immigrants who needed provisioning for the first year or two until they could establish their own farms. Immigrants brought their life savings with them from England in the form of hard currency, which the colony urgently needed to pay for a host of manufactured goods that had to be imported from England (Rutman 1963). Thus, the Bay Colony prospered during its first decade through the steady infusion of new immigrants from England and their accumulated wealth.

The Massachusetts countryside posed a formidable challenge to farming, especially dairy farming. Vast virgin forests covered the entire New England landscape; open land was nonexistent except for salt-marsh lands along the coast, freshwater marshes inland, and scattered open fields that had been cleared by the Indians to raise their crops. As Puritan settlers moved inland and established villages away from the coast they cleared forest and fenced off fields to grow crops, especially wheat. In the short run, however, it was impossible to clear large tracts of pastureland suitable for livestock grazing; therefore, cows and pigs were allowed to roam freely and forage in the woods (Bidwell and Falconer 1941). As villages grew, village herd sizes also increased, and their impact on the surrounding woodlands became a source of constant friction with the neighboring Indians, who relied on the woods for hunting. The cattle drove away wild game that the Indians hunted, and they wandered into unfenced Indian cornfields and orchards, wreaking havoc. The Indians for their part hunted Puritan livestock on what they considered to be their hunting lands, infuriating Puritan farmers (Kulikoff 2000). It was only a matter of time before violence and open conflict erupted, hardening hearts on both sides into mutual distrust and hatred that soon led to war and, ultimately, the large-scale destruction and dislocation of Native Americans by European immigrants and their descendants.

The tragedy of the Indians was further compounded by their introduction to rum, the fiery distilled spirit that rose to prominence in the seventeenth century as a by-product of the vast network of West Indies sugar plantations. Having had no previous experience with alcohol, Indians easily fell prey to its addictive properties and all too often succumbed to alcoholism, poverty, and despair. For the Puritans, the sad irony is that rum became the economic lifeblood of the New England colonies for well over a century and the source of enormous wealth and prosperity. The story of cheese making in America cannot be separated from this tragic chapter of New England history.

Fatal Attraction—The West Indies

The Great Migration ended in 1640 when King Charles I of England yielded to Puritan pressure to reform both church and state. Faced with a much-improved outlook in England, Puritan migration to the New World slowed to a trickle. This devastated the fledgling economy of Massachusetts Bay, leaving farmers without a steady stream of new settlers to purchase their surplus farm produce and furnish the crucial hard currency needed to obtain manufactured goods from England. The colony's burgeoning negative balance of trade quickly led to panic and economic depression (Sprague 1967).

Over the next decade the agricultural economy of Massachusetts was forced to shift from one sustained by internal consumption to one dependent on export markets. During the early 1640s Puritan merchants developed trade relations with Spain and the Canary Islands, where the colony's wood products and wheat and other grains were in demand. By the mid-1640s exports were growing and Boston merchants were keen to establish new markets. Their chance came in 1647 when a plague struck the island of Barbados in the West Indies and ships were dispatched to Boston in search of urgently needed provisions. Boston merchants immediately responded with shipments of wheat and salted fish and beef, which marked the beginning of large-scale agricultural exports to the West Indies that would last for nearly two centuries (Rutman 1963). By 1650, only twenty years after the founding of the Bay Colony, cheese and butter had joined the growing list of provisions sent to the West Indies. Exports of cheese and butter grew rapidly after 1663, when soil exhaustion and blight caused widespread failure of wheat crops, prompting Massachusetts farmers to switch from wheat to livestock raising and dairying (Bidwell and Falconer 1941).

By this time the Puritans of Massachusetts had spread beyond the bounds of the Bay Colony. Winthrop's "City upon a Hill" proved too restrictive, theologically and socially, for some of the Puritan immigrants. Soon splinter groups either voluntarily left Massachusetts or were forced to leave, forming separate colonies to the north in New Hampshire and to the south in Rhode Island and Connecticut. This in turn expanded the reach of Puritan culture, creating an identifiable and homogeneous "New England" that combined a strong merchant class with an agricultural economy based on family farms. Cheese and butter making quickly became important components of the agricultural economies of Connecticut and Rhode Island. Boston dominated maritime trade in New England during the seventeenth century, and surplus farm products from across New England were transported to Boston for shipment to the West Indies. The constant flow of agricultural goods into Boston, in turn, attracted Atlantic shippers to the city for the provisioning of their ships, thereby creating another large market for agricultural products. Thus, farmers and merchants of early New England were mutually dependent, the farmers relying on the merchants to sell their surplus production and the merchants needing the farmers' agricultural surpluses to gain entrance to the vast Atlantic trading network that was crystallizing around sugar production in the West Indies.

The Dutch, French, and English had colonized the West Indies during the early seventeenth century. Initially, the English West Indies were settled by relatively small landholders who drew their labor force from indentured servants recruited from among London's poor to grow tobacco, ginger, indigo, and cotton. However, by midcentury great plantations specializing in the enormously profitable sugarcane began to replace all other crops. Barbados led the way in the transformation to intensive sugarcane production, followed gradually by the rest of West Indies (Sheridan 1973). As the plantations grew in size and their demand for labor increased, the supply of white indentured servants from England could not keep pace with the need and plantation owners turned to slaves kidnapped from Africa as their primary source of workers. Eventually, black slaves constituted up to 90 percent of the population of the English West Indies (Bailey 1990). Intensive production of sugarcane rendered the plantations increasingly dependent on the mainland colonies for their provisioning; New England merchants seized the opportunity, shipping ever-larger quantities of cheese, butter, and other provisions to feed the black slaves and their white overlords (Rutman 1963).

Boston merchants found in the West Indies not only profitable markets for their agricultural, fish, and wood products but also the makings of a New England "cash crop," a high-value-added item of trade that could be produced cheaply and sold dear to a market that seemed almost limitless. The opportunity centered on the massive volumes of molasses that the sugar plantations produced as a by-product of sugar refining. The most profitable use for molasses was to ferment and distill it into rum. Barbados began distilling rum as early as 1647, and during the second half of the seventeenth century New England merchants carried rum back from the West Indies for sale in the American colonies and Newfoundland, where it attained immense popularity. The merchants quickly found, however, that they could obtain raw molasses very cheaply in the West Indies, transport it back to New England, and distill it into rum at a fraction of the cost. By 1661 the Massachusetts Judiciary was compelled to issue a declaration stating that the overproduction of rum represented a menace to society, which indicates that a well-developed distilling industry was already in place in the colony by that time. The warnings evidently went unheeded, and rum distilling spread. Rhode Island's first distillery commenced operation some-time around 1684. By 1770 some 140 rum distilleries in New England were collectively turning out 5 million gallons (19 million liters) of rum annually (Bailey 1990).

With New England's entrance into the rum trade, cheese, butter, and other provisions could now be exchanged in the West Indies for molas-ses, thereby priming the economic pump of the growing rum economy. The West Indies market for New England's agricultural provisions was almost limitless, and the market for New England rum in the mainland colonies, Newfoundland, and eventually England was also immense. Thus, the slave plantations and the rum trade now afforded New England dairy farmers a very stable and lucrative market for their cheese and butter, and Massachusetts, Connecticut, and Rhode Island responded by specializing in dairying.

The most lucrative market for rum by far, however, was situated in Africa where rum had become the premier currency for purchasing African slaves for transport to the West Indies and other colonies. The sugar plantations in particular needed a constant supply of new slaves to maintain their workforce; therefore the English and Dutch established a massive trading network in the early seventeenth century that specialized in human traffick-ing. Massachusetts merchants, well provisioned with rum, entered the slave trade during the second half of the seventeenth century, but their efforts met with limited success. The English Crown had granted the English Royal African Company a monopoly on the west-African slave trade, effectively shutting out Massachusetts merchants from the African west coast where the company was active, forcing them to journey all the way to Madagascar on the east coast of Africa to barter for slaves. Still, the Massachusetts slave trade proved profitable and grew slowly. Most of the slaves were delivered to the southern colonies of America, but a few were brought back to New England. By the end of the seventeenth century, around a thousand slaves were scattered throughout the New England colonies (Greene 1968).

Two developments occurred near the end of the seventeenth century that catapulted the New England colonies into the slave trade on a much larger scale in the eighteenth century. First, Rhode Island distillers devel-oped double- and triple-distilled rums of exceptionally high alcohol content and quality. The concentrated rum could be shipped at lower cost and commanded a higher price for its excellent quality. The second development occurred in 1696 when the English government revoked the English Royal African Company's monopoly on the African slave trade, opening the door for New England merchants to access Africa's lucrative west coast. Massachusetts slave traders seized the opportunity and established a presence in the west-African trade. A few years later, Rhode Island merchants from Newport, bearing their new super-premium rum, joined Massachusetts in the west-African slave trade and quickly overtook their neighbors. Indeed, Rhode Island dominated the American slave trade throughout the eighteenth century, accounting for 60 to 90 percent of the slave trade conducted by the American colonies. In the larger scheme of things, the entire New England slave trade accounted for only a small fraction (less than 5 percent) of the approximately 4.4 million slaves who were transported from Africa to the West Indies and American colonies during the seventeenth, eighteenth, and early nineteenth centuries (Bailey 1990). Nevertheless, slave trading became a vital cog in the New England economy; Newport, Rhode Island, in particular became very wealthy as the slave capital of New England (Coughtry 1981).

The dramatic increase in New England slave trading also brought more slaves to New England. By 1715 the slave population in the New England colonies had increased to 4,150, up from 1,000 at the start of the century; by the time of the American Revolution, the number had increased to more than 16,000. The use of slave labor spread to virtually every segment of the New England economy, including agriculture, and even dairy farmers succumbed to the use of slave laborers (Bailey 1990). Whereas male slaves on dairy farms labored as herdsmen, the women slaves worked as dairymaids, continuing the age-old English custom of cheese making as strictly women's work, even among slave laborers (Berlin 1998). The most dramatic use of slaves in dairying and cheese making occurred in the Narragansett region of Rhode Island. There the acquisition of large tracts of land and wealth by a dozen or so families, coupled with the steady influx of slaves into Newport during the early eighteenth century, led to the formation of the Narragansett Plantations, great landed estates comprising thousands of acres that were worked by up to forty slaves, according to some historical accounts. The estates were located along the coastal salt-marsh lands of the Narragansett Bay and specialized in horse breeding and dairying and cheese making, both for the West Indies markets. The plantations grazed large herds of dairy cattle numbering around 100 to 150 head, and some produced as much 13,000 pounds (6,000 kg) of cheese annually, an enormous volume for the time (Miller 1934).

Cheese making in the Narragansett region already had a long history by the eighteenth century. Richard Smith and his family, who were the first Puritans to settle in Narragansett around 1637, had emigrated from the cheese-making region of Gloucestershire in England. According to family accounts, Smith's wife brought the recipe for making Cheshire cheese with her from England and established the practice in Rhode Island (Updike 1907). By 1676 Rhode Island was exporting cheese and butter to Barbados (Weeden 1910). By the eighteenth century, Narragansett cheese, also called Rhode Island cheese, was widely recognized as New England's finest cheese according to numerous accounts from the time (Miller 1934), and it was highly esteemed in Boston, even alongside imported Cheshire cheese from England (Weeden 1963). Benjamin Franklin featured Rhode Island cheese for sale in his shop in Philadelphia (Miller 1934).

Narragansett or Rhode Island cheese seems to be one the few examples of a colonial New England cheese identified by its place of origin, no doubt because of its exceptional quality and extensive export to major cities such as Boston and Philadelphia. Other New England cheeses seemed to have been hardly noticed by contemporary writers (Weeden 1963). What has not been appreciated in the past is that much, if not most, of the famous Rhode Island cheese during the eighteenth century was made by black slave women who served as the dairymaids on the plantations. One of the largest of the plantation dairies reportedly was staffed by twenty-four black dairymaid slaves who produced twelve to twenty-four cheeses a day, each cheese the size of a bushel, probably around 20 to 30 pounds (9 to 14 kg) in weight (Updike 1907).

All of the New England colonies except Rhode Island had much higher populations of male slaves than female slaves, the males being generally preferred. Rhode Island, however, with its strong emphasis on the use of female dairymaid slaves, had a singularly high ratio of female to male slaves.

Slaves also were used widely on Connecticut farms, though mostly in small numbers (one or two per farm). Interestingly, the gender distribution of slaves varied greatly among counties within Connecticut, with much higher proportions of female slaves occurring in the highly specialized dairying and cheese-making regions of Litchfield, Fairfield, and Windham Counties than elsewhere (Greene 1968). This strongly suggests that slave women may have been used widely as dairymaids in those particular counties, though this has yet to be confirmed through archival evidence. If so, slave women must have played an important role in Connecticut cheese making during the eighteenth century, which included considerable exports to the West Indies; some 150,000 pounds (68,000 kg) of cheese were exported annually from Connecticut to the West Indies during the mid-eighteenth century (Daniels 1980).

In summary, African slaves produced large amounts of cheese in Rhode Island, and probably in Connecticut as well, during the eighteenth century. Much of that cheese was then shipped to the West Indies to feed the slave population there and exchanged for molasses, which was then used to produce rum back in New England. The rum, in turn, was used to purchase slaves in Africa for transport to the West Indies, where they were traded for more molasses . . . and so the cycle continued. Rhode Island became the leader of this so-called triangular trade in the American colonies, but Massachusetts and Connecticut also participated to one extent or another. Indeed, most of the cheese produced in New England for export, whether made by black slave women or white free women, fed into this system from the mid-seventeenth century onward. The great stability and profitably of the Atlantic system encouraged many farmers in Massachusetts, Connecticut, and Rhode Island to specialize in dairy farming. Such was the attraction of the West Indies.

Cheese Technology in Colonial New England

The Puritans left England at a time when commercial cheese making was already solidly established in East Anglia and on the rise in the West Country (Gloucestershire, Berkshire, Wiltshire, and Somerset), where so many of the Puritans had originated. Therefore, Puritan colonists came well equipped with the commercial cheese-making practices of early-seventeenth-century England, which at the time was best exemplified by Cheshire cheese: uncooked (unscalded), moderately pressed, surface-salted technology. Cheshire cheese was very popular in New England and was imported from England on regular basis from the 1630s on (Weeden 1963). Cheshire was probably the most widely produced cheese in New England during the seventeenth and eighteenth centuries and continued to dominate there through the mid-nineteenth (Flint 1862).

As time passed new immigrants to New England brought the latest English cheese-making practices with them, furnishing colonial cheesemakers with an infusion of new ideas and technology from England. Therefore, it is not surprising that the development of cheese making in New England mirrored that in Old England for the most part, with one exception. The much hotter summers of New England, and the tropical heat of the West Indies, presented new technical challenges for New England cheesemakers. Exposure to high temperatures rendered the newly made cheeses susceptible to excessive weeping, drying, and cracking, as well as to unwanted fermentations that led to gas production, bloating, and undesirable flavors. Cracking at the surface was especially troublesome because it rendered the cheese highly vulnerable to maggots, a problem also faced by English cheesemakers, but to a lesser degree. New England cheesemakers must have developed innovations from the beginning to cope with the heat, but unfortunately detailed descriptions of New England cheese-making practices were not compiled until the end of the eighteenth century. Thus little is known of the sequence and timing of any early innovations.

As in England, women served as the cheesemakers in colonial New England. However, it was men at the end of the eighteenth century and beginning of the nineteenth who compiled the first detailed accounts of New England cheese-making practices. By that time farmer husbands began to recognize the growing importance of their wives' cheese- and butter-making enterprises to the overall farm economy. Just as men had infiltrated the world of the English dairymaid during the eighteenth century, men in New England now sought to systemize and improve the "secret arts" that had heretofore been handed down from mother to daughter and mistress to servant or slave (Adams 1813; Deane 1790; Hough 1793; Johnson 1801; Wood 1819). Male American writers also began to assemble recipes from English writers for Cheshire and Gloucester cheese, and later Cheddar cheese, and evidently it was around then that American cheesemakers began to use the English names of Cheshire, Gloucester, and Cheddar to identify their own cheeses.

The New England cheese-making practices that the American writers described at the end of the eighteenth century were indeed very similar to those used contemporaneously in England to make Cheshire (uncooked, pre-salted before pressing or surface-salted, high-pressure pressing) and Gloucester and Cheddar (cooked, pre-salted before pressing, high-pressure pressing). For obvious reasons, the American writers stressed various strategies for dealing with the heat. For example, uncooked, surface-salted, higher-moisture cheeses similar to Cheshire were deliberately held at warm temperatures immediately after pressing to promote "sweating," whereby the cheese exuded whey and liquid fat at the surface (Hough 1793). Sweating lowered the moisture content of the cheese, hardened up the surface, and coated the surface with a film of butteroil that acted as a protective barrier against flies and excessive surface drying and cracking. Aging the cheese in complete darkness offered another strategy to prevent maggots from infesting the cheese surface (Deane 1790).

The most important American innovation, however, was devised for cheeses similar to Gloucester and Cheddar that were cooked (scalded), pre-salted before pressing, and pressed at high pressure. The lower moisture content of these cheeses rendered them especially vulnerable to surface drying and cracking, making them highly susceptible to maggots in hot weather. To combat this, New England cheesemakers "dressed" the cheese. At first this was accomplished by simply smearing the surface repeatedly with melted whey butter (Adams 1813; Johnson 1801), but American cheesemakers soon began to wrap the cheese with cotton bandages after pressing and rubbed melted whey butter onto the bandages to create a more durable coating that protected the surface, reduced the rate of evaporation, prevented cracking, and helped retain the shape of the cheese (Stamm 1991). The dramatic rise of the cotton plantation in the southern states and cotton textile mills in New England during the early decades of the nineteenth century drastically increased the availability and reduced the cost of cotton cloth in America, which made it feasible, probably for the first time, to use greased cotton bandaging as "single service" protective wrap.

Sometimes cheeses also were scalded in hot whey before bandaging to toughen up the surface. Scalding the finished cheese in whey, smearing the cheese surface with butter, and eventually bandaging and greasing the bandage all were used in England in parallel with America, but the combined act of bandaging the cheese and impregnating it with melted butter (later melted lard) may very well have been an American innovation, born of necessity to deal with the hotter climate of America and enabled by the arrival of abundant and inexpensive cotton cloth. Thus it is perhaps not surprising that during the early 1840s when America first began exporting cheese to England, English journalists noted that American cheeses differed from English cheeses in that they were wrapped in bandaging that was "first rubbed over with paste to make it adhere firmly" (Anonymous 1842).

This turned out to be a major technological step forward, because it opened the door to "semi-rindless" and eventually "fully rindless" aged cheeses. Cheeses dressed in greased bandages required less pampering and therefore less labor during aging, retained more moisture, and were less prone to defect formation than traditional rinded cheese. Paraffin wax, a product of the petroleum refining industry, eventually replaced melted butter and lard in dressings during the second half of the nineteenth century; paraffin, in turn, was replaced by multilayer laminate plastic films, also products of petroleum industry, during the twentieth century to create truly rindless cheese. By simplifying the aging requirements, the early use of greased dressings paved the way for Cheddar cheesemakers to vastly increase their scale of production during the second half of the nineteenth century when the factory system came into operation.

The Revolutions

The American Revolution and the founding of the new Republic ushered in sweeping changes to the former British colonies. Throughout the eighteenth century the West Indies continued to serve as a major market for

New England cheese and butter. During the second half of the eighteenth century, however, North American markets expanded dramatically and eventually surpassed those of the West Indies (Bailey 1990). Around the time of the American Revolution twice as much cheese and butter was being shipped to coastal North American destinations, such as Nova Scotia and Newfoundland to the north and South Carolina and Georgia to the south, as was going to the West Indies. By that time the countryside of eastern Pennsylvania around Philadelphia and the adjacent regions of New Jersey, New York, and Delaware had become highly specialized in butter production. Philadelphia usually led the colonies in the export of butter, whereas the New England ports of Boston, Newport, and New London were the major centers for cheese exports (Oakes 1980). The large surpluses of skim milk produced in the "butter belt" around Philadelphia, along with the high concentration of immigrants from Germany that settled in eastern Pennsylvania, encouraged the production there of traditional central European fresh, acid-coagulated cheeses. Eventually, with the help of government promotional efforts aimed at stopping the widespread practice of the dumping of skim milk left over from butter making into rivers and streams, the production of cottage cheese spread during the early twentieth century. It became one of America's most popular cheeses (Pirtle 1926).

The slave trade was abolished by the United States and England in 1808, followed by slavery itself in the West Indies within two decades, bringing an end to New England's large-scale provisioning trade with the islands. However, around the same time England began importing cheese from the new American Republic. Furthermore, the growing urban centers in New England and the mid-Atlantic states, especially New York City, provided expanding markets for New England cheese (Bidwell and Falconer 1941). Thus, the demand for New England cheese continued to be strong at the dawn of the nineteenth century, despite the impending loss of the West Indies market, and would soon become stronger still because of another revolution that was unfolding in America—the Industrial Revolution, which centered on the New England textile industry.

The invention of the cotton gin in 1791 vastly reduced the cost of producing raw cotton for sale to textile manufacturers. This clever invention transformed the American South into a massive and highly specialized cotton-growing region. The rapidity and scale of the transformation was remarkable. In 1790 the United States produced 1.5 million pounds (680,000 kg) of cotton; by 1800, production had risen to 35 million pounds (15.9 million kg); by 1820, 160 million pounds (72.6 million kg); and by 1860, 2.3 *billion* pounds (1 billion kg). The explosive growth of southern cotton plantations breathed new life into the American institution of slavery and created large new markets for northern provisions, including New England cheese, thereby continuing the long-standing complicity of New England cheesemakers with institutionalized slavery (Bailey 1990).

The cotton revolution of the South, in turn, spurred on the Industrial Revolution in New England. Initially, southern cotton was exported to England to fuel the advanced textile industry that had developed during England's own industrial revolution of the eighteenth century. However, during the first decades of the nineteenth century, a number of prominent New England merchants who had amassed great wealth through the rum and slave trades of the eighteenth century invested in new industrial textile manufacturing equipment and infrastructure: water-powered yarn-spinning machines, power looms, and mill facilities. These well-capitalized New England mills produced cotton textiles, the demand for which was virtually inexhaustible. Consequently, the number and size of New England textile factories grew quickly and the mills soon became the backbone of the southern New England economy.

The booming textile mills, in turn, created new employment opportunities and spurred the growth of mill towns, which shifted the demographics of southern New England from rural farming communities to urban centers and created new local markets for New England cheese and butter. Even more important from the standpoint of nineteenth-century American cheese making, the dawn of textile manufacturing marked the end of the homespun age. Now farm women no longer needed to spend long hours spinning and weaving to produce clothing for their families. This meant that they had significantly more time for other pursuits. Women on the dairy farms in southern New England responded by increasing their production of cheese to take advantage of growing markets, both local and distant, while the men increased the sizes of the dairy herds. Thus dairying and cheese making in New England became ever more specialized and commercialized during the first half of the nineteenth century (Bidwell 1921). By 1850 annual cheese production in Massachusetts and Connecticut had increased to 7.1 million and 5.4 million pounds (3.2 and 2.4 million kg), respectively. Amazingly, however, this represented only about 12 percent of the nation's total cheese production: By that time cheesemakers had been leaving New England for almost a century in search of new land and new opportunity, moving north and west. By 1850 New York had become the top-producing cheese state, followed by Ohio and Vermont, with Massachusetts and Connecticut rounding out the top five states. Cheese making in southern New England was indeed in decline and soon would be rendered all but extinct by new competition from the north and especially the west.

The Exodus

By the middle of the eighteenth century, southern New England began to experience a shortage of available farmland to support new farms due to population growth, prompting a growing number of farm families from Connecticut and Massachusetts to move north into New Hampshire and Vermont and west into New York State. This migration remained little more than a trickle during the turbulent and dangerous years of the French and Indian Wars and the Revolutionary War, but surged to a torrent after the American Revolution (Kindstedt 2005).

With the opening of the Erie Canal in 1825, which linked Lake Erie to the Hudson River, there was no turning back from the westward movement of American cheese making or American agriculture in general. The Erie Canal provided the crucial transportation link between the vast fertile farmlands of the Upper Midwest that border the southern shores of the Great Lakes and the urban markets of East Coast and beyond. America's spacious Midwest contained seemingly limitless expanses of high-quality farmland. Furthermore, America had no major North American adversaries to contend with, no enemies capable of disrupting the long supply lines between the food-producing regions of the Midwest and the food-consuming regions of the East Coast. Thus, once suitable transportation links were in place there seemed little reason to preserve agricultural production

Figure 8-1. Cheese production in the United States during 1849. Each dot represents 200,000 pounds (about 91,000 kg) of cheese produced. By 1849 New York was the number one cheese-producing state, with Ohio ranked second. Cheese making would continue to move west during the second half of the nineteenth century. (Source: Bidwell and Falconer 1941, figure 101, p. 423; used by permission of the Carnegie Institution for Science)

capability back east, except for perishable foods that still needed to be produced locally.

The midwestern heartland, therefore, was quickly opened up to commercial agriculture, first through the construction of a network of canals during the 1830s and 1840s that connected the interior to the Great Lakes, followed a decade later by the construction of railroad networks that crisscrossed the Midwest and connected to all points east (Bidwell and Falconer 1941). By 1850 cheese making had decisively shifted west (figure 8-1) along with the production of other nonperishable commodities, a trend that has yet to be reversed in America.

The distribution of cheese production shown in figure 8-1 is instructive on two counts. First, it mirrors the westward movement of New England cheesemakers. Yankee cheesemakers from southern New England and their descendants progressively moved up the Hudson and Mohawk River Valleys, followed the course of the Erie Canal westward to Lake Erie, and then continued westward through New York, Ohio, and beyond along the southern shores of the Great Lakes (Kindstedt 2005). Even more telling is the lack of cheese making in the southern states. Although some small-scale cheese making was carried out by slaves on the southern plantations during the eighteenth century (Wright 2003), the transformation to intense cotton growing throughout much of the South during the nineteenth century put an end to most food production on the plantations. Like the sugar plantations of the West Indies, the southern cotton plantations looked to the North for their provisioning.

Ironically, the settling of the Upper Midwest by Yankee cheesemakers brought an end to cheese making in southern New England. Cheese now flowed east from western New York, Ohio, and beyond, as well as from northern New England, making it impossible for cheesemakers in southern New England to compete. Dairy farmers in southern New England responded by switching to butter production during the nineteenth century (butter being a more perishable product than cheese), and eventually to the production of highly perishable liquid milk to supply the growing urban populations (Bidwell 1921). Dairy farming ultimately withered in southern New England, as did many other agricultural pursuits along the East Coast, victims of the vast productive farmlands to the west and the massive transportation networks that connected East to West.

The westward exodus of agriculture also marked the beginning of the separation of large segments of the American population from the farms that produced the food they consumed each day. The limited farming that remained in southern New England consisted mostly of perishable specialty crops such as fresh fruits and vegetables that could not be transported long distances. This disconnect between food producer and consumer in America was destined to grow ever wider after 1851, when the opening of first cheese factory ushered in the age of factory production and economies of scale into American agriculture.

The Cheese Factory and Economies of Scale

The Industrial Revolution that sparked New England's textile industry during the early nineteenth century also brought changes to the farmhouse dairy. The invention and mass production of new cheese vats, utensils, and other labor-saving equipment made it possible for dairy-farm families to produce larger volumes of cheese with greater consistency, enabling dairy farms that had room for expansion to increase their herd sizes and cheese-production capacities (McMurry 1995). Hence, during the first few decades of the nineteenth century farms with forty or more cows became common in the spacious countryside of New York State (Stamm 1991). The early nineteenth century also witnessed the formation of American agricultural societies that served as clearinghouses for the exchange of agricultural information and best practices, and as conduits for newly emerging scientific knowledge—the applications of which were beginning to percolate down to the practical world of farming (Bidwell 1921). Women still performed the lion's share of cheese making in America, but men, through their better access to education and the growing field of science and technology, gradually acquired and gained control over the cheese-making knowledge that women had accumulated and perfected through the generations. Thus, the early nineteenth century marked the beginning of a process that eventually stripped farm women of their historic and esteemed role as family cheese-maker and mistress of the dairy (McMurry 1995). A similar pattern of male encroachment and gender dislocation in butter making occurred in the region surrounding eastern Pennsylvania during the nineteenth century (Jensen 1988).

The advent of the cheese factory in the mid-nineteenth century propelled American cheese making into a whole new era. Larger scales of production had already pushed cheese making on the larger farms out of the farmhouse kitchen and into separate cheese-making facilities or cheese houses that were still located on the farm. The factory went a step farther and removed cheese making from the farm altogether, transferring production to central facilities dedicated to processing milk from multiple farms. In 1851, two dairy farmers from Rome, New York, Jesse Williams and his son George, became the first to implement the cheese factory concept by building dedicated facilities for making and aging cheese that were separate from their two farms and designed to handle the milk from both of their herds, as well as that from several neighboring farms. During its first season of operation the Williams factory produced more than 100,000 pounds (45,000 kg) of stirred-curd Cheddar cheese, some five times the amount produced by a good-sized farmstead operation of the time. The resulting savings in labor, the ability to buy supplies in bulk at lower cost, and the improved uniformity in cheese quality rendered the Williams's experiment an immediate success that was soon replicated as new factories sprang up across the New York countryside (Stamm 1991).

Almost overnight the factory would come to dominate cheese making in America, and overwhelmingly the new American factories would produce one cheese variety: Cheddar. This was a major shift from the eighteenth century when Cheshire was the most widely produced cheese in New England. During the first half of the nineteenth century, New England and New York State cheesemakers continued to produce large amounts of Cheshire cheese, though by midcentury Cheddar production was on the rise (Flint 1862).

Two key developments in England helped to accelerate America's transformation from Cheshire to Cheddar production. First, around the same time that the Williams factory commenced operation Joseph Harding was gaining notoriety in England for his groundbreaking work in applying scientific principles to Cheddar-cheese making. Harding's scientific approach incorporated defined schedules for time, temperature, and acidity at various steps in the cheese-making process, which opened the door to unprecedented control over cheese quality and consistency (Cheke 1959). It was a huge step forward technologically, and one that caught the attention of Xerxes Willard, a professor and representative of the American Dairyman's Association who visited Harding in England in 1866. Willard brought Harding's Cheddar system back to America and championed its adoption by American cheese factories (Blundel and Tregear 2006). The implementation of Harding's scientific principles in turn gave the new Cheddar factories a robust competitive boost.

Second, and even more important, by this time Cheddar had displaced Cheshire as the preeminent cheese in England. Cheddar now commanded the highest price in the London market, and the English demand for Cheddar was enormous. Hence, the combination of Harding's striking advancements in Cheddar technology and the ascendancy of Cheddar as the leading cheese variety on the London market stimulated sweeping changes in American cheese making that would position Cheddar cheese to become the world's most widely produced variety.

The arrival of the cheese factory also came at a crucial time in American history that helped to kick-start its phenomenal success. The factory system had been in operation for ten years and was just beginning to gain steam when the Civil War broke out. The mass exodus of men from northern farms to fight for the Union army left women on the farms with the over-whelming burden of doing it all . . . raising the crops, herding the cows, milking the cows, making the cheese, selling the cheese, raising the chil-dren, cooking the meals, keeping the home. . . . The local cheese factory provided overstressed farm women with much needed relief from the seven-day-a-week burden of making cheese. The urgency of the times thus made it easier for farm women to make what must have been heart-wrenching decisions in many cases to give up the time-honored profession of cheese making (Kindstedt 2005).

Ironically, at the same time that women were leaving cheese making, the market for cheese had never been better. England was in the midst of a population explosion and unable to feed its own people. Therefore, during the 1840s England reduced tariffs on food products in an effort to stimu-late food imports. This in turn opened the floodgates to American cheese imports during the 1850s. The outbreak of the American Civil War made the English market even more attractive because English merchants paid for goods in gold currency, not American paper currency that was becom-ing worthless through rampant wartime inflation. Consequently, new US cheese factories sprang up overnight, and exports to England rose from 5 million pounds (2.3 million kg) in 1859 to 50 million pounds (23 million kg) in 1863 (McMurry 1995). Production of factory cheese skyrocketed even as on-farm production plummeted (figure 8-2). This trend continued after the Civil War ended and came to be viewed as "progress" by the increasingly male-dominated, factory-dominated cheese industry (McMurry 1995).

Cheese exports to England continued to rise after the war, exceeding 100 million pounds (45 million kg) by 1874 (Blundel and Tregear 2006). Overwhelmingly it was Cheddar cheese that America sent to England. Harding's improved technology helped the new American Cheddar-cheese factories attain great competitive advantages by operating at ever-larger scales, thereby lowering the unit cost of production. American dominance in the English market seemed secure in the early 1870s, and back home in

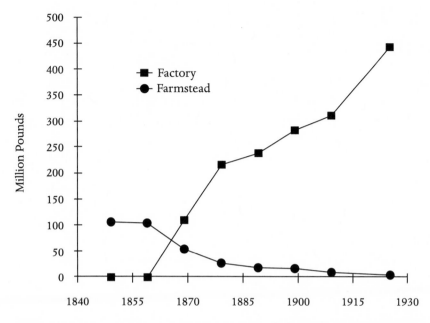

Figure 8-2. Annual production of farmstead and factory cheese in the United States from 1848 to 1925. The factory system for cheese making was introduced in 1851 and quickly came to dominate the US cheese industry. (After Kindstedt 2005; adapted from Pirtle 1926)

the United States domestic demand for Cheddar cheese also rose dramatically as waves of new immigration fueled explosive population growth and urban development. The future seemed bright indeed.

There was a dark side to all of this, however. Though the demand for American-made cheese climbed steadily during the second half of the nineteenth century, production consistently outpaced demand, which placed downward pressure on cheese prices. Cheese factories struggled to make ends meet and many, following in the footsteps of their East Anglian forebears some 250 years earlier, began to skim cream from their cheese milk in order to produce both butter and cheese from the same milk. The temptation to maximize the removal of cream while still producing a salable cheese was enormous, and cheese quality suffered (Stamm 1991).

An even more ominous development emerged in 1869 with the invention of oleomargarine in France. The same technology that enabled milkfat in butter to be replaced by a cheaper source of fat such as lard in the making of oleomargarine could also be used to produce "filled cheese" in which the natural fat from milk was replaced by lard. Production of filled cheese began in New York State in 1871, and soon immense quantities of filled cheese were made at many factories (Stamm 1991). Both skim and filled cheeses were exported to England, generally under the guise of genuine cheese; thus it did not take long for the reputation of American cheese to plummet. Exports to England, which peaked at 148 million pounds (67 million kg) in 1881, declined precipitously thereafter, becoming negligible by the turn of the twentieth century (Pirtle 1926). Although Congress enacted labeling requirements for filled cheese in 1896, the damage had already been done and was irreparable; Canada, and then New Zealand and Australia replaced America as England's main suppliers of Cheddar cheese. The United States would never regain a major presence in the English market for Cheddar.

The regulatory reforms of the late nineteenth century put an end to the fraud and blatant quality lapses of skim and filled cheeses. However, over-production leading to downward pressure on prices continued to plague America's cheese industry during the twentieth century. Factories, in turn, lowered production costs by increasing plant capacities to reap economies of scale, by reducing labor through automation, and by maximizing cheese yield (squeezing the maximum amount of cheese out of each gallon of milk). The key to survival became least-cost production while still producing a salable product; companies that failed to jump on this treadmill largely fell by wayside. Yet amazingly, even though an explosion of scientific knowledge and engineering advances during the twentieth century led to dramatic reductions in the cost of production, they were never large enough to adequately offset the accompanying decline in cheese prices. Cheese factories continued to experience relentless pressure to lower their costs of production through economies of scale, automation, and yield enhancement.

The large changes in manufacturing practices that enabled lower-cost production inevitably affected the character and quality of America's Cheddar cheese. Pasteurization and standardization, technologies that factories used to gain control over the microbiology and chemistry (fat and protein contents) of their milk, drastically reduced the incidence of quality defects in factory cheeses, but also made it more difficult to achieve the full range of flavor and character that are evident in the finest Cheddar cheeses made by traditional methods. American Cheddar became more defect-free and consistent in quality than ever before, but also less intense and complex in flavor.

This trend toward blander flavor accelerated as cheese companies homed in on yield enhancement to reduce unit costs. One of the most effective ways to increase cheese yield is to retain as much water in the cheese as possible. However, as the moisture content of Cheddar cheese increases, the amount of aging time that the cheese can withstand before defects set in generally declines. Therefore, in order to reap the higher yield of higher-moisture cheese, aging times had to be shortened. From the industry perspective, this was a win–win proposition because shorter aging meant significant savings in the cost of aging, as well as the higher yields gained through higher moisture retention. Bottom line: Industrial Cheddar cheese-makers came under considerable economic pressure during the second half of the twentieth century to lower the cost of production by increasing cheese moisture contents and decreasing the length of aging, conditions that favored less intense and less complex cheese flavor.

For the most part, the American public didn't seem to notice. Production and per-capita consumption of Cheddar cheese climbed steadily during the second half of the twentieth century, reaching new records year after year. Cheddar continued to eclipse all other cheeses until 2001, when mozzarella moved into the number one position. Mozzarella, of course, is a relative newcomer to the American scene, brought by Italian immigrants during the nineteenth and early twentieth centuries. Until the middle of the twentieth century, however, mozzarella largely remained an ethnic specialty of modest production. After World War II, the highly mobile, fast-paced suburban culture that unfolded ever so quickly across large swaths of America, with its growing appetite for fast food, provided the perfect context for Americans to embrace the humble ethnic pizza restaurant and transform it into a massive empire fueled by an ever-larger mozzarella industry.

Mozzarella cheesemakers were quickly confronted with the economic realities that Cheddar manufacturers had been battling for a century: over-production leading to downward pressure on cheese prices. For the most part, mozzarella factories had no option but to get larger to gain economies of scale, become more automated to reduce labor costs, and boost cheese yields by retaining more water in their cheese. By the start of the twenty-first century some of the cheese used on pizza had changed to the extent that it no longer met the legal definition of mozzarella cheese and was labeled with the nebulous term pizza cheese. Again, for the most part the American public didn't seem to notice. Production and per-capita consumption of mozzarella and pizza cheese climbed steadily during the second half of the twentieth century and through the first decade of the twenty-first century, reaching new records year after year.

Other immigrant groups brought their own ethnic cheeses with them to America. Besides mozzarella, Italian immigrants brought Parmesan and ricotta; German immigrants brought Limburger, Muenster, and fresh acid-coagulated types; Swiss immigrants brought Emmental and Gruyère; French immigrants brought Camembert, Brie, Neufchâtel, and cream cheese, among others (Apps 1998; Sernett 2011; Stamm 1991). Some of these ethnic cheeses like Swiss (Emmental), cottage, and cream cheese grew into very large industries, in part because technologies were developed that enabled these cheeses to be produced on very large scales at low cost. Cheeses that couldn't be scaled up easily largely disappeared from the American scene by the second half of the twentieth century.

Thus, as the twentieth century drew to a close, cheese production in America stood at historic highs, topping 9 billion pounds (4 billion kg) annually—the overwhelming majority of which was produced in very large manufacturing facilities. This isn't the entire story, however. Against all odds, farmstead and artisan cheese making returned to America during the last three decades of the twentieth century. A new appreciation of traditional cheeses emerged among a growing segment of the American public that challenged the notion that mass production is the only future for cheese making in America (Kindstedt 2005).

This rebirth has been built on the willingness of enthusiasts to accept prices for artisan cheeses that are often two, three, five, even ten times higher than those of conventional mass-produced products. Whether this model is sustainable in the long run remains to be seen. What is crystal clear, however, is that the economics of small-scale traditional cheese making are inescapable. Traditional cheeses are expensive to produce, and somebody will have to pay if they are to survive; either the consumer alone or the consumer in partnership with the public in the form of friendly government policies that encourage traditional cheese making. Will traditional cheeses in America simply be an elitist pastime of the rich who are willing and able to pay $30 for a pound of cheese? Will a growing segment of middle-class Americans choose to limit their discretionary spending in other areas in order to regularly purchase expensive but exquisite traditional cheeses? Will (and should) state and federal governments enact policies to encourage traditional cheese making and help bring down the cost? That history is yet to be written.

CHAPTER NINE

The Cultural Legacy of Cheese Making
in the Old and New Worlds

In 1994 the United States and 116 other nations signed the Uruguay Round Agreement under the General Agreement on Tariffs and Trade (GATT) to reduce trade barriers and to create more comprehensive and enforceable world trade rules. A landmark provision of the agreement was the creation of the World Trade Organization (WTO) to enforce the new rules. The WTO represented a major milestone for the global trade movement; member states were now subject to a common set of standards that theoretically leveled the playing field and were enforceable by law under the WTO. One problem remained, however . . . how to agree on the details of a common set of standards. The Uruguay Round established the framework for the agreement, but the thorny details in areas such as intellectual property rights and product safety regulations were left for future working groups to hammer out in committee proceedings. More than a decade and a half later that process is still being played out over the issues involving cheese and other foods; it has been a painfully slow process that has been hindered at every turn by the cultural legacy of Europe's and America's very different food histories.

Protected Designation of Origin

Much cheese is traded internationally, and soon after the Uruguay Round Agreement went into effect friction between the United States and the European Union surfaced over the standards for intellectual property relating to cheese. At issue was the section of the agreement that offered comprehensive global standards for the protection of geographical indications. A *geographical indication* (GI) is a label of origin indicating that a particular food or beverage is special or unique in quality because of its place of origin. The name of a food that acquires a GI is also unique under GATT and cannot be used for products produced outside the geographic area for which the GI is granted. For example, a GI granted to Roquefort cheese means that the name Roquefort cannot be used for cheese produced outside of Roquefort, France. The purpose of GIs is to prevent the public from being misled into believing that a product originates from somewhere other than its true place of origin, and to protect the genuine food from copies produced elsewhere that unfairly use the same name (Barham 2003).

The agreement contains an exemption, however, for GIs that have become "generic" terms—that is, terms that have come to describe a type of product rather than a place of origin. For example, although the name Cheddar originally designated cheese that was made in the region around Cheddar, England, the term now commonly refers to a style of cheese, not a place of origin; it has become a generic term that is no longer eligible for protection as a GI. According to the agreement, individual WTO member countries can decide for themselves whether a particular term is eligible for GI protection or has become generic. The exemption clause quickly became a flashpoint.

Industry leaders and trade negotiators in Europe and America viewed cheese and GIs differently, their perceptions having been shaped by very different histories. From the American perspective, homesick European immigrants had brought the names and technologies of their favorite cheeses to America from the beginning. There were no legal restrictions on intellectual property at the time, no GIs, thus immigrant cheesemakers were free to continue using the names and recipes that they had used in Europe. Many did, and some of their cheeses eventually achieved widespread popularity. Therefore, the American side argued that many of the traditional cheese names brought to America long ago had become generic over time and no longer referred to a place of origin, but rather to a style of cheese that could be produced anywhere. Entire industries in America had been producing cheese under European names such as Cheddar, Emmental (or Swiss), Parmesan, and mozzarella for many decades, even centuries, and American companies had invested heavily in branding under those names, thereby developing their own intellectual property that was legally protected under the US trademark system. Furthermore, these terms have become an integral part of the legal and regulatory infrastructure that governs cheese making in America. For example, many traditional cheese names were incorporated into the US Federal Standards of Identity for cheese more than half a century ago.

In light of all of this, the American cheese industry and US trade negotiators considered it outrageous that attempts were now being made at the WTO level to restrict the use of traditional cheese names to the regions of Europe where those particular styles of cheese first originated, thus reversing many decades of history. That, however, is exactly what the European Union was seeking to achieve through the GATT standards that govern intellectual property (Anonymous 2003).

The European Union viewed the names of their traditional cheeses quite differently. Europe had a long history with GIs dating back at least to the fifteenth century when Charles VI granted exclusive use of the name Roquefort to cheese made in Roquefort, France. Underpinning the EU's commitment to GIs is the concept of *terroir,* a French term loosely translated as "taste of place" (Trubek 2008). At the heart of terroir is the notion that different geographic regions possess unique environments that uniquely influence the quality and character of the foods produced in each region. Differences may result from a variety of factors such as soil, climate, and topography, as well as the traditional technology and practices developed by the local population over long periods of occupation that were delicately fine-tuned to the local environment (Barham 2003).

Thus, Europeans tend to view their traditional cheeses as one of a kind, products of a unique place of origin where the actions of local cheesemakers have been sculpted by the surrounding environment over centuries to arrive at traditional recipes and practices. The pastures, local animal breeds, environmental microflora, temperature and humidity conditions, topological and geological features, and so forth all contribute to the uniqueness of local traditional cheeses. Such cheese may be imitated but never truly duplicated outside of the region of origin. Therefore, the names of traditional cheeses, like the cheeses themselves, are unique and should never be duplicated. Hence the need for GIs.

The first national system for GIs, the Appellation d'Origine Contrôlée (AOC), was established in France for wines in 1919 and later extended to other foods, including cheeses. Roquefort was the first cheese to be granted AOC status in 1925. In 1992 the EU created a Europe-wide system of GIs modeled after the French AOC system, referred to as Protected Designation of Origin (PDO). Cheeses that are granted PDO status must be produced within a defined geographic region by a prescribed "traditional" cheese-making technology, although some of the highly automated high-tech processing lines and robotic labor-saving devices that are used in the making of some PDO cheeses render the latter provision somewhat meaningless. Currently more than 150 traditional cheeses have been granted PDO status. Not surprisingly, the number of PDO cheeses is generally greater in countries such as France, Italy, Spain, and Greece that retained robust local peasant agriculture into the twentieth century, and where it has persisted to the present, though in weakened form and now fighting for survival. In contrast, countries such as England, the Netherlands, and Denmark that developed specialized commercial agriculture and industrialized cheese making during the late nineteenth and twentieth centuries, generally have fewer PDO cheeses, and those that do exist are usually the result of the revival in traditional cheese making that occurred there, as in America, near the end of the twentieth century.

Although PDO restrictions are enforceable by law within the EU, the Uruguay Round Agreement allows countries outside the EU to ignore the PDO if they determine that the cheese name has become generic. Even within the EU some cheese names are considered generic, such as the terms Cheddar, Gouda, and Edam; others such as Asiago and feta have been granted PDO status in Europe but are considered generic in America. However, the EU has been working tirelessly to eliminate the generic exemption and extend PDO restrictions globally. If the EU has its way, many cheese names that are used routinely by cheesemakers in America will become off-limits for cheese produced in America, and the US industry is dead-set against that happening.

Even more alarming from the American standpoint is the possibility that PDO protection will be extended to names that were once considered generic even within the EU. For example, in 1996 the EU granted PDO status to the name Parmigiano-Reggiano for the genuine Parmesan-style cheese produced in the Parma and Reggio region of northern Italy. However, an enormous amount of cheese labeled Parmesan had been produced in other parts of Europe for many years, so several European countries, especially Germany, considered the term Parmesan to be generic, just as the United States and many other countries outside Europe consider Parmesan to be a generic term. Nevertheless, in 2008 the European Court of Justice ruled that the PDO for Parmigiano-Reggiano also protects the term Parmesan (Anonymous 2010b). Therefore, companies producing Parmesan cheese in Europe outside the PDO region had to rename their products. Similarly, the European Court awarded the term *feta* PDO status over the objections of European countries such as France and Denmark, which produced enormous amounts of feta cheese and considered the term *feta* to be generic. It is radical court decisions such as these that have Americans worried that the European courts may gradually reinterpret other PDOs to include other cheese names that were once considered generic in the EU, such as Cheddar, mozzarella, Brie, Camembert, Swiss, Gouda, and Edam, among others. If that happens, and if PDO status receives global recognition under the WTO, Europe will control the exclusive rights to the names of almost all of the economically important cheeses of the world. In other words, the vast majority of the cheese produced in the United States will have to be relabeled with fanciful names instead of the names that have been used historically. "Vermont Cheddar," for example, will have to be relabeled "Vermont Delight" or some other silly designation, despite the long and proud history of Vermont Cheddar cheese.

Because the economic implications of global PDO enforcement are staggering, a complex chess game is being played out between the EU and America over intellectual property rights. What makes the dispute so intractable and difficult to solve through simple rational compromise are the historical and cultural, and therefore emotional, elements that are vested in the dispute. For the United States, the names of traditional cheeses are simply a link to America's European heritage from the distant past. The names no longer mean what they once did; long ago they were legally transferred to the

US and molded there into vibrant industries with identities all their own. America has its own proud traditions with cheese, forged over centuries. Under these circumstances, Europe has no legal or historical justification to claim exclusive ownership of cheese terminology, only arrogance and self-interest. Even the author, who deeply admires traditional European cheeses and acknowledges the need to protect their identity in the marketplace, and who strongly supports the rural development goals of the PDO system, becomes riled when the future of Vermont Cheddar cheese is called into question. Emotion can be a powerful roadblock to compromise.

In Europe, however, traditional cheeses and other traditional foods still occupy a place in the working landscape and local culture of many regions, still form the basis for local cuisine and cultural traditions, and still contribute to local, regional, and even national identity, and ethnic pride. PDO legislation is viewed as a long overdue means to redress the abuses of past history and return to Europe its rightful cultural and intellectual property. For Europeans the issue has attained a high level of urgency because traditional cheese making there has come under intense economic stress for the same reasons that traditional cheeses all but disappeared in America. Protection of traditional names is viewed in Europe as a vehicle for economic development, a means to differentiate and add value to traditional European cheeses in the marketplace; it also is viewed as a means for preserving cultural continuity (Barham 2003).

Emotions run high on both sides of the Atlantic because both economics and culture are involved. So far European efforts to extend PDO protection globally have failed, but the end is nowhere in sight, and the Americans have their work cut out for them. Indeed, the EU's latest strategy, to inject PDO restrictions into international trade through the back door of bilateral free-trade agreements, represents a new and troubling development from the American perspective (Anonymous 2010b).

Raw Milk and Cheese Safety

Europe's efforts to extend PDO protection globally directly overlap with another area of friction with the United States over the safety regulations that govern cheese, specifically as they relate to the use of raw (unpasteurized) milk. A requirement for virtually all PDO cheeses is that they be made from raw milk, as has been practiced traditionally from time immemorial. In general, the EU has a strong commitment to raw-milk cheeses. The US, on the other hand, has been moving in the opposite direction, toward eliminating raw milk from cheese making, ostensibly to improve product safety. Once again, the confluence of history, culture, and economics has turned this into an emotionally charged, high-stakes issue.

US regulations governing raw-milk cheese date back to 1949 when the Federal Standards of Identity for cheese were enacted. According to the Federal Standards, ten specific cheeses including mozzarella, cottage, Monterey Jack, and cream cheese must be made from pasteurized milk. Other cheese varieties can made from raw milk provided that the cheese is aged for at least sixty days at a minimum temperature of 35°F (1.6°C), what has come to be known as the sixty-day rule. Back in 1949, sixty days of aging was viewed as a reasonable safeguard against food poisoning, the presumption (based largely on previous experience) being that food-poisoning organisms were unlikely to survive in cheese longer than sixty days in high enough numbers to cause problems.

As the second half of the twentieth century progressed, however, the cheese industry increasingly came to view the sixty-day rule as inadequate. Large cheese companies were under intense economic pressure to pursue ever-greater economies of scale. Factories grew to immense capacities, often producing hundreds of thousands of pounds of cheese each day. Cheese making had become very unforgiving: A single day's lapse in product quality and consistency was devastating financially; a single day's lapse in safety was catastrophic. Cheese making at this scale required perfect control over all aspects of the process, and pasteurization came to be viewed as essential to cheese quality, consistency, and safety.

Even as factories massively increased their scales of production, however, small artisan cheesemakers began to spring up in America during the 1970s and early 1980s. The artisans even formed their own grassroots association, the American Cheese Society, in 1983 under the leadership of Cornell professor Frank V. Kosikowski (Kindstedt 2005). These new artisan cheesemakers and their supporters were passionately committed to traditional handmade practices, the use of raw milk, and the making of European cheese varieties that were either new to America or had long since disappeared. They were particularly interested in traditional washed-rind, bloomy-rind, and natural-rind cheeses, cheeses that carry much higher risks of food poisoning than the hard aged varieties such as Cheddar, Swiss, and Parmesan. The conventional cheese industry viewed this new artisan movement as a recipe for disaster, the gateway to an onslaught of food-poisoning outbreaks that would erode consumer confidence in all cheeses.

In 1985 a cheese-borne outbreak of *Listeria monocytogenes*, a deadly new pathogen that had just emerged on the scene, placed raw-milk cheese under the spotlight. The outbreak, which occurred mostly in California, involved 152 cases of listeriosis, and caused fifty-two deaths, was one of the largest cheese outbreaks in the United States and received national media coverage. The source of the outbreak was Mexican-style soft cheese (queso-fresco), which by law must be made from pasteurized milk; however, an investigation of the factory that produced the tainted cheese suggested that improper pasteurization and the mixing of raw and pasteurized milk likely contributed to the contamination (Altekruse et al. 1998; Painter and Slutsker 2007). Even though the tainted cheese should have been produced from properly pasteurized milk, the alleged link to raw milk put all raw-milk cheeses in the spotlight and on the defensive, unfairly so.

George Reinbold, an eminent cheese researcher and former Iowa State University professor, articulated the industry's greatest fears during a 1986 seminar hosted by the National Cheese Institute (NCI), the powerful trade association that represents large cheesemakers in America: "Anyone using raw milk is rolling dice loaded against themselves" (Anonymous 1986). Reinbold was highly respected in the industry, and his alarming assessment of raw-milk cheese making became an urgent call to action. Soon after, the National Cheese Institute commissioned a blue-ribbon panel of scientists from the University of Wisconsin to review the safety aspects of cheese and develop recommendations to enhance safety. The panel published its findings in 1990 and recommended that all milk for cheese making be subjected to either pasteurization or, at a minimum, a heat treatment of 148°F (64.4°C) for sixteen seconds, a time/temperature combination known as *thermization* that is slightly less severe than legal pasteurization, but almost equally effective in destroying pathogens (Johnson et al. 1990a, b, c). Thermization was recommended as an alternative to pasteurization because it allows for fuller and more rapid flavor development than pasteurization in some aged cheeses.

Around this same period, several research studies were published demonstrating conclusively that sixty days of aging does not guarantee that pathogens will die off in a number of different cheeses. Thus, pressure began to mount for the FDA to change the standards that had been in place since 1949 but were now viewed as inadequate. Mandatory pasteurization or thermization seemed to be a simple solution to the dilemma: The science behind the thermal destruction of pathogens was clear and uncontroversial, the equipment readily available, and the process easy to oversee and enforce from a regulatory inspection point of view. Moreover, the cheese industry was solidly in favor of it. Indeed, it seemed the ideal solution, and by the early 1990s a ban on raw-milk cheese making increasingly came to be viewed as inevitable.

Meanwhile, on the international scene the Codex Alimentarius working group, referred to as the Codex Committee, began working out the details of international food-safety regulations under the Uruguay Round Agreement. The committee reached a consensus in 1998 on new safety standards that included the following wording:

> "From raw material production to the point of consumption, the products covered by this standard should be subject to a combination of control measures, which may include, for example, pasteurization, and these should be shown to achieve the appropriate level of public health protection."
>
> (Quoted in Anonymous 1999)

The American side was pleased, having achieved everything that it wanted: the right of individual countries to decide for themselves what constitutes the appropriate level of public-health protection; the option to include pasteurization in national safety standards; and the option to incorporate new technologies that may become available in the future (for example, irradiation treatment), so long as they achieve the appropriate level of public-health protection. The FDA now seemed well positioned to respond to industry calls for new safety regulations and satisfy the new Codex language by replacing the sixty-day rule with mandatory pasteurization.

It was within this context that rumors began to circulate that the FDA was about to make regulatory changes that would likely include mandatory pasteurization. The American Cheese Society (ACS) became alarmed and retained the services of Marsha Echols, an attorney who specialized in food law, to act as a liaison with the FDA and to keep the ACS apprised of regulatory developments. In an electrifying presentation at the 1999 annual meeting of the ACS, Echols reported that the FDA was indeed reviewing the cheese safety regulations and that she had been told that "FDA is just waiting for an outbreak" to ban raw-milk cheeses (Anonymous 1999). The end of raw-milk cheese in America seemed imminent, and the mood at the annual meeting turned to a combination of somber discouragement and fierce defiance.

ACS members weren't the only ones concerned about the signals emanating from the FDA. The Europeans, who annually export millions of pounds of pricey raw-milk cheeses that would be shut out of the American market if mandatory pasteurization became the law of the land, were horrified. They knew, however, that the new Codex language afforded them a powerful tool to counter the FDA. Although the United States was free to establish whatever safety standards it deemed necessary to protect public health, including mandatory pasteurization, other GATT member nations under Codex were entitled to satisfy US requirements using any combination of control measures that provided the same level of public-health protection.

This became known as the Principle of Equivalency. If mandatory pasteurization was the standard in one country, other countries could use measures other than pasteurization to satisfy the standard, provided that the same level of public-health protection was achieved. The EU, led by France, had been developing comprehensive safety regulations for raw-milk cheeses that used a combination of risk-reduction strategies. EU authorities made it a point to stress that the new safety standards had been deliberately configured to be flexible with aim of protecting long-standing cultural traditions. David Byrne, EU commissioner for health and consumer protection, expressed it this way: "Throughout the Union, there are longstanding cultural traditions with regard to food and food preparation that I am keen to protect and encourage" (Anonymous 2002). The message to the United States and other GATT member countries was clear: Traditional raw-milk cheeses in Europe were here to stay, and Europe would fight for them. The question remained, however, whether risk-reduction strategies could match the level of public-health protection provided by pasteurization.

Australia became the testing ground for the Codex Principle of Equivalency. The Australian Food Standards Code required that all cheese be made from milk that was either pasteurized or, alternately, thermized at 144°F (62.2°C) for fifteen seconds provided that the cheese was stored for at least ninety days from the date of manufacture; raw-milk cheeses thus were banned in Australia. In 1998 the Swiss government petitioned Australia to permit the import and sale of Emmental, Gruyère, and Sbrinz cheeses, all made from raw milk (FSANZ 2008). This was the first test case under the Principle of Equivalency in international trade, and the Swiss came well armed with extensive research data to corroborate their claim that these cheeses achieved a level of safety comparable to pasteurization. Upon completing their review, the Australian authorities concluded that Emmental, Gruyère, and Sbrinz cheeses achieved the appropriate level of public-health protection under Australian law.

No doubt anticipating similar petitions from the Italians, the Australians voluntarily undertook a review of extra-hard grating cheeses made from raw milk in 2002. The Australian authorities concluded that these extra-hard grating cheeses, which include Parmigiano-Reggiano, Grana Padano, Romano, Asiago, and Montasio, also achieve the appropriate level of public-health protection (FSANZ 2008).

Australia's actions set an important precedent for the Principle of Equivalency in international trade; they affirmed the view that certain traditional raw-milk cheeses can achieve the same level of public-health protection as provided by pasteurization or thermization combined with ninety-day holding. Any hopes that the FDA might have entertained for a simple one-size-fits-all change in US regulations to require mandatory pasteurization or thermization were now fading because the United States is a lucrative market for many European raw-milk cheeses such as Emmental and Parmigiano-Reggiano, and any attempt to ban all raw-milk cheeses would likely be challenged by Switzerland and Italy, and could possibly lead to litigation in the WTO. It was unlikely that Europe would concede the American market without a fight.

Opposition to Australia's Food Code also was being mounted from within Australia. Like the United States, Australia was experiencing a rebirth of interest in traditional cheeses and cheese making. A leading voice in the movement was Will Studd, author of the award-winning book *Chalk and Cheese,* and later host of the popular television series *Cheese Slices.* Studd owned a wholesale cheese company, and in 2001 he decided to personally undertake an unofficial test case of the Equivalency Principle by importing Roquefort cheese from France. Upon arrival the cheese was seized by the Australian authorities on the grounds that Roquefort violated the code and was held for almost two years while the decision was appealed. Ultimately, the court upheld the ruling that Roquefort violated the Australian Food Code and the cheese had to be destroyed (Studd 2003).

France was not happy with the decision and became the next in line to officially test the Principle of Equivalency with Roquefort cheese in 2004. Roquefort carries a much higher risk of food poisoning than the hard Swiss and Italian types due the lack of heating that occurs during its manufacture, and to its high moisture content and the very high pH that develops during aging. Therefore, Roquefort presented a much greater challenge in designing an effective risk-reduction program. The French government submitted voluminous documentation on the safety of Roquefort; it took the Australians a year to review this and render a decision. In the end Australia agreed that Roquefort, like the hard Swiss and Italian types, achieves the appropriate level of public-health protection (FSANZ 2008). Thus, the momentum for international trade in raw-milk cheeses had shifted decidedly in favor of greater market access and away from blanket prohibition.

As for the FDA, after almost completing a risk assessment of raw-milk cheese, the agency announced in 2010 that the sixty-day rule was inadequate to ensure safety and that the current regulations were being reviewed with an eye to revision (Anonymous 2010a). Thus, little seemed to have changed since 1998 when the demise of raw-milk cheese appeared imminent, except that now the FDA realistically could not consider mandatory pasteurization or sub-pasteurization without risking a flood of petitions for cheeses such as

Emmental, Parmigiano-Reggiano, Roquefort, et cetera, and possible WTO litigation. As of this writing, the FDA has yet to change the US regulations governing cheese safety.

Differences between the United States and Europe over food-safety regulations are by no means restricted to cheese; they extend throughout the entire food system, and cheese is just the tip of the iceberg. The US has a long history of embracing new technology in food production and processing, and of abandoning traditional practices in the name of progress. Europeans, in contrast, have a long history with traditional foods and a much greater suspicion toward new food technologies (Echols 1998). This has led to conflicts in many areas, including bitter disputes over the use of growth hormones and antibiotics in beef cattle raising, growth hormones in milk production, genetically modified crops, the use of other genetically modified organisms (GMOs) in food, and the cloning of farm animals. In the case of hormone-treated beef, the dispute has been festering in WTO litigation for more than a decade and nearly produced an unexpected casualty in Roquefort cheese. In 2009 the US threatened to triple the import duty on Roquefort in retaliation for the European Union's unwillingness to abide by a WTO decision concerning hormone use in beef production; such an action would have sent the price of Roquefort spiraling upward toward the $60 per-pound range at retail (Anonymous 2009). The EU backed down before that happened, thus avoiding all-out cheese warfare. In many ways the issues swirling around cheese and their historical and cultural contexts offer a lens through which to view developments occurring much more broadly throughout the food system.

Where are we headed in the future? Recent history may offer some clues. The resurgence of traditional cheese making in America points to a cultural shift that extends far beyond cheese. A growing segment of the American public is questioning the technology-driven, least-cost model for food production and processing. This is manifested in a number of grass-roots movements that have gained considerable momentum in recent years. Sustainable agriculture, animal welfare, organic foods, artisan foods, free-range chickens, and grass-fed cattle all reflect a growing discomfort with the American least-cost food system. If this trend continues, America's outlook likely will move gradually closer to that of Europe as elected officials and policy makers respond to the changing will of the people. Just how much closer remains to be seen. In the short run at least, somebody will have to pay, and pay dearly, to replace least-cost production and processing with alternatives. Either the consumer alone will have to bear the cost, or the consumer in partnership with the public in the form of friendly government policies that encourage alternatives to the least-cost model. Cultural changes certainly can drive changes in the food system, but in the end economic realities are inescapable and the question remains: Who will pay for change?

ACKNOWLEDGMENTS

I am deeply grateful to Dr. Jean Harvey-Berino, Chair, Department of Nutrition and Food Sciences, and the College of Agriculture and Life Sciences at the University of Vermont for affording this cheese scientist the opportunity to branch out into unchartered territory. I appreciate the efforts of my agent, Angela Miller, in shepherding the project along the way, and of my editor, Ben Watson, whose eye to detail and helpful guidance enabled the manuscript to move to the next level. I especially thank my wife, Christina, for graciously putting up with a husband who has all too often been cranky during the long years of this book project.

The quote from Wainwright (1959) on page 51 is reprinted by permission of The British Institute of Ankara.

The quote from Aeliean: On the Characteristics of Animals, Vol. 3 on page 73–74 is reprinted by permission of the publishers and the Trustees of the Loeb Classical Library from AELIAN: VOLUME III, ON THE CHARACTERISTICS OF ANIMALS, Loeb Classical Library Volume 449, with an English translation by A.F. Scholfield, pp. 307, 309, Cambridge, Mass.: Harvard University Press, Copyright © by the President and Fellows of Harvard College. Loeb Classical Library ® is a registered trademark of the President and Fellows of Harvard College.

The quote from Saint Benedict on page 116 is reprinted by permission of Rowan & Littlefield Publishing Group from *The Rule of Saint Benedict*, translated with an introduction by Cardinal Gasquet,1966, Cooper Square Publishing, NY, p. 84.

The quote from Oschinsky (1971) *Walter Of Henley And Other Treatises On Estate Management And Accounting.* pp. 287, 289 on pages 142–143 is by permission of Oxford University Press.

The photograph in Figure 4-1 on page 77, *Woman grating cheese*, is of a Greek statuette, Late Archaic Period, Early 5th century BC. The terracotta statuette was made in Greece, Boiotia, Tangra. Its dimensions (height × width × length) are 9.5 × 5.6 × 9.4 cm (3 ¾ × 2 ³⁄₁₆ × 3 ¹¹⁄₁₆ in). Photograph courtesy of the Museum of Fine Arts, Boston; Museum purchase with funds donated by contribution, 01.7783.

BIBLIOGRAPHY

Abramovitz, K. 1980. Frescoes from Ayia Irini, Keos. Parts II–IV. *Hesperia* 49(1):57–85.

Achaya, K. T. 1994. *Indian Food: A Historical Companion.* Oxford University Press, Oxford, UK.

Adams, R. W. 1813. *A Dissertation, Designed for the Yeomanry of the Western Country.* American Friend, Marietta, OH.

Adshead, S. A. M. 1992. *Salt and Civilization.* St. Martin's Press, New York.

Alberini, M. 1998. "The Fascinating and Homemade Story of Parmigiano-Reggiano." In *Parmigiano Reggiano: A Symbol of Culture and Civilization,* F. Bonilauri, ed. Consorzio del Formaggio Parmigiano-Reggiano, Reggio.

Algaze, G. 2008. *Ancient Mesopotamia at the Dawn of Civilization.* University of Chicago Press, Chicago.

Altekruse, S. F., B. B. Timbo, J. C. Mowbray, N. H. Bean, and M. E. Potter. 1998. Cheese-Associated Outbreaks of Human Illness in the United States, 1973 to 1992: Sanitary Manufacturing Practices Protect Consumers. *Journal of Food Protection* 61:1405–1407.

Anifantakis, E. M. 1991. *Greek Cheeses: A Tradition of Centuries.* National Dairy Committee of Greece, Athens.

Anonymous. 1842. *American Cheese.* The Penny Magazine of the Society for the Diffusion of Useful Knowledge (March 12). 11(638):98–99

———. 1986. Reinbold Discusses Heat Treatments on Cheese Milk, Pro's and Con's for Cheese. *Cheese Reporter,* January 24, p. 13.

———. 1999. FDA Reviewing Policy That Allows Use of Unpasteurized Milk in Cheese. *Cheese Reporter,* August 27, p. 1.

———. 2002. European Council Adopts More Flexible Hygiene Rules for Traditional Cheeses. *Cheese Reporter,* June 28, p. 10.

———. 2003. Dangers of EU's Proposal to Protect Geographical Indications. *Cheese Reporter,* July 25, p. 1.

———. 2009. Trade Wars Hike Cost of Roquefort to $60 a Pound; Retailers Scale Back on Inventory. *Cheese Reporter,* February 27, p. 1.

———. 2010a. Raw Milk Cheese: FDA Says 60-Day Aging Not Effective, Is Looking for Alternatives. *Cheese Reporter,* February 5, p. 1.

———. 2010b. Dairy Groups Concerned Over EU Efforts to "Claw Back" Common Cheese Names. *Cheese Reporter,* July 11, p.5.

Anthony, D. W. 2007. *The Horse, the Wheel, and Language: How Bronze-Age Riders from the Eurasian Steppes Shaped the Modern World.* Princeton University Press, Princeton, NJ.

Apps, J. 1998. *Cheese: The Making of a Wisconsin Tradition.* Amherst Press, Amherst, MA.

Aubet, M. E. 2001. *The Phoenicians and the West,* 2nd ed. Cambridge University Press, Cambridge, UK.

Bailey, R. 1990. The Slave(ry) Trade and the Development of Capitalism in the United States: The Textile Industry in New England. *Social Science History* 14(3):373–414.

Banning, E. B. 1998. The Neolithic Period: Triumphs of Architecture, Agriculture, and Art. *Near Eastern Archaeology* 61(4):188–237.

————. 2003. Housing Neolithic Farmers. *Near Eastern Archaeology* 66(1/2):4–21.

Barako, T. J. 2000. The Philistine Settlement as Mercantile Phenomenon? *American Journal of Archaeology* 104:513–530.

Barham, E. 2003. Translating Terroir: The Global Challenge of French AOC Labeling. *Journal of Rural Studies* 19:127–138.

Barker, G. 1981. *Landscape and Society: Prehistoric Central Italy.* Academic Press, London.

————. 1985. *Prehistoric Farming in Europe.* Cambridge University Press, Cambridge, UK.

————. 2006. *The Agricultural Revolution in Prehistory: Why Did Foragers Become Farmers?* Oxford University Press, Oxford, UK.

Barker, G., and T. Rasmussen. 1998. *The Etruscans.* Blackwell Publishing, Oxford, UK.

Barker, G., A. Grant, P. Beavitt, N. Christie, J. Giorgi, P. Hoare, T. Leggio, and M. Migliavacca. 1991. Ancient and Modern Pastoralism in Central Italy: An Interdisciplinary Study in the Cicolano Mountains. *Papers of the British School at Rome* 59:15–88.

Bass, G. F. 1991. Evidence of Trade from Bronze Age Shipwrecks. In *Bronze Age Trade in the Mediterranean,* N. H. Gale, ed. Studies in Mediterranean Archaeology, Vol. XC, Paul Åströms Fölag, Jonsered. pp. 69–82.

Beckman, G. 1989. The Religion of the Hittites. *The Biblical Archaeologist* 52(2/3):98–108.

————. 2005. How Religion Was Done. In *A Companion to the Ancient Near East,* D. C. Snell, ed. Blackwell Publishing, Oxford, UK, pp. 343–354.

Bellwood, P. 2005. *First Farmers: The Origins of Agricultural Societies.* Blackwell Publishing, Oxford.

Berlin, A. M. 1997. Archeological Sources for the History of Palestine: Between Large Forces: Palestine in the Hellenistic Period. *The Biblical Archeologist* 60(1):2–51.

Berlin, I. 1998. *Many Thousands Gone: The First Two Centuries of Slavery in North America.* Belknap Press of Harvard University Press, Cambridge, MA.

Bezeczky, Dr. 1996. Amphora Inscriptions—Legionary Supply? *Britannia* 27:329–336.

Bidwell, P. W. 1921. The Agricultural Revolution in New England. *The American Historical Review* 26(4):683–702.

Bidwell, P. W., and J. I. Falconer. 1941. *History of Agriculture in the Northern United States, 1620–1860.* Carnegie Institution of Washington, Publication No. 358. Peter Smith, New York.

Bieber, M. 1957. A Bronze Statuette in Cincinnati and Its Place in the History of the Asklepios Types. *Proceedings of the American Philosophical Society* 101(1):70–92.

Bier, L. 1976. A Second Hittite Relief at Ivriz. *Journal of Near Eastern Studies* 35(2):115–126.

Bikel, H. 1914. Die Wirtschaftsverhältnisse des Klosters St. Gallen: von der Gründung bis zum Ende des XIII. Jahrhunderts, eine Studie. Freiburg im Breisgau: Herder.

Birmingham, D. 2000. *Switzerland: A Village History.* St. Martin's Press, New York.

Birmingham, J. 1967. Pottery Making in Andros. *Expedition* 10:33–39.

Blitzer, H. 1990. KOPΩ NEIKA: Storage-Jar Production and Trade in the Traditional Aegean. *Hesperia* 59(4):675–711.

Bloch, M. 1966. *French Rural History: An Essay on Its Basic Characteristics.* University of California Press, Berkeley.

Blundel, R., and A. Tregear. 2006. From Artisans to "Factories": The Interpretation of Craft and Industry in English Cheese-Making, 1650–1950. *Enterprise & Society* 7(4):705–739.

Bogucki, P. 1984. Ceramic Sieves of the Linear Pottery Culture and Their Economic Implications. *Oxford Journal of Archaeology* 3(1):15–30.

———. 1988. *Forest Farmers and Stockherders.* Cambridge University Press, Cambridge, UK.

———. 1999. *The Origins of Human Society.* Blackwell Publishing, Oxford, UK.

Bostock, J., and H. T. Riley. 1855. *The Natural History of Pliny.* Vol. 3. Henry G. Bohn, London.

Bottéro, J. 1985. The Cuisine of Ancient Mesopotamia. *Biblical Archaeologist* 48(1):36–47.

———. 2004. *The Oldest Cuisine in the World: Cooking in Mesopotamia.* University of Chicago Press, Chicago.

Bowen, E. W. 1928. Roman Commerce in the Early Empire. *Classical Weekly* 21(26): 201–206.

Braund, D. 1994. The Luxuries of Athenian Democracy. *Greece & Rome,* Second Series 41(1):41–48.

———. 1999. Laches at Acanthus: Aristophanes, Wasps 968–969. *Classical Quarterly,* New Series 49(1):321–325.

Brea, L. B. 1957. *Sicily Before the Greeks.* Frederick A. Praeger, New York.

Brehaut, E. 1933. *Cato the Censor on Farming.* Columbia University Press, New York.

Bremer, F. J. 2003. *John Winthrop: America's Forgotten Founding Father.* Oxford University Press, Oxford, UK.

Brown, E. 1960. An Introduction to Mycenology. *Classical World* 53(6):186–191.

Brumfield, A. 1997. Cakes in the Liknon: Votives from the Sanctuary of Demeter and Kore on Acrocorinth. *Hesperia* 66(1): 147–172.

Bryce, T. 2005. *The Kingdom of the Hittites.* Oxford University Press, Oxford, UK.

Burriss, E. E. 1930. The Objects of a Roman's Prayers. *Classical Weekly* 23(14)105–109.

Butler, L., and Given-Wilson, C. 1979. *Medieval Monasteries of Great Britain.* Michael Joseph, London.

Butler, R. D. 2006. *The New Prophecy & "New Visions."* Catholic University of America Press, Washington, DC.

Carrington, R. C. 1931. Studies in the Campanian "Villae Rusticae." *Journal of Roman Studies* 21:110–130.

Carter, C. 1985. Hittite *Hashas. Journal of Near Eastern Studies* 44(2):139–141.

Camden, W. 1586. *Britannia.* London.

Campo, P., and G. Licitra. 2006. I Formaggie Storici Siciliani. Historical Sicilian Cheeses. Officine Grafiche Riunite Palermo.

Casson, L. 1954. The Grain Trade of the Hellenistic World. *Transactions and Proceedings of the American Philological Association* 85:168–187.

Cauvin, J. 2000. *The Birth of the Gods and Origins of Agriculture*. Cambridge University Press, Cambridge, UK.

Chadwick, R. 2005. *First Civilizations: Ancient Mesopotamia and Ancient Egypt*. 2nd ed. Equinox Publishing, London.

Chaniotis, A. 1999. Milking in the Mountains: Economic Activities on the Cretan Uplands in the Classical and Hellenistic Periods. In *From Minoan Farmers to Roman Traders*, A. Chaniotis, ed. Franz Steiner Verlag, Stuttgart.

Charlesworth, M. P. 1970. *Trade-Routes and Commerce of the Roman Empire*. 2nd ed. Cooper Square Publishers, New York.

Chavalas, M. 2005. The Age of Empires, 3100–900 BCE. In *A Companion to the Ancient Near East*, D. C. Snell, ed. Blackwell Publishing, Oxford, UK. pp. 34–47.

Cheke, V. 1959. *The Story of Cheese-Making in Britain*. Routledge & Kegan Paul, London.

Cherry, J. F. 1988. Pastoralism and the Role of Animals in the Pre- and Protohistoric Economies of the Aegean. In *Pastoral Economies in Classical Antiquity*, C. R. Whittaker, ed. Cambridge University Press, Cambridge, UK. pp. 6–34.

Churchill Semple, E. 1922. The Influence of Geographic Conditions upon Ancient Mediterranean Stock-Raising. *Annals of the Association of American Geographers* 12:3–38.

Clark, J. M. 1926. *The Abbey of St Gall as a Center of Literature & Art*. Cambridge University Press, London.

Cline, E. H. 2007. Rethinking Mycenaean International Trade with Egypt and the Near East. In *Rethinking Mycenaean Palaces II*. Revised and Expanded 2nd edition, M. Galaty and W. A. Parkinson, ed. University of California, Los Angeles.

Cooley, A. S. 1899. Athena Polias on the Acropolis of Athens. *American Journal of Archaeology* 3(4):345–408.

Coolidge, A. B. 1889. The Republic of Gersau. *English Historical Review* 4(15):481–515.

Copley, M. S., R. Berstan, S. N. Dudd, S. Aillaud, A. J. Mukherjee, V. Straker, S. Payne, and R. P. Evershed. 2005a. Processing Milk Products in Pottery Vessels Through British Prehistory. *Antiquity* 79(306):895–908.

Copley, M. S., R. Berstan, A. J. Mukherjee, S. N. Dudd, V. Straker, S. Payne, and R. P. Evershed. 2005b. Dairying in Antiquity. III: Evidence from Absorbed Lipid Residues Dating to the British Neolithic. *Journal of Archeological Science* 32:523–546.

Copley, M. S., R. Berstan, S. N. Dudd, G. Docherty, A. J. Mukherjee, V. Straker, S. Payne, and R. P. Evershed. 2003. Direct Chemical Evidence for Widespread Dairying in Prehistoric Britain. *Proceedings of the National Academy of Sciences USA* 100(4):1524–1529.

Coughtry, J. 1981. *The Notorious Triangle: Rhode Island and the African Slave Trade 1700–1807*. Temple University Press, Philadelphia.

Craig, O. E., J. Chapman, C. Heron, L. H. Willis, L. Bartosiewicz, G. Taylor, A. Whittle, and M. Collins. 2005. Did the First Farmers of Central and Eastern Europe Produce Dairy Foods? *Antiquity* 79:882–894.

Cunliffe, B. 1997. *The Ancient Celts*. Oxford University Press, Oxford, UK.

Dalby, A. 2009. *Cheese: A Global History*. Reaktion Books, London.

Daniels, B. C. 1980. Economic Development in Colonial and Revolutionary Connecticut: An Overview. *William and Mary Quarterly*, Third Series 37(3):429–450.

D'Arms, J. H. 2004. The Culinary Reality of Roman Upper-Class Convivia: Integrating Texts and Images. *Comparative Studies in Society and History* 46(3):428–450.

Dausse, L. 1993. Époque gallo-romaine: L'essor de échanges. In *Échanges: Circulation d'objets et commerce en Rouergue de la Préhistoire au Moyen Age*, P. Gruat and J. Delmas, ed. Musée Archéologique de Montrozier.

Davies, R. W. 1971. The Roman Military Diet. *Britannia* 2:122–142.

Deane, S. 1790. *The New-England Farmer, or Georgical Dictionary Containing a Compendious Account of the Ways and Methods in which the most Important Art of Husbandry, in all its various Branches, is, or may be, Practiced to the Greatest Advantage.* Isaiah Thomas, Worcester.

De Angelis, F. 2000. Archaeology in Sicily 1996–2000. *Archaeological Reports* 47(2000–2001): 145–201.

De Shong Meador, B. 2000. *Inanna: Lady of the Largest Heart.* University of Texas Press, Austin.

de Vries, J. 1974. *The Dutch Rural Economy in the Golden Age, 1500–1700.* Yale University Press, New Haven, CT.

———. 1976. *Economy of Europe in an Age of Crisis.* Cambridge University Press, Cambridge, UK.

de Waele, F. J. 1933. The Sanctuary of Asklepios and Hygieia at Corinth. *American Journal of Archaeology* 37(3):417–451.

Dickin, A. 2007. *Pagan Trinity – Holy Trinity.* Hamilton Books, Lanham, MD.

Doehaerd, R. 1978. *The Early Middle Ages in the West.* North Holland Publishing, Amsterdam.

Douglas, D. C., and G. W. Greenaway. 1953. *English Historical Documents 1042–1189.* Eyre & Spottiswoode, London.

Drew, J. S. 1947. Manorial Accounts of St. Swithun's Priory, Winchester. *English Historical Review* 62(242):20–41.

Duby, G. 1968. *Rural Economy and Country Life in the Medieval West.* University of South Carolina Press, Columbia.

Echols, E. C. 1949. "Ea Quae ad Effeminandos Animos Pertinent." *Classical Journal* 45(2):92–93.

Echols, M. 1998. Food Safety Regulation in the European Union and the United States: Different Culture, Different Laws. *Columbia Journal of European Law* 4:525–543.

Edwards, G. R. 1975. Corinthian Hellenistic Pottery. *Corinth* 7(3):1–254.

Ehrenberg, V. 1951. *The People of Aristophanes: A Sociology of Attic Comedy.* Basil Blackwell, Oxford, UK.

Ellerbrock, I. J. 1853. *Die Holländische Rinndviehzucht und Milwirthschaft.* F. Vieweg and Sohn, Braunschweig.

Ellison, R. 1981. Diet in Mesopotamia: The Evidence of the Barley Ration Texts (c. 3000–1400 BC). *Iraq* 43(1):35–45.

———. 1983. Some Thoughts on the Diet of Mesopotamia from c. 3000–600 BC. *Iraq* 45(1):146–150.

———. 1984. The Uses of Pottery. *Iraq* 46(1):63–68.

Emery W. B. 1962. *A Funerary Repast in an Egyptian Tomb of the Archaic Period.* Nederlands Instituut Voor Het Nabije Oosten, Leiden.

Everitt, A. 1967. The Marketing of Agricultural Produce. In *The Agrarian History of England and Wales*. Vol. 4, *1500–1640*. J. Thirsk, ed. Cambridge University Press, London.

Evershed. 2005. Dairying in Antiquity. III: Evidence from Absorbed Lipid Residues Dating to the British Neolithic. *Journal of Archaeological Science* 32:523–546.

Evershed, R. P., S. Payne, A. G. Sherratt, M. S. Copley, J. Coolidge, D. Urem-Kotsu, K. Kotsakis, M. Özdogan, A. E. Özdogan, O. Nieuwenhuyse, P. M. M. G. Akkermans, D. Bailey, R. Andeescu, S. Campbell, S. Farid, I. Hodder, N. Yalman, M. Özbasaran, E. Bicakci, Y. Garfinkel, T. Levy, and M. M. Burton. 2008. Earliest Date for Milk Use in the Near East and Southeastern Europe Linked to Cattle Herding. *Nature* 455(7212):528–531.

Fagles, R. 1996. *The Odyssey/Homer*. Viking, New York.

Faith, R. 1994. Demesne Resources and Labour Rent on the Manors of St Paul's Cathedral, 1066–1222. *Economic History Review* 47(4):657–678.

Farmer, D. L. 1991. Marketing the Produce of the Countryside 1200–1500. In *The Agrarian History of England and Wales*. Vol. 3. Cambridge University Press, Cambridge, UK.

Faust, A., and E. Weiss. 2005. Judah, Philistia, and the Mediterranean World: Reconstructing the Economic System of the Seventh Century BCE. *Bulletin of the American Schools of Oriental Research* 338:71–92.

Ferguson, W. S. 1938. The Salaminioi of Heptaphylai and Sounion. *Hesperia* 7(1):1–74.

Figulla, H. H. 1953. Accounts Concerning Allocations of Provisions for Offerings in the Ningal-Temple at UR. *Iraq* 15(2):171–192.

Finberg, H. P. R. 1951. *Travistock Abbey. A Study in the Social and Economic History of Devon*. Cambridge University Press, London.

Finkelstein, J. J. 1968. An Old Babylonian Herding Contract and Genesis. *Journal of the American Oriental Society* 88(1):30–36.

Finley, M. I. 1968. *A History of Sicily: Ancient Sicily to the Arab Conquest*. Viking Press, New York.

Finsinger, W., and W. Tinner. 2007. Pollen and Plant Macrofossils at Lac de Fully (2135 m a.s.l.): Holocene Forest Dynamics on a Highland Plateau in Valais, Switzerland. *Holocene* 17(8): 1119–1127.

Fisher, F. J. 1935. The Development of the London Food Market, 1540–1640. *Economic History Review* 5(2):46–64.

Fitzgerald, R. 1989. *The Iliad/Homer*. Anchor Books, Doubleday, New York.

Flannery, K. V. 1965. The Ecology of Early Food Production in Mesopotamia. *Science* 147(3663):1247–1256.

Flint, C. L. 1862. *Milch Cows and Dairy Farming*. Crosby and Nicholas, Boston.

Forster, E. S., and E. H. Heffner. 1954. *Lucius Junius Moderatus Columella on Agriculture*. Harvard University Press, Cambridge, MA.

Foster, B. R., and K. P. Foster. 2009. *Civilizations of Ancient Iraq*. Princeton University Press, Princeton, NJ.

Foster, C. F. 1998. *Cheshire Cheese and Farming in the North West in the 17th and 18th Centuries*. Arley Hall Press, Northwich, UK.

Frayn, J. M. 1984. *Sheep-Rearing and the Wool Trade in Italy During the Roman Period*. Francis Cairns, Liverpool.

FSANZ. 2008. Proposal P1007, Primary Production & Processing Requirements for Raw Milk Products (Australia Only), Discussion Paper. Food Standards Australia New Zealand.

Fussell, G. E. 1935. Farming Methods in the Early Stuart Period. I. *Journal of Modern History* 7(1):1–21.

———. 1959. Low Countries' Influence on English Farming. *English Historical Review* 74(293):611–622.

———. 1966. *The English Dairy Farmer*. A. M. Kelley, New York.

Ganshof, F. L., and A. Verhulst. 1966. Medieval Agrarian Society in Its Prime. 1: France, the Low Countries, and Western Germany. Chapter 7 In *The Cambridge Economic History of Europe*. Vol. 1, *The Agrarian Life of the Middle Ages*. 2nd ed., M. M. Postan, ed. Cambridge University Press, London.

Ganz, D. 2008. *Einhard and Notker the Stammerer: The Two Lives of Charlemagne*. Translated with an introduction and notes by David Ganz. Penguin Books, London.

Gasquet, F. A. 1966. *The Rule of Saint Benedict*. Translated with an introduction by Cardinal Gasquet. Cooper Square Publishers, New York.

Gelb, I. J. 1967. Growth of a Herd of Cattle in Ten Years. *Journal of Cuneiform Studies* 21:64–69.

Gill, D. 1974. Trapezomata: A Neglected Aspect of Greek Sacrifice. *Harvard Theological Review* 67(2):117–137.

Goetze, A. 1971. Hittite Sipant. *Journal of Cuneiform Studies* 23(3):77–94.

Goldsmith, J. L. 1973. Agricultural Specialization and Stagnation in Early Modern Auvergne. *Agricultural History* 47(3):216–234.

Gomi, T. 1980. On Dairy Productivity at Ur in the Late Ur III Period. *Journal of the Economic and Social History of the Orient* 23(1/2):1–42.

Grandjouan, C., E. Markson, and S. I. Rotroff. 1989. *Hellenistic Relief Molds from the Athenian Agora*. *Hesperia Supplements,* Vol. 23. American School of Classical Studies at Athens, Princeton.

Grant, A. J. 1966. *Early Lives of Charlemagne: Eginhard & the Monk of St Gall*. Translated and edited by Professor A. J. Grant. Cooper Square Publishers, New York. Pp. 79–80

Grant, M. 2000. *Galen on Food and Diet*. Routledge, London.

Granto, J., R. Inglehart, and D. Leblang. 1996. The Effects of Cultural Values on Economic Development: Theory, Hypotheses, and Some Empirical Tests. *American Journal of Political Science* 40(3):607–663.

Gras, N. F. S. 1940. *A History of Agriculture in Europe and America*. 2nd ed. F. S. Crofts, New York.

Green, M. W. 1980. Animal Husbandry at Uruk in the Archaic Period. *Journal of Near Eastern Studies* 39(1):1–35.

Greene, L. J. 1968. *The Negro in Colonial New England*. Atheneum, New York.

Greenfield, H. J. 1988. The Origins of Milk and Wool Production in the Old World. *Current Anthropology* 29(4):573–593.

Gulley, J. L. M. 1963. The Bruton Chartulary. *British Museum Quarterly* 27(1/2):5–9.

Güterbock, H. G. 1968. Oil Plants in Hittite Anatolia. *Journal of the American Oriental Society* 88(1):66–71.

Hadzsits, G. D. 1936. The Vera History of the Palatine Ficus Ruminalis. *Classical Philology* 31(4):305–319.

Hagan, A. 2006. *Anglo-Saxon Food and Drink: Production Processing, Distribution and Consumption.* Anglo-Saxon Books, Hockwold cum Wilton, UK.

Halbherr, F. 1897. Cretan Expedition III. *American Journal of Archaeology* 1(3):159–238.

Halstead, P. 1981. Counting Sheep in Neolithic and Bronze Age Greece. In *Patterns of the Past: Studies in Honour of David Clarke.* I. Hooder, G. Isaac, and N. Hammond, ed. Cambridge University Press., Cambridge, UK. pp. 307–340.

———. 1996. Pastoralism or Household Herding? Problems of Scale and Specialization in Early Greek Animal Husbandry. *World Archaeology* 28(1):20–42.

Harley, T. R. 1934. The Public School of Sparta. *Greece & Rome* 3(9):129–139.

Harrod, J. B. 1981. The Bow: A Techno-Mythic Hermeneutic: Ancient Greece and the Mesolithic. *Journal of the American Academy of Religion* 49(3): 425–446.

Heiri, C., H. Bugmann, W. Tinner, O. Heir, and H. Lischke. 2006. A Model-Based Reconstruction of Holocene Treeline Dynamics in the Central Swiss Alps. *Journal of Ecology* 94:206–216.

Hickman, T. 1995. *The History of Stilton Cheese.* Alan Sutton Publishing, Stroud, UK.

Hill, J. 2003. *The History of Christian Thought.* IVP Academic, Downers Grove, IL.

Hodges, R. 1982. *Dark Age Economics: The Origins of Towns and Trade AD 600–1000.* St. Martin's Press, New York.

Hodkinson, S. 1988. Animal Husbandry in the Greek Polis. In *Pastoral Economies in Classical Antiquity,* C. R. Whittaker, ed. Cambridge Philological Society, Cambridge, UK.

Hoffner, H. A. 1966. A Native Cognate to West Semitic *GBN "Cheese"? *Journal of the American Oriental Society* 86(1):27–31.

———. 1967. Second Millennium Antecedents to the Hebrew ʾŌB. *Journal of Biblical Literature* 86(4):385–401.

———. 1995. Oil in Hittite Texts. *Biblical Archaeologist* 58(2):108–114.

———. 1998. *Hittite Myths,* 2nd ed. Society of Biblical Literature. Scholars Press, Atlanta.

Hole, F. 1989. A Two-Part, Two-Stage Model of Domestication. In *The Walking Larder: Patterns of Domestication, Pastoralism, and Predation,* J. Clutton-Brock, ed. Unwin Hyman, London.

———. 1996. The Context of Caprine Domestication in the Zagros Region. In *The Origins and Spread of Agriculture and Pastoralism in Eurasia,* D. R. Harris, ed. Smithsonian Institution Press, Washington, DC.

Holloway, R. R. 1975. The Early Bronze Age Village of Tufariello. *Journal of Field Archaeology* 2(1/2):11–81.

Horn, W. W., and E. Born. 1979. *The Plan of St. Gall: A Study of the Architecture & Economy of & Life in a Paradigmatic Carolingian Monastery,* Vol. 3. University of California Press, Berkeley.

Hough, G. 1793. *The Art of Cheese-Making, Taught from Actual Experiments, by Which More and Better Cheese May be Made from the Same Quantity of Milk.* George Hough, Concord, NH.

Hurt, R. D. 1994. *American Agriculture: A Brief History.* Iowa State University Press, Ames.

Itan, Y., A. Powell, M. A. Beaumont, J. Burger, and M. G. Thomas. 2009. The Origins of Lactase Persistence in Europe. *PLoS Computational Biology* 5(8): e1000491. doi:10.1371/journal.pcbi.1000491.

Jacobsen, T. 1983. Lad in the Desert. *Journal of the American Oriental Society* 103(1):193–200.

Jeffery, L. H. 1948. The Boustrophedon Sacral Inscriptions from the Agora. *Hesperia* 17(2):86–111.

Jensen, J. M. 1988. Butter Making and Economic Development in Mid-Atlantic America from 1750–1850. *Signs: Journal of Women in Culture and Society* 13(4):813–829.

Johnson, E. A., J. H. Nelson, and M. Johnson. 1990a. Microbiological Safety of Cheese Made from Heat-Treated Milk. Part 1: Executive Summary, Introduction and History. *Journal of Food Protection* 53(5):441–452.

———. 1990b. Microbiological Safety of Cheese Made from Heat-Treated Milk. Part 2: Microbiology. *Journal of Food Protection* 53(6):519–540.

———. 1990c. Microbiological Safety of Cheese Made from Heat-Treated Milk. Part 3: Technology, Discussion, Recommendations, Bibliography. *Journal of Food Protection* 53(7):610–623.

Johnson, J. 1801. *The Art of Cheese-Making Reduced to Rules, and Made Sure and Easy, from Accurate Observation and Experience.* Charles R. and George Webster, Albany, NY.

Johnson, P. 1976. *A History of Christianity.* Atheneum, New York.

Jones, H. L., and J. H. Sterrett. 1917. *The Geography of Strabo, with an English translation by Horace Leonard Jones.* William Heinemann, London; G. P. Putnam's Sons, New York.

Jones, P. 1966. Medieval Agrarian Society in Its Prime. 2: Italy. Chapter 7 In *The Cambridge History of Europe.* Vol. 1. *The Agrarian Life of the Middle Ages*, 2nd ed., M.M. Postan, ed. Cambridge University Press, London

Kamber, U. 2008a. The Traditional Cheeses of Turkey: Cheeses Common to All Regions. *Food Reviews International* 24:1–38.

———. 2008b. The Traditional Cheeses of Turkey: The Aegean Region. *Food Reviews International* 24:39–61.

Kamber, U., and G. Terzi. 2008. The Traditional Cheeses of Turkey: Middle and Eastern Black Sea Region. *Food Reviews International* 24:95–118.

Kearns, E. 2010. *Ancient Greek Religion: A Sourcebook.* Wiley-Blackwell, Chichester, UK.

Kindstedt, P. S. 2005. *American Farmstead Cheese.* Chelsea Green Publishing, White River Junction, VT.

Knapp, A. B. 1991. Spice, Drugs, Grain and Grog: Organic Goods in the Bronze Age East Mediterranean Trade. In *Bronze Age Trade in the Mediterranean.* N. H. Gale, ed. Studies in Mediterranean Archaeology, Vol. XC, Paul Åströms Fölag, Jonsered. pp. 21–68.

Koebner, R. 1966. The Settlement and Colonization of Europe. Chapter 1 In *The Cambridge Economic History of Europe.* Vol. 1, *The Agrarian Life of the Middle Ages.* 2nd ed., M. M. Postan, ed. Cambridge University Press, London.

Kosikowski, F. V., and V. V. Mistry. 1997. *Cheese and Fermented Milk Foods.* Vol. 1. F. V. Kosikowski, Great Falls, VA.

Kramer, S. N. 1963a. *The Sumerians: Their History, Culture and Character.* University of Chicago Press, Chicago.

————. 1969. *The Sacred Marriage Rite: Aspects of Faith, Myth, and Ritual in Ancient Sumer.* Indiana University Press, London.

————. 1972. *Sumerian Mythology: A Study of Spiritual and Literary Achievement in the Third Millennium BC.* University of Pennsylvania Press, Philadelphia.

Kramrisch, S. 1975. The Mahāvīra Vessel and the Plant Pūtika. *Journal of the Oriental Society* 95(2):222–235.

Kulikoff, A. 2000. *From British Peasants to Colonial American Farmers.* University of North Carolina Press, Chapel Hill.

Lacour-Gayet, J., and R. Lacour-Gayet, R. 1951. Price-Fixing and Planned Economy from Plato to the "Reign of Terror." *American Journal of Economics and Sociology* 10(4):389–399.

Leary, T. J. 2001. *Martial Book XIII. The Xenia.* Gerald Duckworth, London.

Le Glay, M., J.-L. Voisin, and Y. Le Bohec. 2009. *A History of Rome.* 4th ed. Wiley-Blackwell, Chichester, UK.

Leon, E. F. 1943. Cato's Cakes. *Classical Journal* 38(4):213–221.

Lever, K. 1954. Middle Comedy: Neither Old nor New but Contemporary. *Classical Journal* 49(4):167–180.

Lev-Yadun, S., A. Gopher, and Shahal Abbo. 2000. The Cradle of Agriculture. *Science* 288(5741):1602–1603.

Limet, H. 1987. The Cuisine of Ancient Sumer. *Biblical Archeologist* 50(3):132–147.

Liverani, M. 2005. Historical Overview. In *A Companion to the Ancient Near East,* D. C. Snell, ed. Blackwell Publishing, Oxford, UK. pp. 3–19.

Lupack, S. 2007. Palaces, Sanctuaries, and Workshops. In *Rethinking Mycenaean Palaces II.* Revised and expanded 2nd ed. M. Galaty and W. A. Parkinson, ed. University of California, Los Angeles.

Maier, B. 2003. *The Celts: A History for Earliest Times to the Present.* University of Notre Dame Press, Notre Dame, IN.

Marshall, Mr. 1796. *The Rural Economy of Gloucestershire: Including Its Dairy: Together with the Dairy Management of North Wiltshire and the Management of Orchards and Fruit Liquor in Herefordshire.* Vol. 1 and 2. G. Nicol, London.

Martin, H. P., F. Pomponio, G. Visicato, and A. Westenholz. 2001. *The Fara Tablets in the University of Pennsylvania Museum of Archaeology and Anthropology.* CDL Press, Bethesda, MD.

Mastrocinque, A. 2007. The Cilician God Sandas and the Greek Chimaera: Features of Near Eastern and Greek Mythology Concerning the Plague. *Journal of Ancient Near Eastern Religions* 7(2):197–217.

Mate, M. 1987. Pastoral Farming in South-East England in the Fifteenth Century. *The Economic History Review,* New Series 40(4):523–536.

McMahon, A. 2005. From Sedentism to States, 10,000–3000 BC. In *A Companion to the Ancient Near East.* D. C. Snell, ed. Blackwell Publishing, Oxford, UK.

McManis, D. R. 1975. *Colonial New England: A Historical Geography.* Oxford University Press, London.

McMurry, S. 1992. Women's Work in Agriculture: Divergent Trends in England and America, 1800 to 1930. *Comparative Studies in Society and History* 34(2):248–270.

————. 1995. *Transforming Rural Life: Dairying Families and Agricultural Change, 1820–1885.* Johns Hopkins University Press, Baltimore.

Migeotte, Léopold, translated by J. Lloyd. 2009. The Economy of the Greek Cities. From the Archaic Period to the Early Roman Empire. University of California Press, Berkeley

Miller, E., and J. Hatcher. 1978. *Medieval England: Rural Society and Economic Change 1086–1348.* Longman Group, London.

Miller, W. D. 1934. The Narragansett Planters. *Proceedings of the American Antiquarian Society,* New Series 43:49–115.

Monroe, C. M. 2007. Vessel Volumetrics and the Myth of the Cyclopean Bronze Age Ship. *Journal of the Economic and Social History of the Orient* 50(1):1–18.

Morgan, G. 1991. "Nourishing Foods": Herodotus 2.77. *Mnemsoyne,* Fourth Series 44(3/4):415–417.

Muhly, J. D., R. Maddin, T. Stech, and E. Özgen. 1985. Iron in Anatolia and the Nature of the Hittite Iron Industry. *Anatolian Studies* 35:67–84.

Najovits, S. 2003. *Egypt: Trunk of the Tree.* Vol. 1, *The Contexts.* Algora Publishing, New York.

Needham, J., and A. Hughes. 1959. *A History of Embryology.* Abelard-Schuman, New York.

Neils, J. 2008. *The British Museum Concise Introduction to Ancient Greece.* University of Michigan Press, Ann Arbor.

Niblett, R., W. Manning, and C. Saunders. 2006. Verulamium: Excavations Within the Roman Town 1986–88. *Britannia* 37:53–188.

Nicholas, D. 1991. Of Poverty and Primacy: Demand, Liquidity, and the Flemish Economic Miracle, 1050–1200. *The American Historical Review* 96(1):17-41

Noussia, M. 2001. Solon's Symposium. *The Classical Quarterly,* New Series 51(2):353–359.

Oakes, E. F. 1980. A Ticklish Business: Dairying in New England and Pennsylvania, 1750–1812. *Pennsylvania History* 47(3):195–212.

Ó Hógáin, D. 2002. *The Celts: A History.* Collins Press, Cork, Ireland.

Oldfather, W. A. 1913. Homerica: I. akrhton gala, i 297. *Classical Philology* 8(2):195–212.

Olson, L. 1945. Cato's Views on the Farmer's Obligation to the Land. *Agricultural History* 19(3):129–132.

Olson, S. D., and A. Sens. 2000. Archestratos of Gela. *Greek Culture and Cuisine in the Fourth Century BCE.* Oxford University Press, Oxford, UK.

Oschinsky, D. 1971. *Walter of Henley and Other Treatises on Estate Management and Accounting.* Oxford University Press, London.

Outram, A. K., N. A. Stear, R. Bendrey, S. Olsen, A. Kasparov, V. Zaibert, N. Thorpe, and R. P. Evershed. 2009. The Earliest Horse Harnessing and Milking. *Science* 323:1332–1335.

Owen, D. I., and G. D. Young. 1971. Cuneiform Texts in the Museum of Fine Arts, Boston. *Journal of Cuneiform Studies* 23(3):68–75.

Owen, T. 1805. *Geoponika (Agricultural Pursuits),* London. Scanned by the Michigan State University Library; accessed on 3/8/2010 at www.ancientlibrary.com/geoponica. index.html.

Page, F. M. 1936. *Wellingborough Manorial Accounts AD 1258–1323.* Northamptonshire Printing & Publishing, Kettering, UK.

Painter, J. and L. Slutsker. 2007. Listeriosis in Humans. Chapter 4 In *Listeria, Listeriosis, and Food Safety*. 3rd ed., E. Ryser and E.H. Marth, ed. CRC Press, Boca Raton.

Palaima, T. G. 2004. Sacrificial Feasting in the Linear B Documents. *Hesperia* 73(2):217–246.

Palmer, R. 1994. *Wine in the Mycenaean Palace Economy*. Université de Liège, Liège.

Pearson, K. L. 1997. Nutrition and the Early-Medieval Diet. *Speculum* 72(1):1–32.

Pirtle, T. R. 1926. *History of the Dairy Industry*. Mojonnier Bros., Chicago.

Pollock, S. 1999. *Ancient Mesopotamia: The Eden That Never Was*. Cambridge University Press, Cambridge, UK.

Post, L. A. 1932. Catana the Cheese-Grater in Aristophanes' Wasps. *American Journal of Philology* 53(3):265–266.

Potter, T. W. 1976. *A Faliscan Town in South Etruria: Excavations at Narce 1966–71*. British School at Rome, London.

———. 1979. *The Changing Landscape of South Etruria*. St. Martins Press, New York.

Potts, D. T. 1993. Rethinking Some Aspects of Trade in the Arabian Gulf. *World Archaeology* 24(3):423–440.

Pounds, N. J. G. 1994. *An Economic History of Medieval Europe*. 2nd ed. Longman Group, London.

Pourrat, H. 1956. *The Roquefort Adventure. Translated from the French by Mary Mian*. Société anonyme des caves et des producteurs reunis de Roquefort, Roquefort

Prakash, O. 1961. *Food and Drinks in Ancient India (from Earliest Times to c. 1200 AD)*. Munshi Ram Manohar Lal, Delhi.

Procelli, E. 1995. Cultures and Societies in Sicily Between the Neolithic and Middle Bronze Age. In *Ancient Sicily*, T. Fischer-Hansen, ed. Museum Tusculanum Press, Copenhagen.

Rance, P. 1989. *The French Cheese Book*. Macmillan Publishers, London.

Rapp, A. 1955. The Father of Western Gastronomy. *Classical Journal* 51(1):43–48.

Rasmussen, P. 1990. Leaf-Foddering in the Earliest Neolithic Agriculture: Evidence from Switzerland and Denmark. *Acta Archaeologica* 60:71–86.

Reisman, D. 1973. Iddin-Dagan's Sacred Marriage Hymn. *Journal of Cuneiform Studies* 25(4):185–202.

Ridgway, D. 1997. Nestor's Cup and the Etruscans. *Oxford Journal of Archaeology* 16(3):325–344.

Rist, M. 1942. Pseudepigraphic Refutations of Marcionism. *Journal of Religion* 22(1):39–62.

Russell, J. R. 1993. On Mysticism and Esotericism Among Zoroastrians. *Iranian Studies* 26(1/2):73–94.

Rutman, D. B. 1963. Governor Winthrop's Garden Crops: The Significance of Agriculture in the Early Commerce of Massachusetts Bay. *William and Mary Quarterly*, Third Series 20(3):396–415.

Sagona, A., and P. Zimansky. 2009. *Ancient Turkey*. Routledge, New York.

Şahoğlu, V. 2005. The Anatolian Trade Network and the Izmir Region During the Early Bronze Age. *Oxford Journal of Archaeology* 24(4):339–361.

Sansone, D. 2009. *Ancient Greek Civilization*. 2nd ed. John Wiley and Sons, Chichester, UK.

Sauter, M. R. 1976. *Switzerland: From Earliest Times to the Roman Conquest*. Thames and Hudson, Southhampton, UK.

Schon, R. 2007. Chariots, Industry, and Elite Power at Pylos. In *Rethinking Mycenaean Palaces II*. Revised and expanded 2nd edition. M. Galaty and W. A. Parkinson, ed. University of California, Los Angeles.

Schwartz, B. 1938. The Hittite and Luwian Ritual of Zarpiya of Kezzuwatna. *Journal of the American Oriental Society* 58(2):334–353.

Selz, G. J. 2008. The Divine Prototypes. In *Religion and Power: Divine Kingship in the Ancient World and Beyond,* N. Brisch, ed. University of Chicago Press, Chicago. pp. 13–32.

Sernett, M. 2011. *Say Cheese! The Story of the Era When New York State Cheese Was King.* Milton C. Sernett, Cazenovia, NY.

Sharma, R. S. 2005. *India's Ancient Past.* Oxford University Press, New Delhi.

Shaw, B. D. 1993. The Passion of Perpetua. *Past & Present* 139:3–45.

Sheridan, R. B. 1973. *Sugar and Slavery: An Economic History of the British West Indies 1623–1775.* Johns Hopkins University Press, Baltimore.

Sherratt, A. 1981. Plough and Pastoralism: Aspects of the Secondary Products Revolution. In *Patterns of the Past: Studies in Honour of David Clarke,* I. Hooder, G. Isaac, and N. Hammond, ed. Cambridge University Press, Cambridge, UK. pp. 261–306.

———. 1983. The Secondary Exploitation of Animals in the Old World. *World Archeology* 15(1—Transhumance and Pastoralism):90–104.

———. 2004. Feasting in Homeric Epic. *Hesperia* 73(2):301–337.

Sherratt, A., and S. Sherratt. 1991. From Luxuries to Commodities: The Nature of Mediterranean Bronze Age Trading Systems. In *Bronze Age Trade in the Mediterranean.* N. H. Gale, ed. *Studies in Mediterranean Archaeology,* Vol. XC, Paul Åströms Fölag, Jonsered. pp. 351–386.

Simmons, A. H. 2007. *The Neolithic Revolution in the Near East: Transforming the Human Landscape.* University of Arizona Press, Tucson.

Simond, L. 1822. *Switzerland; or, a Journal of a Tour and Residence in That Country in the Years 1817, 1818 and 1819.* Vol. 2. Wells and Lilly, Boston.

Simoons, F. J. 1971. The Antiquity of Dairying in Asia and Africa. *Geography Review* 61(3):431–439.

———. 1991. *Food in China. A Cultural and Historical Inquiry.* CRC Press, Inc., Boca Raton.

Singh, U. 2008. *A History of Ancient and Medieval India: From the Stone Age to the 12th Century.* Dorling Kindersley, Delhi.

Sommer, M. 2007. Networks of Commerce and Knowledge in the Iron Age: The Case of the Phoenicians. *Mediterranean Historical Review* 22(1):97–111.

Spangenberg, J., S. Jacomet, and J. Schibler. 2006. Chemical Analyses of Organic Residues in Archeological Pottery from Arbon Bleiche 3, Switzerland: Evidence for Dairying in the Late Neolithic. *Journal of Archeological Science* 33:1–13.

Sprague, R. W. 1967. Boston Merchants and the Puritan Ethic (1630–1691). In *The Formative Era of American Enterprise,* R. W. Hidy and P. E. Cawein, ed., D. C. Heath, Boston.

Stamm, E. R. 1991. *The History of Cheese Making in New York State.* E. R. Stamm, Publishing Agencies, Endicott.

Steiner, G. 1955. The Fortunate Farmer: Life on the Small Farm in Ancient Italy. *Classical Journal* 51(2):57–67.

Stern, W. M. 1973. Cheese Shipped Coastwise to London Towards the Middle of the Eighteenth Century. *Guildhall Miscellany* 4(4):207–221.

———. 1979. Where, Oh Where, Are the Cheesemongers of London? *London Journal* 5(2): 228–248.

Stone, B. J. 1995. The Philistines and Acculturation: Culture Change and Ethnic Continuity in the Iron Age. *Bulletin of the American Schools of Oriental Research* 298:7–32.

Storr-Best, L. 1912. *Varro on Farming*. G. Bell and Sons, London.

Studd, W. 2003. In Memoriam. *Australian Dairy Foods,* December, p. 15.

Tabbernee, W. 2007. *Fake Prophecy and Polluted Sacraments: Ecclesiastical and Imperial Reactions to Montanism*. Koninklijke Brill NV, Leiden.

TeBrake, W. H. 1981. Land Reclamation and the Agrarian Frontier in the Dutch Rijnland, 950–1350. *Environmental Review* 5(1):27–36.

———. 1985. *Medieval Frontier: Culture and Ecology in Rijnland*. Texas A&M University Press, College Station.

Thirsk, J. 1967. The Farming Regions of England. In *The Agrarian History of England and Wales.* Vol. 4, *1500–1640,* J. Thirsk, ed. Cambridge University Press, London.

Thompson, D. V. Jr., and G. H. Hamilton. 1933. *An Anonymous Fourteenth-Century Treatise, De Arte Illuminandi, The Technique of Manuscript Illumination*. Yale University Press, New Haven, CT.

Thompson, D. W. 1907. Book 3 in *The History of Animals*. John Bell, London.

Thorpe, L. 1969. *Einhard and Notker the Stammerer: The Two Lives of Charlemagne*. Translated with an introduction by Lewis Thorpe. Penguin Books, Harmondsworth, UK.

Tinner, W., and P. Kaltenrieder. 2005. Rapid Responses of High-Mountain Vegetation to Early Holocene Environmental Changes in the Swiss Alps. *Journal of Ecology* 93:936–947.

Tinner, W., and J.-P. Theurillat. 2003. Uppermost Limit, Extent and Fluctuations of the Timberline and Treeline Ecoline in the Swiss Central Alps During the Past 11,500 Years. *Arctic, Antarctic, and Alpine Research* 35(2):158–169.

Trow-Smith, R. 1957. *A History of British Livestock Husbandry to 1700*. Routledge and Kegan Paul, London.

Trubek, A. B. 2008. *The Taste of Place: A Cultural Journey into Terroir*. University of California Press, Berkeley.

Trump, D. 1965. *Central and Southern Italy Before Rome*. Frederick A. Praeger, New York.

Twamley, J. 1784. *Dairying Exemplified, or the Business of Cheese-Making*. J. Sharp, Warwick, UK.

———. 1816. *Essays on the Management of the Dairy; Including the Modern Practice of the Best Districts in the Manufacture of Cheese and Butter*. J. Harding, London.

Updike, W. 1907. *A History of the Episcopal Church in Narragansett Rhode Island*. Merrymount Press, Boston.

Valenze, D. 1991. The Art of Women and the Business of Men: Women's Work and the Dairy Industry c. 1740–1840. *Past and Present* 130:142-169.

van Bavel, B. J. P., and J. L. van Zanden. 2004. The Jump-Start of the Holland Economy During the Late-Medieval Crisis, c. 1350–c. 1500. *Economic History Review* 57(3):503–532.

Vidal, J. 2006. Ugarit and the Southern Levantine Sea-Ports. *Journal of the Economic and Social History of the Orient* 49(3):269–279.

Wainwright, G. A. 1959. The Teresh, the Etruscans and Asia Minor. *Anatolian Studies* 9:197–213.

————. 1961. Some Sea-Peoples. *Journal of Egyptian Archaeology* 47:71–90.

Wallace, S. A. 2003. The Changing Role of Herding in Early Iron Age Crete: Some Implications of Settlement Shift for Economy. *American Journal of Archaeology* 107(4):601–627.

Weeden, W. B. 1910. *Early Rhode Island. A Social History of the People.* Grafton Press, New York.

————. 1963. *Economic and Social History of New England 1620–1789.* Vol. 2. Hillary House Publishers, New York.

Wehrli, M., W. Tinner, and B. Ammann. 2007. 16,000 Years of Vegetation and Settlement History from Egelsee (Menzingen, Central Switzerland). *Holocene* 17(6):747–761.

West, L. C. 1935. *Roman Gaul. The Objects of Trade.* Basil Blackwell, Oxford, UK.

West, M. L. 1988. The Rise of the Greek Epic. *Journal of Hellenistic Studies* 108:151–172.

Whitelock, D. 1955. *English Historical Documents c. 500–1042.* Oxford University Press, New York.

Whittaker, D., and J. Goody. 2001. Rural Manufacturing in the Rouergue from Antiquity to the Present: The Examples of Pottery and Cheese. *Comparative Studies in Society and History* 43(2):225–245.

Wick, L., and W. Tinner. 1997. Vegetation Changes and Timberline Fluctuations in the Central Alps as Indicators of Holocene Climatic Oscillations. *Arctic and Alpine Research* 29(4):445–458.

Wild, J. P. 2002. The Textile Industries of Roman Britain. *Britannia* 33:1–42.

Williams, C. H. 1967. *English Historical Documents 1458–1558.* C. H. Williams, ed. Oxford University Press, New York.

Winthrop, J. 1630. A Modell of Christian Charity. In *The Role of Religion in American Life, An Interpretive Historical Anthology,* 1982, R. R. Mathisen, ed. University Press of America, Lanham.

Wood, J. 2007. A Re-interpretation of a Bronze Age Ceramic: Was It a Cheese Mould or a Bunsen Burner. In *Fire as an Instrument: The Archaeology of Pyrotechnologies,* D. Gheorghiu, ed. Oxford University Press, Oxford, UK.

Wood, M. 1986. *Domesday: A Search for the Roots of England.* BBC Books, London.

Wood, S. 1819. *The Progress of the Dairy; Descriptive of the Method of Making Butter and Cheese for the Information of Youth.* Samuel Wood & Sons, New York.

Woolley, L., and P. R. S. Moorey. 1982. *Ur "Of the Chaldees."* Cornell University Press, Ithaca, NY.

Wright, D. P. 1986. The Gesture of Hand Placement in the Hebrew Bible and in Hittite Literature. *Journal of the American Oriental Society* 106(3):433–446.

Wright, G. 2003. Slavery and American Agricultural History. *Agricultural History* 77(4):527–552.

Wycherley, R. E. 1956. The Market of Athens: Topography and Monuments. *Greece & Rome,* Second Series 3(1):2–23.

Wypustek, A. 1997. Magic, Montanism, Perpetua, and the Severan Persecution. *Vigiliae Christianae* 51(3):276–297.

Yeo, C. A. 1946. Land and Sea Transportation in Imperial Italy. *Transactions and Proceedings of the American Philological Association* 77:221–244.

———. 1948. The Overgrazing of Ranch-Lands in Ancient Italy. *Transactions and Proceedings of the American Philological Association* 79:275–307.

Yoffee, N. 1995. Political Economy in Early Mesopotamian States. *Annual Review of Anthropology* 24:281–311.

Zaky, A., and Z. Iskander. 1942. Ancient Egyptian Cheese. *Annales du service des antiquités de l'Egypte* 41:295–313.

Zarins, J. 1990. Early Pastoral Nomadism and the Settlement of Lower Mesopotamia. *Bulletin of the American Schools of Oriental Research* 280:31–65.

Zohary, D., and M. Hopf. 2000. *Domestication of Plants in the Old World*. Oxford University Press, Oxford, UK.

INDEX

Abel. See Cain and Abel

Abraham, 17–18

Achaeans. *See* Mycenaean civilization

acid-coagulated cheeses, 12–13, 129, 199

acid/heat-coagulated cheeses, 12–13, 31, 37–38, 83–84

ACS. *See* American Cheese Society

aged cheeses, 38–39, 50, 101, 103, 105, 108, 183, 198

aged soldier cheeses, 45, 51

agriculture. *See also* cheese making; cultivation
    per Cato, 96–98
    per Columella, 100–102
    cotton growing, 199–200
    cultivation and domestication, 6–8
    Dutch reclaimed land and, 176–79
    Inanna and, 23–29
    irrigation and, 15–16, 19–20, 22
    nineteenth century US, 200–204
    origins of, 3–5
    plows and, 20, 22, 43, 52, 55–56
    of the Roman Empire, 93–95, 117–22
    per Varro, 98–100

alpine cheese production, 146–57

alpine milk production, 57–58

America. *see* United States

American Cheese Society (ACS), 218, 221

American Revolution, 198–99

amphoras, 49–50

Anatolia, 6–7, 9–10, 21, 41–43, 58–61

animal sacrifice, 67–68

animal transport, 21–22

AOC. *See* Appellation d'Origine Contrôlée

Aphrodite, 67

Appellation d'Origine Contrôlée (AOC), 215

Appenzeller cheeses, 148

Aristotle, 63, 111

Arnuwanda, 51

artisan cheeses. *see* farmhouse/farmstead cheeses

Aryan people, 37

Asia. *see* southwest Asia

Asiago cheese, 215, 222

Asklepios, 70, 72

Australia, 222–23

Austria, 152

Babylonians, 66

Balkan peninsula, 16, 56

bandaging, 171–72, 197–98

Beaufort cheese, 106

Benedictines, 116–17, 123–24, 155–56, 158

biblical stories
    Abraham, 17–18
    Cain and Abel, 3
    David and Goliath, 40–41, 62
    Job, 63–64

bloomy-rind cheeses, 128–29, 219
blue cheese, 133
Botai people, 59
Brie cheese, 125, 129, 133, 210
brined cheeses, 49–50
Bronze Age
    cheese making advances in,
        47–51
    end of, 58–62
    in Europe, 54–58
    Italy and, 83
    overview, 40–43
    rennet-coagulated cheeses
        and, 45
bubonic plague, 159
butter. *See also* ghee
    in Anglo-Saxon times, 140,
        144–45
    as a dressing on cheese, 171–72,
        197–98
    East Anglian, 163–64
    Inanna and, 23–29
    Mesopotamian production of,
        28–33
    Neolithic period and, 16
    origins of, 12
    spiritual practice and, 18

Cain and Abel, 3
Calvin, John, 158–59
Camembert cheese, 210
Canaan, 40, 47–51, 65
Cantal cheese, 108, 153, 168
caprino cheeses, 50, 76–77, 80, 89
Caprino d'Aspromonte, 50, 76
Carthage, 66, 92–94
Cato, Marcus Procius, 96–98
cattle
    cultivation and, 20, 55–56
    domestication of, 7–8

    in Egypt, 33–34
    milk production and, 9–10
    Uruk herders and, 27–28
Celts, 60, 89–92, 105, 108–9, 138
ceramic shipping jars, 49–50
ceramic sieves, 31, 37, 82. See also
    pottery
chariots, 59
Charlemagne, 132–33
Cheddar cheeses, 153, 169–72, 197,
    204–6, 208–9, 213, 215
cheese. *See also* cheese making;
    spiritual practices; *specific types,*
    such as Gouda
    farmhouse, 163, 174–75, 207,
        210–11, 218–19
    grated, 13, 51, 77–80, 87–89
    in Greek diet and commerce,
        72–80
    Inanna and, 23–29
    as religious sacrifice, 44–45,
        68–72
    soft-ripened, 125–34
    spiritual practice and, 8, 18,
        63–64
cheesecakes, 97–98
cheese making. *See also* cheese
    alpine, 146–57
    per Cato, 96–98
    by the Celts, 60, 89–92, 105,
        108–9
    cheese molds, 119
    in China, 39
    coagulation techniques, 12–14
    per Columella, 100–102
    of Cyclops, 74–77
    in Egypt, 33–35
    in factories, 174–75, 203–11, 218
    filled cheeses, 208
    in Holland, 180–84

in the Indus River Valley, 36–39
large *vs.* small cheeses, 103–9,
      137–38, 142–43, 167–69
manorial, 121–22, 125–46
in Mesopotamia, 28–33
milk boilers and, 83–85, 88
by the Minoans, 52–53
monastic, 122–25, 130–34,
      137–40, 145–48, 155–56, 160
Neolithic period and, 16, 82
origins of, 9–10
pottery and, 10–12
by Puritans, 185–90
Roman military and, 117–22
scalding technique, 169–70,
      182–84
in Sicily, 76–79
in the US, 195–98, 200–203
per Varro, 98–100
by women, 139, 142–43, 160,
      172–75, 194–95, 196, 204, 206
cheese molds, 119
cheese presses, 168
Cheshire cheeses, 153, 165–72, 196,
      197, 205
Chian cheeses, 74
China, 39
Christ. *See* Jesus Christ
Christianity, 81–82, 109–15, 122–24.
      See also Benedictines
Cistercians, 124, 154–56, 158
climate
      of Bronze Age Europe, 55–60
      Mediterranean, 5, 126–27
      of the Neolithic period, 5–6
      of the Paleolithic period, 4
coagulation techniques. *See also*
      specific
      techniques, such as rennet-
      coagulated cheeses

discovery of, 12–14
      fig sap and, 46, 71–72, 75, 100
      of French cheeses, 127–28
      of the Greeks, 70–71
      religious theory and, 63, 111
Codex Committee, 220–21
Çökelek cheese, 12, 30
Columbanus, 123
Columella, Lucius Junis Moderatus,
      100–102, 126–27
commerce. *See* trade in cheeses
Constantine, 115, 120
Copper-Stone Age, 41–42, 82–83
coryneform bacteria, 130, 152
cottage cheese, 199, 210, 218
cotton, 199–200
cradle of civilization, 17–18
cream cheese, 210, 218
Cretan civilization. *See* Minoan
      civilization
Crottin cheese, 125, 129
cultivation. *See also* agriculture
      cattle and, 19–20
      by cattle/oxen, 20, 55–56
      defined, 6
      in the Neolithic period, 6–8
cuneiform tablets, 27–29, 52
curds
      ceramic sieves and, 31, 37
      in the Indian diet, 38
      milled curd technique, 153
      Neolithic pastoralists and, 11
      as a religious offering, 18
      salting of, 107–8, 168
Cyclops, 74–77
Cythnian cheeses, 74

dairying. *See* milk production
dairywomen/maids. *See* women in
      cheese making

David and Goliath, 40–41, 62
demesne cheeses, 121–22, 125, 134–46,
   160. *See also* manor system
diet and nutrition, 72–73
Diocletian, 114–15, 120
Docetists, 110–12
domestication, 6, 20
Double Gloucester cheese, 170
dry-salting, 49–50, 168
Dumuzi-Inanna cult, 23–29, 32–33

East Anglian cheeses, 161–65
Edam cheese, 164, 181–83, 215
Edict of Milan, 115
Egypt, 33–35, 43, 60–61
Emmental cheese, 152, 210, 222, 224
England
   Cheshire cheeses, 165–72
   demesne cheeses, 134–46, 160
   East Anglian cheeses, 161–65
   southern cheeses, 169–72
   yeoman farmers in, 159–61
Eridik cheese, 31
Eridu, 22
Etruria, 82–83, 86–87, 89–91, 92
Europe/European Union. *See also*
   specific countries, such as France
   Bronze Age era, 54–58
   geographical indications, 213–15
   Protected Designation of
      Origin, 215–17
   raw milk/cheese safety
      regulations, 217–25

factory cheese making, 174–75,
   203–11, 218
farmhouse/farmstead cheeses, 163,
   174–75, 207, 210–11, 218–19
FDA, 221–23
Federal Standards of Identity, 218

Felicity, 113
Fertile Crescent, 6, 9, 12, 15
feta cheeses, 49–50, 215
fig sap, 46, 71–72, 75, 100
filled cheeses, 208
Flanders, 135, 137–38, 140–41, 145, 176
flett cheese, 164
food safety, 217–25
France, 127–31, 134–35, 137–38, 141,
   145, 152–55, 223

General Agreement on Tariffs and
   Trade (GATT), 212–17
Genesis (Bible), 3, 17–18
geographical indications (GI), 213–15
ghee, 12, 21, 37
Gloucester cheese, 170, 197
Gnostic Christianity, 110
goats
   Balkan peninsula and, 56
   domestication of, 6–7
   milk of, 31
   Ubaid herders and, 20–21
   Uruk herders and, 27–28
Gouda cheese, 180, 183–84, 215
grain production, 93–94
grana cheeses, 155–157
Grana Padano cheese, 155, 222
graters/grated cheeses, 13, 51, 77–80,
   87–89
Greek civilization
   cheese and commerce in, 72–80
   cheese and religion in, 67–72
   decline of, 80
   Etruria and, 86–87, 89–91
   prominence of, 43, 64–67
Gruyère cheeses, 149–50, 152, 210, 222

Halaf people, 19
Hallstadt culture, 90

Harappan civilization, 16, 36–39
Harding, Joseph, 205
Hattusa, 43–52
Hittite Empire
    cheese making in, 45–46
    cheese trading by, 46–51
    rennet-coagulated cheeses in,
      45, 46–47, 49–51
    spiritual practices of, 43–45
Holland
    Edam cheese, 181–83
    Gouda cheese, 183–84
    growth of cheese making,
      175–81
    spice cheese, 181
Homo sapiens, 4, 8
horses, 59, 90

Inanna, 23–29
India, 36–39
Indus River Valley, 36–39
Industrial Revolution, 199–201
iron production, 58, 65, 87
irrigation, 15–16, 19–20, 22
Israel, 81
Italy, 57–58, 60–61, 83–87, 93–95, 152,
    155–56. *See also* Roman Empire

Jesus Christ, 81, 109. *See also*
    Christianity
Job, 63–64
Jordan River Valley, 6

Kish, 22

lactose tolerance, 10–11, 14, 18
Laguiole cheese, 107
large vs. small cheeses, 103–9, 137–38,
    142–43, 167–69
latifundia, 95, 118

leaf foddering, 57
Levant, 6–7, 9, 17–18, 60
Limburger cheese, 210
Listeria monocytogenes, 219
Livarot cheese, 125
livestock. *See* pastoralism
London
    Cheshire cheeses and, 165–72
    East Anglian cheeses and,
      161–65
    southern cheeses and, 169–72
Lor cheese, 12–13, 31
Luna cheese, 103, 107–8

Madduwattaš, 51
Magna Graecia, 92
manor system, 121–22, 125–46,
    159–60. *See also* demesne cheeses
maritime trade, 47–51
marketing of cheeses. *See* trade in
    cheeses
Maroilles cheese, 130
Martial (Marcus Valerius Martialis),
    102–3
Massachusetts Bay Colony, 161, 188–90
Mediterranean climate, 5, 126–27
Mesopotamia
    Anatolia and, 43
    butter and cheese production,
      28–33
    Egyptian civilization and, 34
    Inanna and, 23–29
    milk and cheese consumption
      in, 17–18
    Neolithic period and, 15–16
    rise of, 19–23
Middle Ages, 125–34
milk boilers, 83–85, 88
milk production. *See also*
    transhumance

alpine, 57–58
    in Egypt, 33–35
    in Europe, 56–58
    in Holland, 175–76
    from horses, 59
    Minoan civilization and, 52–53
    Neolithic period and, 16
    origins of, 9–10
    in southwest Asia, 9–14
    Ubaid people and, 20–21
milled curd technique, 153
Minoan civilization, 52–53
Minzi cheese, 31
monastic cheese production, 122–25,
    130–34, 137–40, 145–48, 155–56, 160
Montanism, 112–14
Montasio cheese, 222
Monterey Jack cheese, 218
mountain cheeses. *See* alpine cheese
    production
mozzarella cheese, 209–10, 218
Muenster cheese, 130, 210
Mycenaean civilization, 53–54, 60, 64,
    86–87

Narragansett cheese, 194
Natufians, 5
natural-rind cheeses, 219
Near East. *See* southwest Asia
Neolithic period, 5–8, 15–16, 32
Neufchâtel, 125, 210
New England, 195–98, 200–201
Nile River Valley, 33–35
Nippur, 22
Normandy, 140–41

oleomargarine, 207
oxen, 20, 55–56. *See also* cattle
Oxygalaktinos cheese, 106

Paleolithic period, 4–5
Palestine, 40–41, 61–62
paneer, 38
Parmesan cheese, 155–57, 164, 210, 216
Parmigiano-Reggiano cheese, 155,
    216, 222
pastoralism, 9, 20–21
PDO. *See* Protected Designation of
    Origin
Pecorino Bagnolese, 50, 76
pecorino cheeses, 50, 76–77, 80, 89,
    109, 118
Pecorino Romano cheese, 136
Penicillium roqueforti, 154
Perpetua, 113–14
pharaohs, 34–35
Philistines, 40–41, 61–62, 65
Phoenicians, 65–66
pigs, 85–86
placenta cakes, 97–98, 103
Pliny the Elder, 103–4, 107–8
plows, 20, 22, 43, 52, 55–56
polis, 67
Pont-L'Evêque cheese, 125, 130
pottery
    ceramic shipping jars, 49–50
    ceramic sieves, 31, 37, 82
    cheese making and, 10–12
    cheese molds, 119
    milk boilers, 83–85, 88
    origins of, 10
Po Valley, 155–56
preservation techniques, 12–13
Principle of Equivalency, 221–23
propionibacteria, 152, 156
Protected Designation of Origin
    (PDO), 215–17
Punic Wars, 92–94
Puritans, 185–90, 194, 195–96
pyrotechnology, 10

queso fresco, 219

raw milk/cheese safety regulations, 217–25
religion. *See* spiritual practices
rennet-coagulated cheeses
    in Anatolia, 41
    Aristotle and, 63, 111
    in the Bronze Age, 45
    per Columella, 100–102
    of Cyclops, 74–77
    of Greece, 71–72
    in the Hittite Empire, 45, 46–47, 49–51
    in India, 37–38
    of Italy and Sicily, 60–61
    Job and, 63
    of Medieval France, 127–29
    in Mesopotamia, 32–33
    in the Neolithic Period, 13–14, 32
    of the Roman Empire, 89
    spice cheese, 181
    Tertullian and, 111
    per Varro, 99
Rhode Island cheese, 194
ricotta cheeses, 83–86, 99, 210
Roman Empire
    agriculture and, 93–95, 96–102
    ascendance of, 91–93
    Celts and, 89–92
    Christianity and, 81–82, 115, 122–24
    colonization and, 117–22
    founding of, 82–83
Romano cheese, 222
Romulus and Remus, 82
Roquefort cheeses, 153–55, 213–15, 223–24
rum, 189, 191–93, 195

sacrificial cakes, 69, 97
safety considerations, 217–25
Saint Gall monasteries, 146–48, 156
Saint Maure cheese, 125, 129
Saqqara Tomb, 34–35
Sbrinz cheeses, 222
scalding technique, 169–70, 182–84, 198
scoured cheeses, 45
sea peoples, 60–61, 65, 86
secondary products revolution, 20
semi-rindless cheeses, 171–72, 198
sheep
    Balkan peninsula and, 56
    demesne cheeses and, 134–37, 145–46
    domestication of, 6–7
    milk of, 31
    Ubaid herders and, 20–21
    Uruk herders and, 27–28
Sicily, 60–61, 76–79, 94, 98
sieves, 11, 31, 37, 82
slaves, 191–95, 199–200
small vs. large cheeses, 103–9, 137–38, 142–43, 167–69
smear-ripened cheeses, 130
smoked cheeses, 103
soft-ripened cheeses, 125–34
Somerset cheeses, 165
southwest Asia
    milk and cheese production, 9–14
    Neolithic period, 5–8, 15–16
    Paleolithic period, 4–5
spice cheese, 181
spiritual practices
    Benedictines, 116–17
    cheese and, 8, 18, 63–64
    Christianity, 109–15
    in Egypt, 34–35

of the Greeks, 67–72
of the Hittite Empire, 43–52
Inanna and, 23–29
of India, 38–39
of the Mycenaeans, 53–54
syncretism, 110
Ubaid people and, 21
Stilton cheeses, 171
Studd, Will, 223
Sub-Boreal period, 55–58
Suffolk cheeses, 165–66
Sumerian civilization, 19–20, 22–28
sweating cheeses, 197
swine. *See* pigs
Switzerland, 56–57, 152, 222–23
syncretism, 110

Templars, 154–55
terroir, 213
Tertullian, Septimius Florens, 110–12
thermization, 219–20
trade in cheeses
by the Celts, 105
East Anglian cheeses, 161–65
geographical indications, 213–15
Greek civilization, 74–80
Hittite Empire, 47–51
in Holland, 179–81
in the Medieval English demesnes,
135–36
Protected Designation of Origin,
215–17
by the US, 189–95, 198–99, 206–7
transhumance, 20–21, 52, 56–58,
83–86, 148–49. *See also* milk
production
Trebula cheese, 103
turnsole, 183

Ubaid people, 15, 19–22

United States
colonial New England cheese making,
195–98
factory cheese making, 174,
203–11, 218
geographical indications, 213–15
Industrial Revolution, 199–201
nineteenth century cheese making,
200–203
Protected Designation of Origin and,
215–17
Puritan cheese making, 185–90, 194,
195–96
raw milk/cheese safety regulations,
217–25
semi-rindless cheese, 171–72, 198
trade in cheeses, 189–95, 198–99,
206–7
unpasteurized milk, 217–25
Ur, 17–18, 22, 25, 28–29
Ur III dynasty, 23, 30
Urnfield culture, 86, 89–90
Uruguay Round Agreement, 212,
215, 220
Uruk, 19, 22–28, 42–43

Varro, Marcus Terentius, 98–100
Vatusican cheese, 106
Velabrum cheese, 103
Vermont Cheddar, 216–17
Vestine cheese, 103

washed-rind cheeses, 129–31, 219
West Indies, 189–95, 198–99
white cheeses, 32
Williams, Jesse and George, 204–5
Winthrop, Adam, 161
Winthrop, John, 185, 188
women in cheese making, 139, 142–43,
160, 172–75, 194–95, 196, 204, 206

wool textiles, 21–22, 25–26, 42–43, 53,
    135–36, 145–46
World Trade Organization (WTO),
    212–17
worship. *See* spiritual practices
WTO (World Trade Organization),
    212–17

yeoman farmers, 159–61
yogurt, 31

Zagros Mountains, 6–7, 21
Zoroaster, 80

ABOUT THE AUTHOR

Paul Kindstedt is professor of food science in the Department of Nutrition and Food Sciences at the University of Vermont. He has authored numerous research articles and invited conference proceedings on dairy chemistry and cheese science, as well as many book chapters. He is also the coauthor of *American Farmstead Cheese* (2005) with the Vermont Cheese Council, and has received national professional recognition for both his research and teaching. Kindstedt currently serves as the codirector of the Vermont Institute for Artisan Cheese at the University of Vermont.

"This logo identifies paper that meets the standards of the Forest Stewardship Council.® FSC® is widely regarded as the best practice in forest management, ensuring the highest protections for forests and indigenous peoples."

Chelsea Green Publishing is committed to preserving ancient forests and natural resources. We elected to print this title on 30-percent postconsumer recycled paper, processed chlorine-free. As a result, for this printing, we have saved:

16 Trees (40' tall and 6-8" diameter)
6 Million BTUs of Total Energy
1,541 Pounds of Greenhouse Gases
6,945 Gallons of Wastewater
440 Pounds of Solid Waste

Chelsea Green Publishing made this paper choice because we and our printer, Thomson-Shore, Inc., are members of the Green Press Initiative, a nonprofit program dedicated to supporting authors, publishers, and suppliers in their efforts to reduce their use of fiber obtained from endangered forests. For more information, visit: www.greenpressinitiative.org.

Environmental impact estimates were made using the Environmental Defense Paper Calculator. For more information visit: www.papercalculator.org.

the politics and practice of sustainable living

CHELSEA GREEN PUBLISHING

Chelsea Green Publishing sees books as tools for effecting cultural change and seeks to empower citizens to participate in reclaiming our global commons and become its impassioned stewards. If you enjoyed *Cheese and Culture,* please consider these other great books related to food, gardening, and sustainable agriculture.

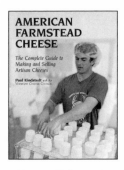

AMERICAN FARMSTEAD CHEESE
The Complete Guide to Making and Selling Artisan Cheeses
PAUL KINDSTEDT, with the
Vermont Cheese Council
9781931498777
Hardcover • $40.00

CHEESEMONGER
A Life on the Wedge
GORDON EDGAR
9781603582377
Paperback • $17.95

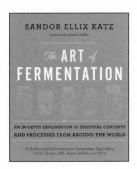

THE ART OF FERMENTATION
An In-Depth Exploration of Essential Concepts and Processes from Around the World
SANDOR ELLIX KATZ
9781603582865
Hardcover • $39.95

MEAT
A Benign Extravagance
SIMON FAIRLIE
9781603583244
Paperback • $24.95

For more information or to request a catalog, visit **www.chelseagreen.com** or call toll-free **(800) 639-4099**.

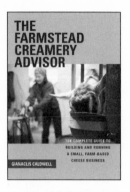
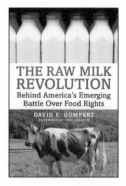

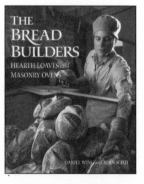